Lost Films of the Fifties

Five (1951)

Lost Films
of the Fifties

By DOUGLAS BRODE

A Citadel Press Book
Published by Carol Publishing Group

To
DOROTHY JOHNSON
My Friend

ACKNOWLEDGMENTS:

With thanks and appreciation to Norman Keim, film bibliographer extraordinaire, and Robert Polonsky, a fine film critic whose suggestions for titles were all taken to heart.

Appreciation also to those people and establishments so helpful in the gathering of the beautiful stills found here: Mary Corliss and the Museum of Modern Art Film Archives, Jerry Ohlinger's Movie Material Store, Collector's Originals, Larry Edmond's Bookstore, Collector's Bookstore, and Movie Star News.

Finally, a word of thanks to the movie studios—those still existing and those that are themselves "lost"—who turned out the films which delighted us during the fifties and left an indelible mark on the minds of those who love film dearly: Paramount, 20th Century-Fox, Universal, Universal-International, Columbia, Eagle-Lion, Metro-Goldwyn-Mayer, R.K.O. Radio Pictures, Republic, Romulus Films, Lippert Pictures, London Films, J. Arthur Rank Productions, Aspen Pictures, Buena Vista (Walt Disney Films), BrynaProd, Batjac, United Artists, Warner Brothers, Allied Artists, Holiday Films, Globe Enterprises, Mark VII, Horizon Pictures, Heath Productions, Dino De Laurentiis Productions, Highroad Pictures, Schulberg Productions, Kingsley International.

First Carol Publishing Group Edition 1991

Copyright © 1988 by Douglas Brode

A Citadel Press Book
Published by Carol Publishing Group

Editorial Offices
600 Madison Avenue
New York, NY 10022

Sales & Distribution Offices
120 Enterprise Avenue
Secaucus, NJ 07094

In Canada: Musson Book Company
A division of General Publishing Co. Limited
Don Mills, Ontario

Citadel Press is a registered trademark of
Carol Communications, Inc.

Manufactured in the United States of America
ISBN 0-8065-1092-7

Designed by A. Christopher Simon

Carol Publishing Group books are available at special discounts
for bulk purchases, for sales promotions, fund raising, or
educational purposes. Special editions can also be created to
specifications. For details contact: Special Sales Department,
Carol Publishing Group, 120 Enterprise Ave., Secaucus, NJ 07094

10 9 8 7 6 5 4 3 2

5,000 Fingers of Dr. T (1953)

Contents

Patterns (1956)

Introduction: Lost and Found

In the fifties, we spent much more time watching Richard Egan and Rhonda Fleming than we did James Dean and Marilyn Monroe.

That may be hard to believe, but it happens to be true. It's also the premise of this book. More than twelve years ago, Citadel Press published my first book, *Films of the Fifties*. As one's first book is for every author, that was a joyous occasion for me. But it was a difficult one, too, for as I'd worked on the book—a hundred representative movies from that decade—I grew ever more frustrated by the realization I would not be able to include many titles I wanted to. Movie buffs, after all, come to such a book with expectations, and I believe it's the author's responsibility to understand that and accommodate them. So I included the films that had to be included: *The Wild One, Rebel Without a Cause, The Seven Year Itch, From Here to Eternity, A Place in the Sun, Singin' in the Rain, High Noon, Vertigo.* Like other fans of fifties films, I love those classics. But as I wrote, I experienced a nagging sense that grew even stronger after the book was in print, a fear I was misrep-

resenting the experience of going to the movies back then by emphasizing those films that were considered great then and have, with the passing of time, come to be considered (quite rightly) landmarks in movie history. Which is why any movie made today about the fifties will show the teenage characters wandering into a theater where they watch *Rebel Without a Cause,* just as TV anthologies invariably represent the fifties by including a shot of the wind from the subway blowing Marilyn Monroe's skirt up.

Dean, the anguished teenager, and Marilyn, the giggling goddess, have passed beyond being actors or even superstars and become popular icons: their faces can be seen decorating everything from T-shirts to coffee mugs. And, for that matter, the cover of my previous book on the fifties. In fact, the myth of what going to the movies back then was like has all but supplanted the reality. Which is why I wanted to write this book, and have been rolling the idea for it over and over in my mind since the day I finished work on *Films of the Fifties.*

The Movies—like any other art or entertainment

ALL THE ANGRY (YOUNG) MEN: Following
in the style of Montgomery Clift, other ultra-
serious practitioners of the Stanislavski
method invaded Hollywood, bringing with
them a fresh acting approach as they embodied the alienated loners so characteristic of
the era. Marlon Brando (1) made his film
premiere as an emotionally scarred vet (opposite Teresa Wright) in *Battle Stripe*; young
James Dean (2) debuted feeding ammunition
to Gene Evans in *Fixed Bayonets*; Jack Webb
(3) (before going aesthetically stiff and politically superstraight) portrayed an intense,
troubled paraplegic in *The Men*; Montgomery Clift (4) is captured in a characteristically
introspective mood while waiting to shoot a
scene for *Two Corridors East*.

1

3

2

4

form—are subject to a natural selection process. There is what lasts, and what doesn't last, which can have precious little to do with the attitudes at the time when the work first appeared. It's the same in music as it is in the movies: the play and the film *Amadeus* are about how a Salieri—winning the accolades of his day—could be all but forgotten a short time later, while a Mozart—damned in his time as an immature artist—could create works that would survive the passing of centuries. More recently, think back less than twenty years, and imagine the response if you had told people that Donovan (perceived as a poet, a seer, and a major artist for all time) would in two decades be forgotten, while Jim Morrison and The Doors (thought of as an appealing if unimportant band) would have established a cult following that continues to grow each year; people would have laughed, called you crazy. But that in fact is what has happened.

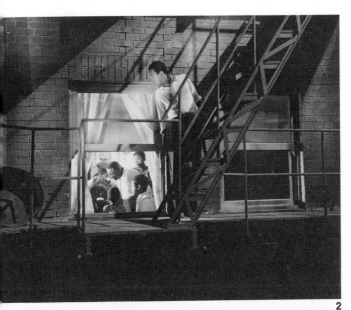

THE EFFECT OF THE CIVIL RIGHTS MOVEMENT: As, in mid-decade, the theme of Civil Rights became ever more prevalent, great novels about the black experience which had not previously reached the screen were now adapted. Canada Lee (1) portrayed the protagonist of Alan Paton's *Cry, The Beloved Country*, while Richard Wright (2) played his own hero "Bigger Thomas" in *Native Son*.

THE GREAT SPORTS HEROES: Many of the decade's greatest athletes portrayed themselves in films, including Jackie Robinson (1) in *The Jackie Robinson* Story, and Bob Mathias (2) in *The Bob Mathias Story*.

9

2

1

3

5

6

BABES IN BAGDAD: As the Production Code grew passé, daring stars revealed considerable decolletage, getting away with ever scantier costumes by having their stories set in exotic locales. Joan Collins (1) was the Egyptian Alexis in *Land of the Pharoahs*; Rita Hayworth (2) admires herself in *Salome*; Kathryn Grayson (3) drove the Foreign Legion wild in *The Desert Song*, while Gina Lollobrigida (4) did the same to Yul Brynner in *Solomon and Sheba*; as evil, irresistible seductresses, Virginia Mayo (5) and Lana Turner (6) needed only to recline for proper effect in *The Silver Chalice* and *The Prodigal*; closer to home, Kim Novak (7) and Rhonda Fleming (8) portrayed real-life hoochie-koochie dancers in *Jeanne Eagels* and *Little Egypt*; but it was Irish spitfire Maureen O'Hara (9) who went all the way for history's most erotic ride in *Lady Godiva*.

7

8

9

And it happens with film. It's difficult to believe that in its day *Battle Cry* made more money at the box-office than *From Here to Eternity*, but it's true. People saw something in that film then, or perhaps in the advertising campaign and aura that surrounded the film. But the enchantment didn't last long, as no one bothered to watch *Battle Cry* when it was released to TV a few years later. Yet *From Here to Eternity* goes on and on, revived endlessly on cable TV, a hit on videocassette. Its appeal reaches beyond the interest surrounding the film's immediate release.

But why did we go to see *Battle Cry* at all? Why were we briefly attracted to some awful films, and why also to some excellent movies (*Tea and Sympathy*, *The Shrike*) that nonetheless failed to speak to us only a few years later? I've always been fascinated by the weeding-out process, trying to determine what it is about a work that allows it to last or dooms it to disappear. Of course, there's a catch, and a fascinating one: just when you think a film is gone for good, it may suddenly reemerge as a cult movie.

FROM BROADWAY TO HOLLYWOOD, PART ONE: Julie Harris was the great theatrical performer of the fifties, bringing two of her most famous stage roles to the screen. In *Member of the Wedding* (1) (with Ethel Waters and Brandon de Wilde), she played a sensitive child growing up in the South; in *I Am a Camera* (2) (with Laurence Harvey), she was Sally Bowles, the free-living, sexually enlightened pre-war Berlin prostitute.

FROM BROADWAY TO HOLLYWOOD, PART TWO: A number of popular Broadway stars, given the opportunity to do the film versions of their stage hits, failed to score a similar success onscreen. John Raitt (1) shared pajamas with pert Doris Day in *the Pajama Game*; Gwenn Verdon (2) seduced ballplayer Tab Hunter in *Damn Yankees*.

1

2

FUN COUPLES: Moviegoers enjoyed seeing their favorite celebrity-newlyweds together onscreen, though sometimes the directors had to rush to get the film completed before divorce proceedings began. Eddie Fisher and Debbie Reynolds (1) cuddled in this publicity shot for *Bundle of Joy*; Janet Leigh seems delighted that Tony Curtis (2) appears about to drown in *Houdini*.

2

1

ANIMAL ANTICS: In the fifties, moviegoers fell in love with offbeat pets and their silly masters, as Donald O'Connor (1) sang with his beloved mule in *Francis Goes to West Point* (Francis's voice courtesy Chill Wills), Charles Drake (2) served lunch to the most appealing chimp this side of Cheetah in *Bonzo Goes to College* (proving there is indeed life after Ronald Reagan).

One example of that is 1953's *Invaders from Mars*. That film has become a part of my own family's mythology, the centerpiece of a tale my mother still invariably tells at the Thanksgiving table. According to the story, many years ago, after a morning of hide-and-seek and cowboys and Indians, I was sent packing to a Saturday matinee with a group of my friends. My mother, catching her breath, sat down to relax when who should appear at the door but yours truly, screaming with terror as I described the onscreen monsters that had sent me running up the aisle, out of the theater, and off for home only minutes after the movie began. "But," my mother kept insisting, "you're ten years old! Terry Rowse is still there, and he's three years younger than you are!" "Yeah," I'm reported to have said, "but he's sitting on Morris Hodkin's lap!"

THE OVERLOOKED ASPECT OF BURT LANCASTER: Though he's warmly remembered for energetic performances like *The Crimson Pirate*, Burt Lancaster alternated such robust roles with more serious parts. All but forgotten are his incarnations of a bitter alcoholic in William Inge's *Come Back, Little Sheba* (1) (opposite Shirley Booth) and a swaggering stud in Tennessee Williams' *The Rose Tattoo* (2) (opposite Anna Magnani). The perfect foil, Lancaster made the ladies look so good (though in fact neither needed much help) that both won Best Actress Oscars.

At that point in the proceedings, everyone in the family howls with laughter. And I'm too polite to mention that Morris Hodkin wasn't even there that day: It was Alan Cohen's lap. Does it really matter whose Jewish lap a terrified Irish kid huddled on? Probably not. What matters is that movies—even modest movies like *Invaders*—exist beyond the frame of reference during which we watch (or, in my case that time, fail to watch) them in the theater. They become a part of us, connected (much like the pop music we hear on the radio) to incidents in our lives, and quite inseparable from those incidents. I can't think about any of the kids I grew up with without thinking of *Invaders*; I can't think about *Invaders* without my mind also wandering to those kids.

A few years later, I finally saw the film all the way through on TV, and was stunned (as a teenager) to realize that what had seemed the most realistically created monsters were just tall men in leotards and Halloween masks. Then, the film disappeared from view for so long I actually reached a point where I wasn't altogether sure if it had ever existed, or if I'd merely dreamed I'd seen it, like the little kid dreaming of the invasion in the movie itself. Like him, I eventually woke to realize the dream was real: there *Invaders* was one night, on cable TV, a lost film that had resurfaced. And what had been treated, in its time, as a junk movie, struck me as being a sensitive, perceptive, aesthetically impressive study of a representative 1950s child's nightmare-scenario of the adult world around him carried to its logical if horrifying extreme.

If I had written *Lost Films of the Fifties* a few years ago, I certainly would have included *Invaders from Mars* as one of the movies. But—like the lost Hitchcock films or the lost episodes of *The Honeymooners*—what had been so long "gone" suddenly came back with a vengeance. A big-budget (if disastrously misguided) remake of *Invaders* hit theater screens, causing enough interest in the old movie that it was re-released on home video and, despite its modest production values, was found to be far superior to the overblown remake, which featured state-of-the-art special effects but totally missed the essence of the original's quirky charm. Still, because of the resurgence of interest in *Invaders*, I felt it necessary to eliminate it from this book, though it was one of the films I'd originally planned to include. Another was *The Trouble With Harry*, which for years was one of the five "lost" Hitchcock films, until it resurfaced with the others (*Vertigo, Rear Window*, etc.) and soon enjoyed enough publicity that it seemed wrong to refer to it as a lost film.

"How do you define forgotten?" That's a question more than one friend and fellow movie buff has asked after learning I was working on this project. The question is a difficult one, to be sure. Certainly, some films are

REMEMBRANCE OF WAR: Throughout the fifties, films continued to revise our vision of the previous decade's war. In *Up Front* Bill Mauldin's cartoon-characters Willie and Joe were vividly brought to life by David Wayne and Tom Ewell.

1

Many social critics likened the paranoia of the fifties to that of Germany before the rise of Hitler, which perhaps accounts for the numerous American remakes of classic films from that era. May Britt and Curt Jurgens subbed for Marlene Dietrich and Emil Jannings in *The Blue Angel*.

2

FIRST PERSON SINGULAR: In the fifties, most monster movies were autobiographical. Michael Landon (1) played a typical James Deanish teenager with a crush on Yvonne Lime until he became hairy as well as horny in *I Was a Teenage Werewolf*; Tom Tryon (2) leaves wife Gloria Talbott trying to comprehend his anguish before likewise revealing his true appearance in *I Married a Monster From Outer Space* (where else?).

more lost than others: when I mention *Donovan's Brain*, *The Young Stranger*, *The Goddess*, or *Underwater!*, people (other than hardcore film buffs, for whom no movie is ever forgotten!) usually stare at me uncomprehendingly; but mention *The Bad Seed*, *Written on the Wind*, *The Moon is Blue*, or *Helen of Troy*, and usually even a non-buff's eyes light up with recognition of a film that once was all the rage but, somehow, some way, got lost, and hasn't been seen in years. I opted for a combination

A RECURRING POSE: In the late fifties and early sixties, beautiful women were constantly being menaced by bug-eyed monsters from outer space. Elegant Nicole Maurey revealed considerable cleavage while facing a deadly tree in Philip Yordan's big-budget English import, *Day of the Triffids*.

THE TV TRAUMA: Realizing the immense challenge posed by television, some Hollywood studios tried to cope by featuring the most popular TV stars in major movies. Ozzie, Harriet, David and Ricky (1) were joined by Rock Hudson for *Here Come the Nelsons*. Gertrude Berg and Philip Loeb (2) (shortly to commit suicide after his career was ruined by the blacklist) were seen in *The Goldbergs*. Though the public dearly loved them all, they quickly proved less than willing to pay for what they could catch at home for free on a weekly basis.

BEACH BLANKET BINGO: Long before the swimsuit issue was a gleam in the eyes of *Sports Illustrated*'s editors, Hollywood showed off its leading ladies in lethal beachware. Jayne Mansfield (1) proved M.M.'s chief competitor as Hollywood's favorite blonde. Among the imports was England's Diana Dors (2).

of the two: certainly, most readers will take exception to several choices, and perhaps think of some gem that ought to have been included. A "lost film," to my mind, is a movie that has yet to evolve as a cult film, but which has the potential to. Perhaps this book will, ironically, serve the purpose of making some long forgotten films a part of the public consciousness once again.

Not that I expect people to suddenly become Edmond Purdom freaks and search out all his old pictures. Still, his career—like that of, say, Sal Mineo or Jayne Mansfield—is one that belonged to the fifties, part of the actual (rather than mythic) experience of going to the movies then. Simply, we did not spend all our time ogling Marilyn or cheering on Jimmy as he raced Corey Allen toward a California cliff. Richard Carlson, Jean Peters, John Payne, Arlene Dahl, Sterling Hayden—they are only a few of the people who seemed so important for a time, but were unable to keep alive our interest in them. A few, like Van Heflin and Robert Ryan, were marvelous actors, worthy of far more attention than they

THE WIDE WORLD OF THE MOVIE MUSICAL: Following the heights of *Singin' in the Rain* and *An American in Paris*, the MGM musical factory ran out of steam, incestuously remaking their own earlier hits *(The Desert Song, Kismet, Rose Marie)*. But various studios did provide some offbeat experiments in the musical genre. The Broadway hit *Li'l Abner* (1) was colorfully transported to the screen, as Leslie Parrish and Julie Newmar compete for Peter Palmer and unbilled guest star Jerry Lewis; Mamie Van Doren (2) taught the Beatniks how to shimmy in the low-budget *Untamed Youth*.

END OF THE TRAIL FOR THE B WESTERN: With TV offering cheaply made westerns on a nightly basis, the theatrical B western faced the last sunset. Before the genre ground to a halt, Lee J. Cobb, Marie Windsor, and Lloyd Bridges calmly watched a companion take an arrow in the back (1). Alan Ladd spent less time with his shooting iron than he did helping his son David (with the aid of Olivia de Havilland) overcome his muteness in *The Proud Rebel* (2).

17

The Forgotten American Folk Hero: Though in real life the cowboy was an overworked, underpaid day-laborer, he has been mythologized by dime novels and movies into a fantasy image of the great American hero. Yet the mountain man—who really did live out an epic adventure in the wilds—has been all but overlooked. In the fifties, there were hundreds of movie and TV cowboy films, but only a precious few pictures explored the far more fascinating but virtually untapped world of the trapper. In Howard Hawks' *The Big Sky* (1), Arthur Hunnicutt and Kirk Douglas were early explorers on a fateful keelboat trip upriver to trade with Indians; in William Wellman's *Across the Wide Missouri* (2), Clark Gable portrayed a "hivernant" caring for his infant child after his Indian wife dies.

have ever received; others, like John Derek or Jeff Chandler, were not terribly good, but still summon up warm memories when we recall that, in truth, they were the people we shared our Saturday matinees with. They may be gone, but it's time they were no longer forgotten.

For that reason, one rule of thumb in compiling the hundred films I write about here (and the selection process was a long, painful one) was that I would severely limit the number of films featuring big stars. There had to be exceptions, of course: you'll find here lost films starring Robert Mitchum, Burt Lancaster, John Wayne, Ava Gardner, Frank Sinatra; I even allowed myself the luxury of including two from my all-time favorite, Kirk Douglas. But I did keep in mind that they are either already the subject of a *Films of . . .* type of book, or eventually will be. So I put a high priority on emphasizing movies that ought to be anthologized but which probably never would be unless I included them here. In my mind, it was time somebody sat down and wrote about *Unchained, The Woman on Pier 13,* and *The Search for Bridey Murphy,* though neither the stars nor the directors of those films are likely to ever warrant books of their own.

Directors were as important for the selection process as were the actors whose careers I wanted to represent. It's worth noting that in the late sixties, the sudden popularity of the auteur theory in general and Andrew

18

Sarris's book *The American Cinema* in specific had a resounding influence on the way films from the fifties were perceived. Certain serious-minded filmmakers (Fred Zinnemann, Elia Kazan, and, most of all, Stanley Kramer), who had in their time been heralded for courageously approaching touchy social issues, were disparaged; on the other hand, flamboyant stylists (Nicholas Ray and Samuel Fuller chief among them), who had been considered intriguing if insignificant directors of florid genre pieces, were hailed as the true artists of the cinema, since their impact lay not in such things as dialogue (the least "cinematic" element of film) but in the way they filled the frame, the way they edited from one frame to the next, the way they supervised set design and the relationship of music to the images; that, is, the way in which they created "pure cinema," stamping their work with an unmistakable "signature."

There is, of course, a certain truth to all that and a

2

INVASION OF THE B GIRLS: While some sci-fi filmmakers offered more realistic projections of space travel, others featured retrograde visions harkening back to Flash Gordon; Marie Windsor (ironically looking more feline, even without costume, than her abductors) was captured by *The Cat Women of the Moon* (1); Susan Shaw's sacrificing of a virgin to the gods is interrupted by a hungry creature in *Fire Maidens of Outer Space* (2); Zsa Zsa Gabor was not the title character but an Amazon revolutionary who aids the earthlings in *Queen of Outer Space* (3).

3

19

THE TWO SIDES OF SAL MINEO: This two-time Oscar nominee balanced a pair of careers during the fifties, as a wholesome rock 'n' roll singer of the sort mothers hoped their daughters would bring home on a date, and as a surly, cigarette smokin' street punk of the sort they feared their daughters were secretly seeing.

legitimate justification for close study of work by too-long-overlooked filmmakers. Quickly, though, it went too far; Sarris's influence spread wider than he likely ever intended (a puckish fellow, Sarris apparently assumed some of his more outrageous statements would be taken with a grain of salt). Only a few years after he'd caused film buffs to wonder if perhaps John Huston wasn't awfully overrated, Sarris himself began wildly praising some (at best) mediocre Huston films in the mid-seventies, as if to make up for the harm he'd done to the man's reputation. This book does herald the finest "expressive esoteric" work by Fuller and my old friend Ray. Also, though, its intent is to revive interest in filmmakers who were praised in the fifties, then dismissed as standing for "strained seriousness" after the publication of *The American Cinema* in 1968. Perhaps we appreciate their seriousness now more than ever because the vast majority of new American films are so unrelentingly frivolous.

Still, it wasn't until I began work on this book that I realized just how significant one trend of the early fifties was. That, as you will read in the body of the text, was the emergence of reality-based narratives or, as they're more commonly (and somewhat incorrectly) called, "docudramas." Common knowledge has it that an influx of Italian neorealist films so influenced American filmmakers that they set out to make their own socially-conscious movies, shot on actual locations, with *On the Waterfront* standing as the grand example of the type. That's certainly true, but it wasn't until I began to research the bulk of movies made during the fifties, to actually watch them once again, that the full impact of the Italian (and, less known but just as significant, British) concept of dramatized documentaries on the first half of the decade hit me full force. Many of those films—so characteristic of the moviegoing experience as it existed in the early fifties, though all but gone today—

20

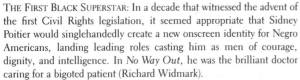

THE FIRST BLACK SUPERSTAR: In a decade that witnessed the advent of the first Civil Rights legislation, it seemed appropriate that Sidney Poitier would singlehandedly create a new onscreen identity for Negro Americans, landing leading roles casting him as men of courage, dignity, and intelligence. In *No Way Out*, he was the brilliant doctor caring for a bigoted patient (Richard Widmark).

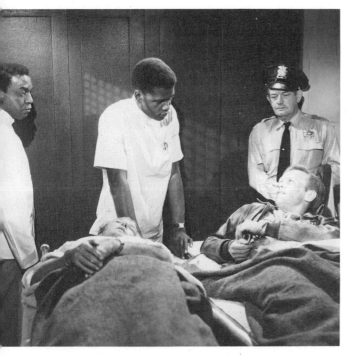

FORGOTTEN OSCAR WINNERS: Several performers achieved superstardom as well as Academy Awards with movies seldom revived today, including William Holden as the snide P.O.W. in *Stalag 17* (1), Susan Hayward as a belligerant death row cellmate in *I Want To Live* (2), Jose Ferrer as a man with the soul of a poet but the schnoz of Durante in *Cyrano de Bergerac* (3), Dorothy Malone as a nymphomaniac obsessed with Rock Hudson in *Written On the Wind* (4).

make up the bulk of choices for the first half of this book.

One last note: there are several movies missing from the list that fans of films from the fifties will immediately note: *Night of the Hunter, High School Confidential, The Littlest Fugitive, Sincerely Yours, Calloway Went Thataway.* The reason is simple: they can be found in my first book, *Films of the Fifties.* As I mentioned earlier, I've always been an admirer of those little movies that linger in my memory but seem to have escaped the ongoing public conception of what we used to watch back then.

True, Richard Egan will never replace James Dean in our hearts, nor should he. And far from being an icon like Marilyn, Rhonda Fleming—haughty, provocative, seemingly the ready-made but invariably unfaithful mistress of some millionaire—remains something of an acquired taste. These two—like so many of the others you will either meet or reacquaint yourself with here—spoke for their times without, like Dean or Monroe, being able to speak about those times after the era was over. But in recalling them, and what it was we (however fleetingly) saw and appreciated in them, we can come to a more realistic assessment of what we, as well as the movies, were truly like in the fifties.

SUPERSTARS ARE SURVIVORS: Most of the leading ladies of the thirties and forties disappeared from the screen or retired to character roles, but the true superstars scratched out new images and continued their careers unabated. Katharine Hepburn (1) played a neurotic spinster surrendering to sexual passion while on vacation in Venice in *Summertime*; Joan Crawford (2) was the aging beauty who realizes the man she's married to is psychologically anguished in *Autumn Leaves*; Bette Davis (3) portrayed a softspoken but courageous career woman, a librarian who fights censorship in *Storm Center*.

UP AND DOWN WITH THE DUKE: In the fifties, John Wayne starred in several forgotten films, including a disastrous turn as Genghis Khan in the cardboard costume epic *The Conqueror* (1), and far more appropriately cast as the rawboned hero of Louis Lamour's *Hondo* (2), the first major western to be shot in 3-D.

1

1

2

THE GOLDEN AGE OF ROCK 'N' ROLL: In 1956–57, rock 'n' roll hit the airwaves, and inexpensive movies were turned out to capitalize on the new phenomenon, allowing screaming teen fans across the country (who could not, like New York kids, attend Alan Freed's lavish shows) to see their favorite stars in action. Fats Domino (1) warbled "Blueberry Hill" in *Shake, Rattle and Rock* while Little Richard (2) bebopped to the tune of "Tutti-Frutti" in *Mr. Rock and Roll*.

As Danny, Montgomery Clift observes firsthand the poverty-stricken life of Germans in the postwar era.

The Big Lift

A 20th Century-Fox Film (1950)

CREDITS:

Produced by William Perlberg; directed by George Seaton; screenplay by Mr. Seaton; running time: 120 minutes.

CAST:

Montgomery Clift (Danny MacCullough); Paul Douglas (Hank); Cornell Borchers (Frederica); Bruni Lobel (Gerda); O. E. Hasse (Stieber); Danny Davenport (Private); Fritz Nichlisch (Gunther); Capt. Dante V. Morel (Himself); Capt. John Mason (Himself); Capt. Gail Plush (Himself).

Like just about every other filmmaker in Hollywood, writer-director George Seaton was highly impressed by the Italian neorealist films imported during the late 1940s. By the early fifties, Seaton, having absorbed this approach, attempted to assimilate the naturalistic techniques and socially conscious themes into the new, emerging American cinema. Such concepts were clearly on Seaton's mind when he took his crew to Berlin to film The Big Lift on the actual locations and employed actual servicemen to play themselves whenever possible.

Seaton—having observed the lift in operation during several months in 1948, when the idea of airlifts developed as a means of circumventing the Russian blockade—fashioned a melodramatic love story concerning two American servicemen who would represent opposing points of view. On the one hand, there is Danny, an idealistic sergeant romancing a pretty German girl, Frederica, believing she sincerely loves him. On the other, there's his abrasively cynical buddy Hank, who likewise has an affair with a lovely fraulein, Gerda, but harbors no such illusions. So far as Hank is concerned, the girl means nothing to him but sex; he insists that if he appears to be using her, she would certainly use him if given the chance. The hero is offended by his friend's contemptuous attitude, until he discovers that Frederica is in fact coldly manipulating him.

This resolution to the tale leaves a bitter aftertaste. The ordinary American movie approach for such a story is the one developed by Frank Capra during the 1930s and forties, in which an innocent, idealistic character gradually proves to a cynical older friend that his negative view of life is wrongheaded. But the darker point-of-view which emerged during the fifties allowed for the opposite approach, as the hero accepts the fact that the woman he trusts is a self-serving Machiavellian.

Not a pretty picture, but one which typifies the mindset then metamorphosing in popular American thought as well as popular American motion pictures. The real-

(Opposite page) Shots like this, featuring actual airlift transports rather than Hollywood facsimiles, helped establish the new realism that entered American films in the early fifties.

Hank enjoys the favors of pretty Gerda, a poor German girl, though he never romanticizes his relationship with her.

as he left behind such polished, pleasant diversions as *Billy Rose's Diamond Horseshoe, Junior Miss,* and *Miracle on 34th Street* and moved on to the grim, gritty movies that would authentically reflect life with all its emotional turmoil: *Little Boy Lost, The Country Girl,* and *The Hook,* among his more memorable endeavors.

The Next Voice You Hear...

A Metro-Goldwyn-Mayer Film (1950)

CREDITS:

Produced by Dore Schary; directed by William A. Wellman; screenplay by Charles Schnee, suggested by a story by George Sumner Albee; running time: 83 minutes.

CAST:

James Whitmore *(Joe Smith)*; Nancy Davis *(Mrs. Joe Smith)*; Gary Gray *(Johnny Smith)*; Lillian Bronson *(Aunt Ethel)*; Art Smith *(Mr. Brannan)*; Tom D'Andrea *(Hap Magee)*; Jeff Corey *(Freddie)*.

life canvas Seaton employed was crowded with densely portrayed details of the lift itself, the everyday operation of the planes by the men who ran them, as well as the more exceptional situations including the way planes landed during heavy fog. High points of the film featured a confrontation of Danny and his girl with several Russian soldiers on a subway, and a conflict that develops over the precise location of the border. Like the neorealist films that inspired him, Seaton's movie works as an accumulation of dramatic episodes and comic anecdotes rather than hewing to the more conventional studio-film storyline. Even today, we can learn more about the workings of the Berlin Airlift from this vivid movie representation than we can from any textbook, since casual viewers are sucked in by the love stories. Entertainment and education do not necessarily have to be at odds with each other.

Montgomery Clift had already emerged, thanks to Howard Hawks's *Red River* and Fred Zinnemann's *The Search* in 1948, as the first of a new breed of screen actors: intense, alienated, existential. His combination of a traditional leading man's good looks and a method actor's mumbling manner helped establish him as the ideal fifties' screen presence for everyone from teenage girls to highbrow aficionados of serious cinema. And while Paul Douglas's career is less vividly remembered than that of his cultish costar, he worked regularly during the fifties playing gruff but savvy characters, a kind of Broderick Crawford with class. For George Seaton, this was a significant transition point in his directorial career,

The name Schary was synonomous with high-minded projects at MGM; the name Wellman has always been associated with serious movies devised around socially relevant themes; the name Albee is a hallmark in American theatrical history. Any film featuring a combination of these talents necessarily had to boast an ambitious premise, as they gathered to create a morality play for the media-addicted population of the early fifties. But the movie they turned out remains one of the most curious oddities ever released by a major studio. Whether they created an inspirational drama or a sacrilege is still difficult to determine. The only thing critics and moviegoers have ever agreed on about this movie is that it is indeed unique.

In *The Next Voice You Hear . . .,* God decides to address the nation over the radio waves. The impact of this event on a single, typical American family (suitably named Smith) provides the film's focus. In a manner both quaint and freakish, featuring a tone alternately sentimental and solemn, assuming a point of view that can be interpreted as critical or condescending, the filmmakers concentrate on the reactions of "the little people" to this modern miracle, as they scurry about an urban area of Los Angeles, adjusting to what's happened,

The Smith Family: as Joe, "Mrs. Joe," and little Johnny, James Whitmore, Nancy Davis, and little Gary Gray created a convincing image of an American family facing the unthinkable: radio remarks from God himself.

trying to comprehend how the normal hustle and bustle can possibly go on after this vocal intrusion from The Great Beyond.

The audience for the movie never actually gets to hear the voice of God, only the reactions to it expressed by the Smith family. In the early portions of the film, Schary and Company introduce Joe as a factory worker, his wife as a reserved and dutiful lady preoccupied with her own pregnancy, their 11-year-old son as a regular gum-chewing, comic-book-reading kid. Then, like every other family in the area, in the country, and in McLuhan's global community, they receive nightly broadcasts from God, a situation which initially sparks fear that the end may be near. Instead, God reminds everyone that in their wild rush for wealth and fame, the secular postwar society has moved dangerously far from the old faiths that once gave their lives meaning. Miracles still do occur, God insists, though man has become the Lord's instrument for presenting them: even the remarkable concept of radio, when carefully considered, is "miraculous," if only one appreciates the quality of the medium even now bringing them all the voice of God. At first, this is too much for Joe: he goes out and gets drunk. By the week's end, though, he has reversed himself, and what initially made him feel insecure brings him a sense of the goodness of life, a realization that even in an age of scientific advancements, the old-fashioned notion of faith is not necessarily gone; in fact,

Despite claims from some quarters that the film was sacreligious, the basic theme was piety.

the former can actually be interpreted as evidence of the latter.

Schary wisely conceived of the film as a trim little project, shooting it in two weeks' time in order to keep expenses down. In many respects, this offbeat drama

Reaffirming their lost faith in church.

The Woman on Pier 13

An RKO Radio Picture (1950)

CREDITS:

Produced by Jack J. Gross; directed by Robert Stevenson; screenplay by Charles Grayson and Robert Hardy Andrews, from a story by George W. George and George F. Slavin; running time: 73 minutes.

CAST:

Laraine Day (Nan Collins); Robert Ryan (Brad Collins); John Agar (Don Lowry); Thomas Gomez (Vanning); Janis Carter (Christine); Richard Rober (Jim Travis); William Talman (Bailey); Paul E. Burns (Arnold); Paul Guilfoyle (Ralston); G. Pat Collins (Charles Dover); Fred Graham (Grip Wilson); Harry Cheshire (Mr. Cornwall).

resembles—in terms of scope and conception, as well as running time and medium star-level of the cast—the kind of experimental teleplays which shows like *Playhouse 90* were regularly featuring in the early days of live television. Still, the film medium—however limited in budget—allowed for a more realistic depiction of the neighborhood than would have been possible on "golden age" television, where settings had to be suggested rather than actualized.

Much of the conviction came from the acting: James Whitmore appeared as a kind of B-budget Spencer Tracy, neatly representing the average guy confronting the Almighty; Nancy Davis likewise assumed an effective low-key approach in playing Joe's dutiful wife, which helped make the bizarre premise seem somewhat believable. But was the movie's message conservative or liberal? That's hard to say: *The Next Voice You Hear . . .* is one of those difficult films that clearly want to disturb an audience (and, in its time, definitely did just that), though precisely toward what end is hard to say. In an age as irreverent as our own, it's remarkable to realize the controversy this offbeat but nonetheless intentionally respectful film caused. Certainly, this is one for the time capsule: a film designed to either anger or appease the moviegoing audience of its time, and which clearly could have been made in no other era but the paranoid fifties.

Laraine Day and Robert Ryan as the harried couple.

During the late forties, RKO Pictures enjoyed considerable success with their *film noirs*, including *Crossfire* and *Out of the Past*, powerful if tawdry tales set in dingy places, perfectly capturing the morally gray, emotionally confusing postwar world. In the early fifties, that successful formula was updated slightly and shifted to a more political point-of-view. The femmes fatales who lured lone wolves down dark streets to their doom were still present; now, "evil" was not organized crime but the Communist Party.

An example of suspense melodrama fashioned specifically for the McCarthy era, *The Woman on Pier 13* seems extraordinarily dated today. Despite the professional filmmaking, excellent cast, and the sustained mood of mystery that pervades the story, it's difficult for

Brad considers packing a gun.

viewers who did not experience the early fifties first-hand to conceive that such blatant propaganda was ever possible within the confines of commercial entertainment. Perhaps, though, that's why this film ought to be seen. We may choose to remember the fifties as the "Happy Days" of Fonzie, but in reality it was an era of rampant suspicion. Movies such as this reflected the pervasive paranoid mentality while adding further fuel to the fire. Originally titled *I Married a Communist*, it presented its heroine Nan as an average young lady, who has married a successful, attractive executive, Brad, the vice president of a San Francisco shipping company. Their life together is almost ideal, as Brad appears to be the American Dream incarnate: he was not born into such a prestige position, but worked his way up from the docks, where he began as a humble longshoreman.

But the past comes back to haunt them in the form of Christine, a dangerous beauty from Brad's youth. Shortly, we realize they were more than mere lovers; preying upon Brad's naivete, Christine operated as a red Black Widow, luring Brad not only into her bed but into the Communist Party—The Red Menace!—as well. Brad has since come to see the error of his ways, as his sincere, effective striving to climb the corporate ladder makes clear. He came to see that the American way—the democratic ideal of giving every man a chance to struggle to the top—is far preferable than the Russian way—the socialist ideal of keeping the working class happy in their prescribed lot in life. Now, though, the communist boss Vanning wants to infiltrate labor and

stir the men up to strikes. He dispatches Christine to use Brad's secret past—and the threat of a revelation of his half-forgotten youth—in order to win Brad over to their side.

The movie operated on a reactionary level by convincing viewers that labor disputes were the machinations of the Communist Party; viewers of the film were thus less

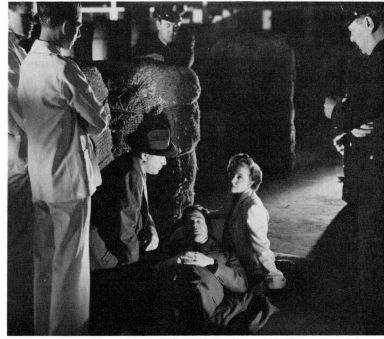

At least he dies happy! Brad is lovingly stroked by his faithful wife, who thought that he'd been slipping out to see another woman.

29

inclined in the future to feel any sympathy for striking workers, having been "educated" by the movie that these were only pawns being manipulated by the Reds. By employing Nan as the focal character, the film was able to effectively present a generalized, representative female lead with whom most women in the audience could identify. The film's tearjerker effectiveness grows directly from this clever ploy, as each female moviegoer looked askance at her own husband as they exited the theater, wondering if he might harbor a similar secret.

For the men, the film threw in some heroic gunplay, as in the final confrontation when Brad redeems himself for "past sins" by shooting it out with the commies, dying a hero. Today, it's almost impossible to view the film without laughing—not at the craftsmanship of moviemaking (which proves most sturdy), but at the widespread fears and frustrations this film embodied. (Its TV equivalent, *I Led Three Lives*, was a weekly counterpart.) If those few who do get to see the movie at first guffaw at the many absurdities, they may finish in a cold sweat of understanding: in the seemingly pleasant fifties, this is the kind of paranoid thinking to which we were susceptible.

Seven Days to Noon

A London Film (1950)

CREDITS:

Produced by Roy Boulting; directed by John Boulting; screenplay by Frank Harvey and Roy Boulting, from an original story by Paul Deher and James Brand; running time: 93 minutes.

CAST:

Barry Jones (Professor Willingdon); Olive Sloane (Goldie); Andre Morell (Superintendent Folland); Sheila Manahan (Ann Willingdon); Hugh Cross (Stephen Lane); Joan Hickson (Mrs. Peckett); Ronald Adam (The Prime Minister).

In 1963, Stanley Kubrick subtitled his doomsday thriller, *Dr. Strangelove*, "How I Learned to Stop Worrying and Love the Bomb." Audiences snickered knowingly; throughout the 1950s, we had worried constantly about the possibility of nuclear holocaust. Rather than take our mind off such troubles, movies regularly distilled them for us, as films ranging in style from *On The Beach* to *The Beast from 20,000 Fathoms* employed the

nightmare possibilities of our atomic age as their starting points. But none did so with quite the impressiveness of this grim British import which won a deserved Oscar for its writers.

The question posed by the film was this: What would happen amid the hubbub of London if a scientist, one who'd been working on the development of England's own atomic bomb, suddenly went over the edge, threatening to use one to blow up the entire city unless his demand—the banning of all atomic weaponry—be met immediately? When that proves quite impossible, a crack team of police and special investigators attempts to track down the illusive Professor Willingdon, to learn the whereabouts of the explosive before it sends the city up in a mushroom cloud.

The audience watching the movie experienced terror on the most complex level imaginable. Certainly, they could associate with the people of the city, menaced by the sudden announcement they might all be obliterated at any moment; but still, they could not help finding this film's diminutive anti-hero a most sympathetic soul, for he went through with his self-proclaimed mission not out of self-interest but owing to a desperate belief that only such an extreme occurrence could wake the world up to the implications of the atomic age—and, hopefully, stir them to do something to end the madness.

If we cannot agree with what Professor Willingdon does, we can certainly appreciate what he is trying to say. So there is a double reaction to the film's suspense: we alternately root for the authorities as they close in on the little man, and for the little man as he again and again escapes them. The film itself divides its time

30   Barry Jones as Professor Willingdon.

In a typical British pub, Willingdon must listen as ordinary British men and woman spout all sorts of misinformation about the current state of affairs of our atomic world.

The total evacuation of London.

almost equally between images of those authorities (from the Prime Minister to the lowliest official) attempting to prevent the explosion, the ordinary people on the streets and in the pubs as they try and adjust to what is about to happen, and Willingdon himself, as he willfully darts around the city's side streets, an enemy of the people who ironically has only the greater good of mankind foremost in his mind.

The film initially moves at a deliberate pace, as one calm Monday morning a note is dropped through a slot on the Prime Minister's door. Once its contents are made clear, there is the quiet investigation to determine whether this is merely a crank's joke. But things gradu-

The sad, lonely little man who plans to blow up the entire city for totally altruistic reasons.

The government goes about tracking him down.

Mr. 880

A 20th Century-Fox Film (1950)

CREDITS:

Produced by Julian Blaustein; directed by Edmund Goulding; screenplay by Robert Riskin, based on articles in *The New Yorker* by St. Clair McKelway; running time: 90 minutes.

CAST:

Burt Lancaster (*Steve Buchanan*); Dorothy McGuire (*Ann Winslow*); Edmund Gwenn (*Skipper Miller*); Millard Mitchell (*Mac*); Minor Watson (*Judge O'Neill*); Howard St. John (*Chief*); Hugh Sanders (*Thad Mitchell*); James Millican (*Olie Johnson*); Howard Chamberlin (*Duff*); Larry Keating (*Lee*); Kathleen Hughes (*Secretary*).

Edmund Goulding is usually written off as an undistinguished director who unaccountably made a handful of highly distinguished films; the classy soap opera *Grand Hotel*, the wartime aviation melodrama *Dawn Patrol*, a pair of terrific tearjerkers (*Dark Victory* and *The Old Maid*), a literary adaptation of *The Razor's Edge* and the cult classic *Nightmare Alley* are all well remembered movies from a director long since forgotten. But in the fifties, even as Goulding's career wound down, he turned out one spritely and brittle comedy suggesting that, given the opportunity, this filmmaker might have emerged as a comic auteur in the tradition of Frank Capra and Preston Sturges. *Mister 880*, though seldom revived, combines charm and satire in an impressively understated manner.

Based on a true story, this tells the tale of Secret Service File # 880, a noted case in which an elderly New Yorker cranked out, over a ten-year period, precisely the amount of counterfeit one dollar bills he needed to maintain his humble existence. He did not do this out of greed (or else he would have opted for considerably higher denominations) but because he could not find other work, and wanted to support himself without being a burden on others. So in the movie, on his beloved printing press, which he affectionately refers to as his "Cousin Henry," Skipper Miller knocks out the singles, then "shoves" them on an unsuspecting public. Mac, a tough old federal agent, has for a decade tried to discover where these counterfeit singles come from. To impress his boss, a diligent young Treasury Man, Steve Buchanan, manages (with the aid of Ann Winslow, a translator at the United Nations who becomes involved in the search) to track down this elusive fellow. After catching him, though, Steve is reluctant to turn the man over to

ally accelerate as the reality of the situation becomes clear, until finally the film moves at a fevered pace as it enters into the ever more tense, frantic search for the professor and his weapon during the final minutes of the seventh day.

Barry Jones is superbly nondescript as the little man with the big troubles, the big responsibility, the big bomb. The Boulting Brothers—who would eventually be associated with a string of silly, saucy comedies—here employed the distinctive fifties style, docudrama (or "dramatized documentary," as it was more correctly called in England) to lend a newsreel-style authority to this representation of an actual event that had not yet occurred. This is most obvious in the sequence depicting the total evacuation of London, as the plans and then the process of the mass exodus are portrayed with what most critics referred to as a journalistic approach. Afterwards, the vision of crack military units patrolling the deserted streets offered images resembling a Kafka nightmare turned into reality.

Early on, Willingdon sits in a pub as a drunk loudly insists a bomb ought to be dropped on the Russians before they can drop one on us. "I believe," the sad, strange, sensitive Willingdon mutters, "that man ought to be made to think about the things he says." That's precisely what he will accomplish; it's also what the movie managed to do.

Ann Winslow (Dorothy McGuire) and Steve Buchanan (Burt Lancaster) find romance while apprehending the world's most charming counterfeiter, Skipper Miller (Edmund Gwenn).

the government for punishment, since he's quite taken with this gentle, self-effacing, harmless old gent, and cannot see what end jailing him will serve.

Like most fine comedies, then, *Mister 880* confounds all our preconceptions about morality, allowing us to share the point of view of a normal hero who finds everything he believes challenged by a situation unique enough to be beyond his frame of reference. Essential to the success was the casting of Edmund Gwenn, recently the winner of a Best Supporting Oscar for playing Santa Claus in the seasonal favorite *Miracle on 34th St.* Gwenn brought something of his Kris Kringle characterization with him to the role of this lovable codger who likewise is an aged iconoclast. Skipper, in his self-defined existence, forces those who come in contact with him to question their own conventionality.

The screen identity of Burt Lancaster had not, at this time, been clearly established. Having played a Humphrey Bogart type hero in *Desert Fury*, Lancaster here tried on the guise of a light comedy leading man and did nicely by the part, though with later films like *The Crimson Pirate* and *From Here to Eternity* he would establish the more robust popular image audiences would come to associate with him. A word ought to be said for Dorothy McGuire, too, whose terrific screen presence is too rarely recalled. In the fifties, Miss McGuire excelled at playing bright, snappy, pseudo-sophisticated career women who find themselves in complicated situations which force them to seriously reconsider their lifestyles. These are the kinds of roles Barbara

Steve is badly beaten during a "sting."

Stanwyck and Rosalind Russell played in the forties. To say that the sweet-faced but extremely saucy Miss McGuire played not only in their league but equalled them in class is to pay her the highest (and long overdue) compliment.

Much of this film's warm, whimsical and utterly winning sensibility can be credited to screenwriter Robert Riskin, who had penned *Mr. Deeds Goes to Town* for

33

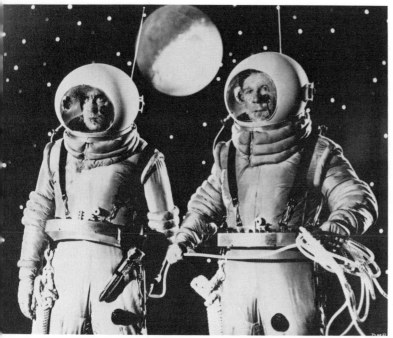

Barnes (John Archer) and Cargraves (Warner Anderson) explore the surface of the moon.

Capra and here created a similar combination of sentiment and cynicism. The dialogue is snappy, the situations poignant. But even the finest script cannot click without the presence of a director who implicitly understands how to pace the proceedings. Though he never worked in this genre before or after, with *Mister 880* Goulding proved his touch was nothing less than golden.

Destination: Moon

An Eagle-Lion Release (1950)

CREDITS:

Produced by George Pal; directed by Irving Pichel; screenplay by Rip Van Ronkel, Robert Heinlein, and James O'Hanlon, from the novel by Robert Heinlein; running time: 91 minutes.

On the moon's surface, the astronauts set up a base of operations.

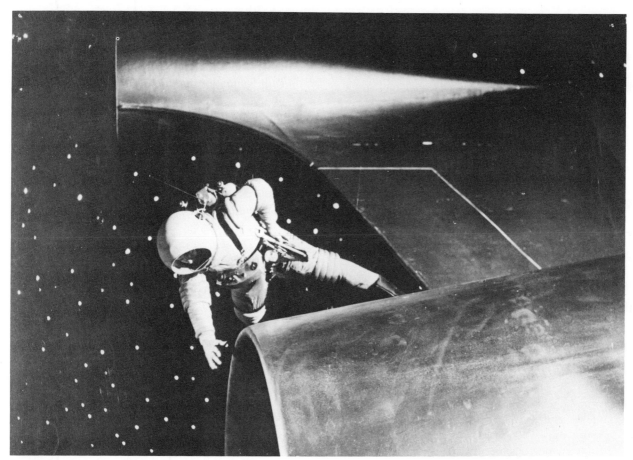

Refueling in space.

CAST:

John Archer *(Barnes)*; Warner Anderson *(Cargraves)*; Tom Powers *(General Thayer)*; Dick Wesson *(Sweeney)*; Erin O'Brien Moore *(Mrs. Cargraves)*.

The race for space began in the early fifties; when the Russians eventually managed to put their Sputnik into the sky before the U.S. had such a missile ready, the competition accelerated. In time, we would win, though the first manned trip to the moon would not be accomplished until 1969, at which point the public would have the opportunity to decide whether two decades of work and untold millions of dollars had been invested for a possible future of economic exploration of space or merely for ego-gratification, of knowing that America had successfully achieved an impractical goal before anyone else. Be that as it may, the fifties was the period when space travel, as portrayed on film, understandably shed its more fantastic aspects; the Buck Rogers/Flash Gordon vision of winged warriors, bug-eyed monsters, and scantily clad space princesses remained with us,

though now it had to share the sci-fi stage with more serious projections of what the universe might actually hold in store.

That was clearly the intention of George Pal, whose *Destination Moon* related, with near documentary technique, a vision of what the first manned trip to the moon might well be like. While certain aspects of the flight—the ship itself, the uniforms worn, the procedures for launching—turned out not to be precisely what reality held in store, the film remains impressive for its unromanticized (and, in many ways, on-target) notions of the inevitable trip. Understandably, the special effects would at year's end win the film a much-deserved Oscar in that category. More important still, *Destination Moon* established not only a key substance of fifties films, but also a characteristic style. While we became obsessed with space travel, we also drifted toward movies with a dramatized documentary approach to their subjects, however fanciful.

Pal and his team researched the project carefully before moving ahead with production. This is evident in the wealth of scientific information presented both visu-

35

Hugh O'Brien, Osa Massen, and Lloyd Bridges provided the conventional romantic-triangle for what was otherwise a most unconventional work of science-fiction.

Dick Wesson played the kind of snappy talking comic relief character he became famous for, and certainly his wise-guy delivery was anything but "realistic" for an astronaut. But the repair work on the damaged ship, the difficult landing on the moon's surface, and the exploration of its craters and crevices were performed without benefit of little green men or any other fanciful intrusions. Even the televised broadcast from the moon to the earth seems a fitting forerunner of what reality would hold in store. Previous pictures dealing with a trip into space had provided frivolous entertainment; *Destination Moon* opted instead for educating its audience as to the possible and probable event we collectively anticipated.

Rocketship X-M

A Lippert Picture (1950)

CREDITS:

Produced, directed, and written by Kurt Neumann; running time: 77 minutes.

CAST:

Lloyd Bridges *(Floyd Oldham)*; Osa Massen *(Lisa Van Horn)*; John Emery *(Karl Eckstrom)*; Noah Beery Jr. *(William Corrigan)*; Hugh O'Brien *(Harry Chamberlin)*; Morris Ankrum *(Dr. Fleming)*.

ally (in the relatively realistic depiction of the astronauts' hardware and software) and in the dialogue heard as scientists discuss the upcoming launch during the slow (at times ponderous) opening half hour. At times, the movie inadvertently reveals its fifties paranoia: without naming the name of any other nation, one scientist does make clear the then-immediate justifications for the space program by insisting the first country to land on the moon will be able to set up a base for launching nuclear missiles at its foes. At the time, more than one critic cynically noted the film casually revealed this "well-kept military secret" to the mass audience viewing it.

There were obligatory stabs at suspense, as when a sheriff attempts to legally halt the launching and the four-man team just barely manages to get off the ground before the program is shut down. Mostly, though, writer Heinlein (who would become one of the nation's leading sci-fi writers with his classic *Stranger in a Strange Land*) kept the "drama" as low-key as possible and the "document" as close to the eventual actuality as could be projected at that time. Perhaps the film seems less impressive today for an audience that has literally seen real-life astronauts dealing with the non-gravitational life inside a space craft and the realities of "free orbit" movement; but for viewers whose only conception of space travel had been Buster Crabbe in a cape surrounded by pretty blondes in brief outfits, *Destination Moon* proved an eye-opener and mindblower.

Throughout the seventies, the rumor circulated that *Rocket Ship X-M* was about to be remade by a major Hollywood studio, this time with an immense budget. For in the seventies, the generation that had been teenagers in the fifties, addicted to low-budget science-fiction flicks, were now affluent adults who enjoyed seeing the fantasies of their youth remounted by filmmakers who had likewise cut their teeth on such fare. How else

36   Realizing they have landed on Mars by mistake, the crew study the planet's surface.

explain the success of the lavish stage and screen versions of *Little Shop of Horrors?* Then again, considering the disappointment that the remakes of *The Thing, Invaders of the Body Snatchers, Invaders From Mars* and TV's *Twilight Zone* engendered, perhaps it's best *Rocket Ship* never did receive its lavish redo. Perhaps the warmly (if dimly) remembered sci-fi films of our collective experience owed much of their appeal to their humble origins. *Rocket Ship* was indeed released in a home video version containing newly shot footage, though the additional material seems unnecessary: the original nicely stands on its own.

The film opens in much the same manner as George Pal's *Destination Moon*, with a team of astronauts, at some unspecified but none too distant point in the future, ready to leave on a scientific journey. But this film quickly abandons any documentary approach, and for good reason: Kurt Neumann's virtual one-man production quickly drops the detailed, realistic, low-key approach, turning first into melodrama, then message movie. Though Neumann's initial approach is to provide yet another version of the space launch story, he redirects his theme (along with his spacecraft) toward a cautionary fable about nuclear proliferation.

As in Pal's picture, there is some obligatory comic relief: Noah Beery as Corrigan, the silly Texan with an extreme drawl and a joking attitude toward everything. But Neumann adds the key soap opera element Pal's docudrama resisted: the pretty female scientist, a fuel expert who also fuels the attentions of the ship's men, creating some interesting sexual chemistry. Even though the film opens with the space program's spokesman, Dr. Fleming, dutifully informing the press about the first trip to the moon, the ship nonetheless gets blown off course, landing on Mars by mistake. Today, that stands out as a whopper, as hard to swallow as if in a western a cowboy headed for the shootout at the O. K. Corral but somehow ended up at Custer's Last Stand.

Yet audiences of the time didn't mind, because the film then created a mounting sense of suspense as the astronauts explored the hostile surface of the planet, gradually realizing that a civilization had once existed on Mars but was now gone. All the while, the viewer notices moving shadows, as creatures silently surround our intrepid band. In a terrifying moment, still able to scare an audience today, the astronauts realize a tribe of Neanderthal-like creatures, the surviving members of the once advanced Martian race, are upon them. By then, they have discovered what it is that destroyed civilization on Mars: an all-out atomic war.

The surviving astronauts barely manage to blast off for earth, knowing they are short on fuel; while they have enough to enter the earth's atmosphere, there isn't enough left to pull off a proper landing, meaning they will be sucked in by the gravitational force and crash. Desperately, they try and radio back the horrible truth they have learned: if mankind doesn't quickly control the escalating weapons of destruction, it will inevitably find itself in the same position as the Martians. They are us, or what we will be if we don't learn from their mistake.

In the film's unforgettable climax, the lovers (Lloyd Bridges and Osa Massen) decide not to wake their wounded comrade (Hugh O'Brien) but let him sleep through the crash. As they kiss, we see the approaching earth over their shoulders and through the ship's window. The film concludes as it began, with Dr. Fleming, insisting that, despite the terrible loss of the entire crew, the mission cannot be considered a failure, owing to the remarkable information he received via radio just before the crash. Dr. Fleming is looking directly out at the audience, making clear that he stands in for filmmaker Neumann, directly addressing the audience of the fifties.

Silvana Mangano as Silvana.

Bitter Rice

A Lux Film (1950)

CREDITS:

Produced by Dino de Laurentiis; directed by Giuseppe De Santis; screenplay by Signor De Santis, Carlo Lizzani, and Gianni Puccini, from a story by Signors De Santis and Lizzani; running time: 107 minutes.

Where does neorealism end and sexploitation begin?

CAST:

Silvana Mangano *(Silvana)*; Doris Dowling *(Francesca)*; Vittorio Gassmann *(Walter)*; Raf Vallone *(Marco)*; Checco Rissono *(Aristide)*; Nico Pepe *(Beppe)*; Adriana Sivieri *(Celeste)*; Lia Corelli *(Amelia)*; Maria Grazia Francia *(Gabriella)*; Dedi Ristori *(Anna)*; Anna Maestri *(Irene)*; Mariemma Bardi *(Gianna)*.

The arthouse circuit came into being during the aftermath of World War II, when we had experienced too much of the world's darker side (the concentration camps, Hiroshima following the atomic bombing) to retreat into reassuring tinseltown formulas. Initially, the new art films were mostly neorealist items from Italy—*Open City, Paisan, The Bicycle Thief*—portraying life in all its raw and random ugliness. But by the early 1950s, "arthouse" had come to mean something quite different. Some imports, made without the Production Code restrictions, featured casual nudity for the sake of realism; when these proved box-office successes with a voyeuristic portion of the public, distributors began booking any foreign picture with a nude scene (regardless of quality) into the arthouses. If in the late forties the arthouse was a place to experience films of quality and integrity, by the mid-fifties it had degenerated into a derogatory term for theaters that purveyed titillation, defending such explicitness under the auspices of "art."

The single movie that provided the transitional bridge between the two meanings of the term was *Bitter Rice.* This was a strange amalgam of sexploitation and serious social commentary, blending an authentic, earnest portrait of poor people in their misery with heavy doses of unabashed, ultra-earthy eroticism. Like so many of the

With the exception of Miss Mangano and America's Doris Dowling *(left),* all the girls were actual rice field workers.

Silvana readies herself for work.

An argument in the rice fields explodes into open rebellion.

other quasi-Marxist tracts coming out of a depressed and devastated Italy, *Bitter Rice* finds a poignant heroism in the suffering of simple working people attempting to survive a failed social system that cannot provide for basic needs. In particular, it tells the story of one indomitable but carnally inclined woman, Silvana, who like her peasant sisters seeks out a humble existence as a migrant worker in the Po Valley rice fields. Turgid is the term that comes to mind when describing the endless incidents piled upon one another, as the filmmakers portray a wide range of women and their reactions to the system that exploits their potential for the sake of the rich few.

A melodramatic romantic storyline manages to convey co-author/director Giuseppe De Santis' politics: Silvana, aware her loyalty should be toward her fellow workers, nonetheless befriends a scab (Doris Dowling, an American actress cast as an Italian in hopes of making the movie more marketable Stateside) among their company. She then allows her passion for the scab's brother (Vittorio Gassman) to destroy her true love for a working class boyfriend (Raf Vallone), leading directly to Silvana's doom. The sado-masochistic quality of the seduction scene—in which Silvana is both attracted to and repulsed by a man who's part of the system which has stripped away her dignity—is powerful, though always edging toward pornography. The depiction of Silvana's surroundings (filmed completely on location, with actual migrant workers playing the supporting characters) captures the tawdry lifestyle of such degraded women with an unsparing camera's eye, yet the positioning of that camera to always emphasize the lovely legs and ample bustline of the leading lady can only be described as exploitative. In particular, the shot of Mangano emerging from the rice fields—defiant but vulnerable, somehow looking quite chic in her cheap clothes—must be credited with making the film a sensation, and establishing Miss Mangano as an overnight star.

Strangely, sadly, and surprisingly, it was a star that would swiftly dim. Mangano may have been the first of the earthy Italian beauties to be seen on these shores, but by mid-decade, she was overshadowed by Sophia Loren and Gina Lollobrigida. Though Miss Mangano married her famous producer, Dino de Laurentiis, he was never able to do for her career what Carlo Ponti managed for Loren. Shortly, Mangano was appearing in such second-rate items as *Mambo* (1954), though she did have a field day as both the faithful Penelope and the seductress Circe in *Ulysses* (1954), opposite Kirk Douglas.

Teresa

A Metro-Goldwyn-Mayer Release (1951)

CREDITS:

Produced by Arthur M. Loew; directed by Fred Zinnemann; screenplay by Stewart Stern, from an original story by Mr. Stern and Alfred Hayes; running time: 102 minutes.

CAST:

Pier Angeli *(Teresa)*; John Ericson *(Philip)*; Patricia Collinge *(Philip's Mother)*; Richard Bishop *(Philip's Father)*; Peggy Ann Garner *(Susan)*; Ralph Meeker *(Dobbs)*; Bill Mauldin *(Grissom)*; Ave Ninchi *(Teresa's Mother)*; Edward Binns *(Brown)*; Rod Steiger *(Frank)*; Aldo Silvani *(Prof. Crocce)*; Tommy Lewis *(Walter)*.

The most significant trend of the late 1940s and early fifties was the importing of foreign films into this country on a far greater scale than ever before; most in demand were the neorealist classics from Italy. American moviemakers, influenced by what they saw in arthouses, set out to create similarly realistic films on our own shores: stark pictures about social injustice, like *On The Waterfront* and *The Defiant Ones*, were the result. But with *Teresa*, director Fred Zinnemann went a step further, creating a fascinating hybrid of Italian and American cinema: a realistic movie shot entirely on location, half in Italy, half on New York's East Side.

The story is simple and unsentimental, with a journalistic look that was the hallmark of so many fine films of this era, when fewer of our pictures were shot within the confines of the studios, as more directors insisted on going out into the real world. *Teresa* is about a young Italian woman who falls in love with an American GI,

Pier Angeli as Teresa.

then follows him home to New York, a place considered a dreamworld by the starving multitudes in Italy. For Teresa, though, America will be less a dream come true than a nightmare realized.

For she is subjected to extreme psychological torture (however unconscious) from her mother-in-law, with whom she must share a sparse tenement apartment not much better than the one where she lived with her own mother. If the style of *Teresa* is the documentary realism that pervaded in the early fifties, then the substance of the film is the in-depth psychological approach to confused, believable characters which likewise characterized the period. Both the young leads, Teresa and Philip, are, we learn, arrested adolescents because of the sharp influence of strong mothers and weak fathers. The story follows their awkward attempts to move beyond the mother-love that's left them emotional cripples, to find themselves as individuals and as a couple.

Like Silvana Mangano, Pier Angeli was one of the lovely and talented Italian actresses who arrived on these shores before Sophia and Gina, but were unable to parlay early arrival into lasting stardom. At least Silvana enjoyed a prosperous life as the wife of producer De Laurentiis; Angeli played leads in several major films (opposite Paul Newman in both the cardboard costume film *The Silver Chalice* and the gritty biopic *Somebody Up There Likes Me*), briefly dated James Dean and

This shot of the peasants in Teresa's village reveals how completely Zinnemann, like other significant directors of his time, was influenced by the neorealist films.

A troubled marriage: shadows and textures merge to suggest the complex gray shadings of the relationship itself.

41

(reportedly) threw him over for singer Vic Damone. She then committed suicide when she came to believe both her career and private lives were in an irreparable shambles. John Ericson received favorable reviews for this performance, and was compared to Brando for creating a method-acting image of a "disturbed, inarticulate" Beat Generation youth in search of himself. But he was unaccountably unable to follow up on his only major success, eventually ending up in B pictures like *Pretty Boy Floyd*, and playing second-lead to Anne Francis in her female private eye TV series, *Honey West*.

Some of the supporting actors were of great interest too: Ralph Meeker, as Philip's sergeant, would prove the screen's best Mike Hammer ever in Robert Altman's vitriolically violent *Kiss Me Deadly*, then enjoy a long career as a first-rate character actor. Bill Mauldin, wartime cartoonist-correspondent, who would shortly switch his focus to politics, was Philip's pal, and played a similar role as Audie Murphy's sidekick in the Civil War drama *The Red Badge of Courage*. Rod Steiger, who played the psychiatrist (a profession that would take center stage in movies of the fifties) here made his film debut in a small but noteworthy part. Director Zinnemann had worked on uninspired projects throughout the forties, but found his metier in the postwar realism: *The Search, Act of Violence, The Men, High Noon, Member of the Wedding, From Here to Eternity, A Hatful of Rain,* and *The Nun's Story* compose the finest body of work any one filmmaker turned out during the decade. Though his career went into decline early in the sixties, he deserves recognition as the most characteristic director of the fifties.

Death of a Salesman

A Columbia Picture (1951)

CREDITS:

Produced by Stanley Kramer; directed by Laslo Benedek; screenplay by Stanley Roberts, adapted from the stage play by Arthur Miller; running time: 115 minutes.

CAST:

Fredric March *(Willy Loman)*; Mildred Dunnock *(Linda Loman)*; Kevin McCarthy *(Biff)*; Cameron Mitchell *(Hap)*; Howard Smith *(Charley)*; Royal Beal *(Ben)*; Don Keefer *(Bernard)*; Jesse White *(Stanley)*; Claire Carlton *(Miss Francis)*; David Alpert *(Howard Wagner)*; Elizabeth Frazer *(Miss Forsythe)*; Patricia Walker *(Letta)*.

The great American play of the postwar era (some would say *the* great American play!) was brought to the screen with surprising success by Stanley Kramer's company, an outfit more noted for its high-minded liberal ideals and serious social intentions than any inherent understanding of the unique qualities of cinematic storytelling. Yet with this impressive adaptation, they did themselves proud, despite the apparent pitfalls of turning a stage vehicle into a movie script. Working in their favor was the fact that Miller's drama was already cinematic in conception, employing flashbacks through dissolves in a manner difficult to pull off in the live theatre, but which readily lent themselves to a movie version. In many

Fredric March as Willy Loman.

him on toward a confrontation with his own sense of failure. The key tragic theme—that knowledge has the capacity to save or destroy a man—is effectively reset in a working class household. Director Laslo Benedek effectively played the stylized drama on realistic sets to anchor Miller's semi-surreal conception in the everyday.

Amazingly, Benedek enjoyed only one other great success—*The Wild One*, with Marlon Brando—before

Willy recalls that high-point of years gone by when Biff (Kevin McCarthy) was a budding football star; the bookish Bernard (Don Keefer) and the wisecracking Hap (Cameron Mitchell) look on in awe.

respects, *Death of a Salesman* is a play that longs to be a movie, which helps explain why it made for such a superlative film.

Retained is the notion of a Greek tragedy given a modern American interpretation: the unities of time are obeyed as, in a 24-hour period, Willy Loman—the man who has lived by the American Dream all his life without ever being blessed by its promised rewards—finds himself dragged down by a combination of the machinations of fate and his own inner flaws. The past—his own mistakes, especially a sexual indiscretion with a long forgotten slut that cost him the love and respect of his favored son Biff—comes back to haunt Willy relentlessly, driving

In better days, Willy referees a mock fight between Biff and Uncle Ben (Royal Beal), while Willy's dutiful wife Linda (Mildred Dunnock) looks on.

43

drifting into mediocre work (*Bengal Brigade, Affair in Havana*), then dropping out of film directing altogether. Such an abrupt end seemed strange indeed for the man who had so effectively guided a masterpiece to the screen. Like him, his film has been criminally overlooked. Perhaps that's due, in part, to the casting of Fredric March as Loman. Columbia felt that March, despite his years, was still a box-office draw, whereas Lee J. Cobb, who mesmerized audiences as Broadway's Willy Loman, had never emerged as anything more than a character actor in films, and was passed over for the part so closely associated with him. There was, understandably, much bitterness resulting from that decision.

In retrospect, though, the decision was clearly right. Cobb's larger than life quality, which could fill a theatre with electric excitement, never translated particularly well to the film medium, where he seemed bombastic and overwrought. March, on the other hand, was the film actor *par excellence*: subtle and understated. Besides, he came physically much closer to the Willy Loman that Arthur Miller first envisioned (Dustin Hoffman's acclaimed 1980s revival of the play wisely chose to emulate the March depiction of Loman as a slight man).

Losing control, Willy assumes a fighting stance on a subway as confused riders stare on.

Neatly blending reality and dream: Willy recalls his sordid hotel tryst with a hooker (Patricia Walker) even though he's actually in the living room with wife Linda only a few feet away.

Mildred Dunnock, one of those rare performers who seemed equally comfortable on stage and in film, did have the opportunity to repeat her role as the long suffering wife who insists, at the end, that "attention must be paid"; Dunnock effortlessly brought her gestures down to the milder range required for the larger than life movie image. Cameron Mitchell also repeated his comical role as the kid brother Hap, while Kevin McCarthy sat in for his look-alike Arthur Kennedy, who had played Biff on Broadway.

Ultimately, though, this is Willy's drama, and March won a much-deserved Oscar nomination for the part. Willy is Miller's non-condescending portrait of the little man in all his pain, the fellow who subscribes to the American ideal of rugged individualism without ever realizing—at least not until too late—that he may not prove fit enough to survive in the social Darwinistic jungle. There are those who achieve success through hard work, but Willy's diligent years of striving earn him nothing, and that's the tragic side of the American Dream, ably illustrated in Miller's play and this formidable film version.

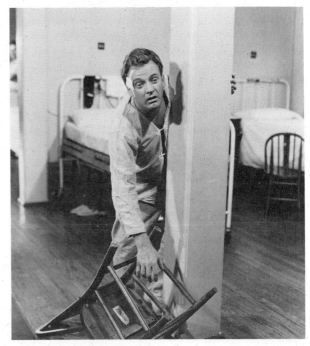

Arthur Kennedy as Larry Nevins.

Bright Victory

A Universal-International Presentation (1951)

CREDITS:

Produced by Robert Buckner; directed by Mark Robson; screenplay by Mr. Buckner, from the novel by Baynard Kendrick; running time: 97 minutes.

CAST:

Arthur Kennedy (Larry Nevins); Peggy Dow (Judy Greene); Julia Adams (Chris Paterson); James Edwards (Joe Morgan); Will Geer (Mr. Nevins); Nana Bryant (Mrs. Nevins); Jim Backus (Bill Grayson); Minor Watson (Mr. Peterson); Joan Banks (Janet Grayson); Richard Egan (Sgt. Masterson).

When Larry is out on a date with his old flame Chris (Julia Adams), he becomes enraged as everyone tries too hard to help.

Another of the fine social problem pictures of the fifties, realistically portraying life in the postwar era through low-key acting and understated direction, *Bright Victory* offered an unsentimentalized depiction of attempts by returning GIs to readjust following particularly difficult homecomings. Arthur Kennedy—best known in movies as an acerbic supporting actor who has graced countless pictures, including the classics *Elmer Gantry* and *Lawrence of Arabia*—has been best at playing journalistic observers. Ironically, in his only Hollywood lead, Kennedy played a man who could not see.

In a sparse, no-nonsense style, the film related the story of Larry Nevins, who is at first engulfed with anger, frustration, and despair over the blindness that is his war legacy. In time, he manages, with the love of a fine woman, Judy Greene, to overcome self-destructive emotions, accepting himself for what he is by acknowledging that he can live a productive life, if far different from what he previously imagined. Larry's courage during the fight to reform his identity, his learning how to deal with the defeats he experiences during his long and difficult passage to a new lifestyle, his final triumph as he finally redefines himself and his goals . . . all this effectively establishes an emotional pitch many films strive for but few achieve. This is, in the end, absolutely inspirational.

Director Mark Robson achieves what he does mainly by sidestepping the histrionic approach which might have aimed too obviously at the audience's heartstrings. By not playing up the hassles Larry has to face, but rather maintaining a decidedly frank and at times almost matter-of-fact approach to the proceedings, Robson managed to win a more honest and nonmanipulative audience response. It's almost impossible to finish this film with dry eyes, yet the viewer never feels "had," because we do believe that any tears we shed have been honestly won.

The screenplay, based on the novel *Lights Out*, did rely a bit heavily on a routine ploy: the man torn between two women, the girl he meets after his accident and who has never known Larry in any other form, and Chris, the woman he left behind, who waits for him at home but who will always be torn between her acceptance of

Larry as he is and her recollections of the way he used to be. Other than that one conventional line, the film is an exemplar of those postwar pictures which left the confines of the studio behind, instead venturing out into the real world for a sense of documentary realism. The movie is half drama, half document; though the key players in the romantic triangle are fictionalized characters enacted by professional actors, those glimpsed in the background are all real inmates and doctors at General Hospital in Valley Forge, Pennsylvania, where the film was shot. Balancing dramatic entertainment with educational documentary, the filmmakers insist Larry's unique story share screen time with newsreel style footage revealing the up-to-the-minute techniques used in the treatment of the afflicted, as well as the training programs through which instructors attempt to rehabilitate their charges.

The key fifties theme of civil rights is effectively added, as the blind hero gradually comes to understand that a new friend, Joe, is a black; there's a poignant moment in which Larry realizes his blindness actually frees him of petty bigotries other people are susceptible to. Joe is played by James Edwards, the all-but-forgotten actor who, in Stanley Kramer's *Home of the Brave* (1949), preceded Sidney Poitier as the first Negro to achieve leading-man status in the postwar period. If Peggy Dow and Julia Adams are a bit too predictable in their performances, that's because their roles are more functional than three-dimensional; they exist mainly to facilitate our understanding of Larry's problem and his eventual growth. Arthur Kennedy's performance, so convincing in its presentation of a blind man's manner that many viewers assumed he was indeed blind, won him an Academy Award nomination, though an overdue Oscar went that year to Humphrey Bogart for *The African Queen*. But however briefly, a top character actor shined brightly as a star.

The breakthrough: Larry opts for a new life with Judy.

Ace in the Hole

A Paramount Picture (1951)

CREDITS:

Produced by Billy Wilder; directed by Mr. Wilder; screenplay by Wilder and Lesser Samuels and Walter Newman; running time: 112

CAST:

Kirk Douglas *(Charles Tatum)*; Jan Sterling *(Lorraine)*; Bob Arthur *(Herbie)*; Porter Hall *(Boot)*; Frank Cady *(Federber)*; Richard

Kirk Douglas as Charlie Tatum.

Billy Wilder's *The Apartment* is one of the small handful of comic films to win an Academy Award as Best Picture, which explains why film historians have tended to tag him as a comic auteur. With such definitive Marilyn Monroe vehicles as *The Seven Year Itch* and *Some Like It Hot*, the writer-director defined his decade in topical comedies. But that seems a limiting analysis of Wilder's work, considering the breadth and depth of his films: suspense thriller *(Five Graves to Cairo)*, film noir *(Double Indemnity)*, message movie *(The Lost Weekend)*, Hollywood in-joke *(Sunset Boulevard)*, biopic *(Spirit of St. Louis)*, courtroom melodrama *(Witness for the Prosecution)*. In each, Wilder offered cynical assessments of characters caught in confining situations. Certainly, no Wilder film displays his characteristic concerns more devastatingly than *Ace in the Hole*.

Briefly titled *The Big Carnival*, the film's name had to be changed when audiences showed up expecting a

A striking shot that reveals why filmmaker Billy Wilder originally chose to call this *The Big Carnival*.

47

While people party up above, Leo Minosa (Richard Benedict) lies near death under the ground.

an issue Wilder was the first to tackle in a film that must be considered far ahead of its time.

His understanding not only of journalistic morality but also of mob psychology makes this a darkly disturbing movie, one far too upsetting to ever have been a popular hit. But Kirk Douglas, as the heel who works out a deal with the sluttish wife (Jan Sterling, the thinking man's Mamie Van Doren) of the victim in order to monopolize and manipulate the tragic situation, found the role that allowed him to distinguish himself as an on-screen embodiment of the anti-heroic fifties. If the ending (in which the cynical hero gets his just deserts) seems a tad contrived, that was the bargain Wilder had to strike to get the movie made at all. *Ace in the Hole* remains one of the most distinctive and representative films of its cynical era, though unaccountably one of the least often revived.

circus picture. It's a different type of circus Wilder was concerned with—the media circus, which in our time comes to attend any incident with the potential to grab hold of the public's imagination for a short if intense period. In this case, a New Mexico mining disaster in an old Indian cave causes a hapless man (Richard Benedict) to be trapped. Rescue teams set to work in a desperate attempt to extricate Minosa before he runs out of oxygen, while the local populace gathers around, attracted to the situation as they would be to a bear-baiting or a cockfight. And a callous, sleazy newspaperman named Tatum senses this is the story that might land him in the big time. Completely unconcerned with the fate of the poor fellow but starved for the journalistic superstar status coverage of the situation can earn him, Tatum quickly realizes a rapid extrication would only close down what might prove to be a Pulitzer Prize winner. Tatum senses that, to properly exploit the more sensational aspects, he must make sure the final rescue is put off as long as possible, so he can reap the full benefits of its commercialization. That evidences Tatum's absolute amorality, for in not only manipulating and monopolizing but also extending the problem, he increases the odds the victim will not emerge alive.

Since the making of this film, many events—personal, public, and tragic—have brought to a head an issue— the rights vs. the responsibilities of a free press in a democratic society—which has emerged as problematically characteristic of our media-dominated society. It's

Fourteen Hours

A 20th Century-Fox Film (1951)

CREDITS:

Produced by Sol C. Siegel; directed by Henry Hathaway; screenplay by John Paxton, from a *New Yorker* magazine story by Joel Sayre; running time: 92 minutes.

CAST:

Paul Douglas (*Patrolman Dunnigan*); Richard Basehart (*Robert Cosick*); Howard da Silva (*Deputy Chief Moksar*); Barbara Bel Geddes (*Virginia*); Agnes Moorehead (*Mrs. Cosick*); Robert Keith (*Mr. Cosick*); Martin Gabel (*Dr. Strauss*); Debra Paget (*Girl in Street*); Jeffrey Hunter (*Boy in Street*); Grace Kelly (*Lady in Lawyer's Office*); James Warren (*Man in Lawyer's Office*).

Fans of Henry Hathaway argue that he's the great overlooked American filmmaker, who like Howard Hawks worked effectively in virtually every genre while keeping his distinctive directorial signature so subtle that it proved invisible to all but those who take the trouble to look closely. In truth, Hathaway has done well by the historical film (*Brigham Young*), the costume picture (*Lives of a Bengal Lancer*), wartime propaganda (*A Wing and a Prayer*), docudrama (*House on 92nd Street*), and gangster flick (*Kiss of Death*). His best (and most characteristic) work has come in sensitive screen treatments of Americana, small subcultures of our democratic society that would otherwise have gone without fitting film

The Man on the Ledge: Richard Basehart considers coming back inside as Barbara Bel Geddes implores him to.

representations: *Trail of the Lonesome Pine, The Shepherd of the Hills, Spawn of the North, Home in Indiana, Ten Gentlemen from West Point, Down to the Sea in Ships.* On rare occasions, though, he involved himself with the suspense genre, and if his westerns (*North to Alaska, From Hell to Texas, True Grit*) have caused critics to compare him with John Ford, his thrillers equal those of Hitchcock: *Niagara* with Marilyn Monroe is the best remembered, but *Fourteen Hours* is the best.

Like so many strong films of the early fifties, this is reality-based, for the story is derived from an actual incident in which a man did climb out of a hotel window and stand precariously on a cornice. What's amazing is that, while the incident took place in 1938, a film version was not considered until the early fifties. In a way, that makes sense; the fifties was the period when filmmakers became hungry for an opportunity to depict reality, especially any freak incident which is turned into a media circus by overzealous reporters. That was the theme of Billy Wilder's *Ace in the Hole,* and again here.

Economical and unsparing, the film begins when Robert Cosick slips out onto the ledge, and continues as Patrolman Dunnigan attempts to talk him into returning to the safety of the building. Most critics correctly labelled Hathaway's style as "journalistic," precise in describing not only the movie but the reigning Hollywood style at the time. The film equals Hitchcock's *Vertigo* in terms of effectively communicating a fear of

An intriguing off-angle shot, as the police try and lasso Robert Cosick (Richard Basehart).

Another intriguing angle shot, as the situation grows tenser still.

falling, but whereas the later Hitchcock classic uses that sense only intermittently throughout what's otherwise a weird romantic film, Hathaway sustains the feeling of vertigo for a full ninety minutes. In retrospect, it's remarkable that Hitchcock did not direct this film about one of his pet phobias.

But if the fifties was the period of cinematic journalism, it was also the era when psychology made itself felt on the screen. And that's certainly basic to the screenplay John Paxton developed from Joel Sayre's *New Yorker* reminiscence of the original ordeal. The film not only analyzes the suicidal character himself (Richard Basehart, considered a serious actor before TV's comic strip level *Voyage to the Bottom of the Sea*, was never better) but also the effect that the possible fall might have on a wide variety of people, including the character's neurotic mother and father, who we realize are responsible for the young man's condition. The film was not content to simply exploit the pathetic situation, but insisted on enlightening us as to how disturbed parents and the modern big city lifestyle could push a man beyond his limit.

The situation becomes a kind of big carnival, just as the man in the well (also based on an actual case) did in the Wilder film. The real subject of *Fourteen Hours* is the way radio and television reporters seize on a situation that can be sensationalized for the modern media, and the effect of all this on the "lonely crowd" of 1950s

onlookers, who gaze up, hoping the man will jump so their time will not have been wasted.

In small parts as onlookers, Fox cast two young studio hopefuls, Jeffrey Hunter and Debra Paget, who were receiving studio grooming for big things; more significant, Grace Kelly makes her film debut as the lady in the lawyer's office, though her brief scene seems something of an intrusion on a film that is otherwise flawlessly tight.

Pandora and the Flying Dutchman

A Romulus Film (1951)

CREDITS:

Produced by Albert Lewin; directed by Mr. Lewin; screenplay by Lewin, suggested by the legend of the Flying Dutchman; running time: 123 minutes.

Ava Gardner as Pandora.

50

One of Lewin's marvelously textured shots: the mirror image allows us to see Pandora's split personality, while the window—looking quite like an alternative mirror—reveals, in the Dutchman's ship, her subconscious desire to share his fate.

CAST:

James Mason *(Hendrick van der Zee)*; Ava Gardner *(Pandora Reynolds)*; Nigel Patrick *(Stephen Cameron)*; Sheila Sim *(Janet)*; Harold Warrender *(Geoffrey Fielding)*; Mario Cabre *(Juan Montalvo)*; Maurius Goring *(Reggie Demarest)*; John Laurie *(Angus)*; Pamela Kellino *(Jenny)*; Patricia Raine *(Peggy)*.

Of all film directors, Albert Lewin may have been the most literary in orientation: he mounted impressive screen adaptations of works by Somerset Maugham *(The Moon and Sixpence)*, Oscar Wilde *(The Picture of Dorian Gray)*, and Guy De Maupassant *(The Private Affairs of Bel Ami)*, in the process presenting George Sanders with some of his finest opportunities to project civilized nastiness and high-culture cruelty. But Sanders was replaced by James Mason for the more lyrical, more romantic film Lewin himself constructed out of two

great literary myths, and the work that this obscure filmmaker here turned out stands as his most intriguing and exasperating, a curious and irresistible if ultimately unsuccessful project. *Pandora and the Flying Dutchman* could have been a joint effort by Jean Cocteau and Michael Powell, featuring the surrealistic flourishes of the former's *Orphée* and the lilting, balletic dreaminess of the latter's *Red Shoes*. But only one filmmaker could have ever made it on his own, and that was Albert Lewin.

The subject of his art is art itself, so he turned to painting to make his points about all artists, poets, and directors; the hero is a painter in *Moon and Sixpence*, whereas the hero is painted in *Portrait of Dorian Gray*. Lewin's Flying Dutchman is a painter, too, one who creates a portrait of the woman of his dreams; for, having met the perfect beauty in Pandora, the Dutchman then feels the need to further idealize her on canvas. Andrew

Sarris has written perceptively of the moment when Pandora, resenting the reduction of her living beauty to an aesthetic contemplation, defaces the portrait, only to have the artist casually observe that his too technically perfect work is now all the richer for having the element of accident introduced into it. That is the ultimate Lewin moment, distilling all the ideas of his brief career and abbreviated canon (six films between 1942 and 1957) into self-expression.

"A legend is a story that's true for all time," Cocteau wrote concerning his decision to update the Greek myth of Orpheus to postwar France. That's an epigram Lewin would have had little trouble subscribing to, as this fanciful but never frivolous updating of two old tales, here crisscrossed in complex ways, makes clear. "What a great adventure it would be to die," Peter Pan sadly comments on his immortality in James M. Barrie's most popular play; Lewin worked in a similar vein. The story begins abruptly in 1930, as simple fishermen discover on their Spanish coast the bodies of a man and woman. We then hear a narration, spoken by a British archaeologist, Fielding, explaining who and what these semblances are. The elegant, enigmatic Hendrick van der Zee visited the village in his yacht; in fact, he is the spirit of the famed Flying Dutchman who, in the 1600s, killed his wife owing to unfounded jealousy, and was cursed by God to roam the seven seas until he discovers a woman who loves him enough to die for him. In the village, he meets the popular American singer Pandora Reynolds, who finds herself so attracted to the brooding presence of this other-worldly man that she happily agrees to love him to death, insuring her own demise as well.

Narcissistic and necrophiliac, this is—to put it mildly—a strange movie. It's also a beautiful movie, photographed in stunning colors by Jack Cardiff to convey a lush loveliness that, in its overripe exquisiteness, suggests the awful fate hovering over these characters. And it is a pretentious movie, the attempts at poetic dialogue too often spilling over into purple prose. Langorously slow, the film details Pandora's willful romantic destruction of such men as the race car driver Cameron, the bullfighter Montalvo, and the wastrel Demarest with a fascination that borders on obsession, implying they long to be destroyed by an emotional vampire every bit as much as she desires to surrender her life for the sake of the one lover she can never possess.

Gardner never appeared more radiant, while Mason—quite possibly, the finest English language actor of our century—projected the proper Heathcliffian aura of doomed sensitivity. This is a one of a kind film; perhaps that's for the best, though we are nonetheless richer for the experience of it.

The Great Caruso

A Metro-Goldwyn-Mayer Film (1951)

CREDITS:

Produced by Joe Pasternak; directed by Richard Thorpe; screenplay by Sonya Levein and William Ludwig, suggested by Dorothy Caruso's biography of her late husband; running time: 109 minutes.

CAST:

Mario Lanza (Enrico Caruso); Ann Blyth (Dorothy Benjamin); Dorothy Kirsten (Louise Heggar); Jarmila Novotna (Maria Selka); Richard Hageman (Carlo Santi); Carl Benton Reid (Park Benjamin); Eduard Franz (Giulio); Ludwig Donath (Alfred Brazzi); Alan Napier (Jean de Reszke); Paul Javor (Antonio Scotti); Carl Milletaire (Gino); Blanche Thebom (Operatic Performer).

In the minds of many opera fans, Mario Lanza exhibited the potential to emerge as the greatest tenor since Enrico Caruso. It made sense, then, that in designing a perfect musical vehicle for Lanza, MGM would fashion a fictionalized biography, loosely based on Caruso's life, thereby allowing Lanza to make clear his comparable talent by performing the numbers that had turned Caruso into a legend. *The Great Caruso* may have little to

52

An all-encompassing love: Pandora reveals she'd gladly give up her luxurious but empty life to find adventure in eternity with the Dutchman.

Mario Lanza as Enrico Caruso.

Caruso and his new wife, Dorothy (Ann Blyth), receive flowers in congratulation of their marriage and his resounding success onstage.

Caruso pledges his undying love to Dorothy.

do with the actual life of its ostensible subject, adapted, as it is, from a glowing and self-serving aggrandizement by Caruso's widow. Further embellished by several Dream Factory writers, it's calculated to perpetuate the myth, rather than realistically depict the man. But as colorful musical entertainment, it served its purpose admirably, making grand opera accessible to the masses. And Lanza was indeed in a class with Caruso; his interpretations of the fifteen songs proved as striking as those of the predecessor whose memory he here enshrined.

As drama, the film is nothing more than a charming collection of timeworn clichés. Caruso and the woman in his life, Dorothy Benjamin, are not developed as unique human beings set against a particular moment in the history of their country or the world at large, but as romanticized and simplified stereotypes. Director Richard Thorpe, never particularly known for a subtle style, responded to the script by playing the love story for as much pizzazz as possible, whipping up a cinematic helping of confectionary sugar, all very colorful to look at and lovely to listen to, though quite lacking any in-

Caruso makes clear his strong religious orientation by singing in church.

54

depth understanding of the operatic world in general or Caruso's contribution to it in particular.

Instead, the movie concentrates on young Enrico's arrival in New York City where, as a green and naive immigrant right off the boat, he quickly falls in love with the youthful daughter of the man he must win over for career purposes as well as in his personal life: the director of the Metropolitan Opera House. Park Benjamin resists this brash boy more adamantly as a match for his daughter than as a future star, though in time Park is forced to accept Enrico in both roles. Caruso becomes a star, a husband, and a father, in that order, then expires at a tragically young age.

The filmmakers did attempt some interesting integration of the traditional operatic music into the storyline they concocted. When, for instance, Dorothy stands Enrico up for a date (we know, as he does not, that she was locked in her room by her father), he performs the appropriate Pagliacci aria, appearing very much the incarnation of a broken-hearted clown. At the very end, when we sense Enrico will die shortly, he sings "The Last Rose of Summer" from *Martha*, the oncoming death intoned in that number neatly paralleling and foreshadowing his own demise. If such decisions on the part of the screenwriters seem somewhat florid and facile, they are nonetheless effective. *The Great Caruso* works as a gorgeous tearjerker, while serving as an opportunity to let not only Lanza but also Dorothy Kirsten and Blanche Thebom perform their versions of magnificent music immortalized thanks to the movie medium.

Sadly, Lanza's career would parallel Caruso's in its briefness. The Hollywood contract, accompanied by vast amounts of money and the attentions of endless beautiful women, were seemingly more than this man could handle. Lanza ate too much, drank too much, caroused and womanized too much. Only scant years later, the extraordinarily handsome star of this 1951 film looked so dreadful that he could not possibly appear in *The Student Prince* (1954), so he only lent his still superb voice to the project, with Edmond Purdom standing in for him onscreen. Not long after, Lanza was dead, the victim of his own inability to deal with celebrity status and the attending life-style it offered him.

Still, the legacy of his music remains rich. And in bringing to vivid life this colorful myth about the earlier Caruso, MGM was able to offer the world a film that today stands as an ironic tribute to two ill-fated stars of the operatic world.

Kon-Tiki

An RKO Radio Picture (1951)

CREDITS:

Presented by Sol Lesser, as an Artfilm; photographed by Thor Heyerdahl and members of the *Kon-Tiki* trans-Pacific expedition; running time: 73 minutes.

CAST:

Thor Heyerdahl and members of the *Kon-Tiki* expedition; narrated by Mr. Heyerdahl, with an introduction by Ben Grauer.

Thor Heyerdahl as Thor Heyerdahl.

During the fifties, practically every eighth grader was required to read *Kon-Tiki* in English class, for the book proved perfect for such purposes—intelligent enough to rate as a worthwhile reading experience for young people, exciting enough so they could work up interest in the required work. Documenting the story of six Scandanavians, who in 1947 travelled on a 40-foot balsa and bamboo raft from Peru to Tahiti to validate Thor Heyerdahl's premise that in days preceding recorded history sailing boats of ancient people had made just such a journey, *Kon-Tiki* rated as a popular bestseller with a patina of scientific purpose.

It proposed that South Americans may well have been ancestors of the Polynesian cultures, having travelled across the Pacific Ocean and navigating the Humboldt

Current, as well as the Easterly Trade Winds. That would explain why aspects of the diverse cultures are remarkably similar. But such an attitude, when first expressed, seemed radical enough to elicit loud expressions of doubt. To at least prove the possibility of his theory, Heyerdahl set off on his adventure, one that was perceived as quixotic (to successfully make the crossing would not actually prove he was right, only that he wasn't necessarily wrong) but which, perhaps for that very reason, captured the imagination of the world.

Though lesser known than the book, the film allowed audiences to witness a visualization of the trip, and won an Oscar in the documentary category for its vivid presentation of the undertaking. Heyerdahl and his people shot footage at unlikely moments, while failing to get some of the shots one might expect. Some incidents of their daily routine are depicted, though surprisingly enough others are not; likewise, the most famous moments in the book—the truly dangerous storms that came out of nowhere and threatened to decimate the boat and its crew—could not be recorded, simply because everyone on board was too busy struggling to try

The Kon-Tiki at sea.

The film was more able to detail daily life aboard the *Kon-Tiki* than it was the more extreme moments.

and stay alive to even consider taking pictures at such a time. So the film, while a record of the same trip that inspired the book with which it shares the title, is in fact a very different work, one that focuses on some of those happenings the book naturally glanced over. That disappointed some moviegoers of the time, though in fact it served as a fine complement to the book. Simply, the book perfectly told that portion of the story which lends itself to reflective writing; the film—in some ways, more a home movie record of the trip than a documentary in any sophisticated sense of the term—tells the story as only a spontaneous on-the-spot record can. After reading the book, one recalls the high points of the trip, as they are unforgettably described; after seeing the film, one understands more completely than words could ever convey the lifestyle that emerged among the voyagers.

Also fascinating is the fact that the film stock was almost lost when the *Kon-Tiki* crashed onto a reef, and the footage—kept sealed tightly in waterproof cans—was exposed to the raging surf. But the movie, like the expedition itself, was apparently meant to be. After considerable reconstruction in the editing room, the surviving footage of course does not capture every aspect of the journey, but it does manage to give an overview, however sketchy, along with vividly realized depictions of specific moments of the trip.

It also stands as a strong illustration of effective non-fiction filmmaking, for the narration Heyerdahl speaks carefully avoids telling us what we can already see for ourselves from the images onscreen, instead filling us in verbally on what could not be made visual. Heyerdahl's voice proved to be quite appropriate for the chore, as he relates the story with a terse tone and an effective undercurrent of self-deprecating humor.

The film was not without its onscreen drama; the men become as vivid as characters in any strong story. It's not without action and adventure: the whales and sharks that slip by remind us of the ever-present danger just beneath the seemingly tranquil surface of the sea. If the book *Kon-Tiki* is no longer as widely read as it once was, the Academy Award-winning movie has all but disappeared from sight; it's nonetheless recommended for anyone interested not only in this unique adventure but in the documentary form, its limitations and its possibilities.

Five

A Columbia Release (1951)

CREDITS:

Produced, directed, and written by Arch Oboler; running time: 93 minutes.

Arch Oboler's films featured lobby cards and marquee displays suggesting something far more exciting than the shoestring budgeted film could deliver.

Susan Douglas, Earl Lee, Charles Lampkin, and William Phipps were four of the "five" who survive the atomic war.

57

As Roseanne, Susan Douglas recalls the world that used to be.

CAST:

William Phipps *(Michael)*; Susan Douglas *(Roseanne)*; James Anderson *(Eric)*; Charles Lampkin *(Charles)*; Earl Lee *(Mr. Barnstaple)*.

Arch Oboler was the Orson Welles of Poverty Row. Whereas Welles came to fame with his cataclysmic *War of the Worlds* broadcast, which terrified the citizenry thanks to a convincingly suggestive portrayal of a Martian invasion, Oboler managed on a weekly basis to scare the wits out of practically everybody with his eerie *Lights Out*, macabre fables that were obviously fictional but still had the potential to strike terror into the hearts and souls of Americans addicted to radio. Welles made the transition to the big screen with what may be the greatest movie ever made, *Citizen Kane*, in 1941; no one has ever ventured such a claim for Oboler's premiere film, *Bewitched* (1946), or any of his later mini-epics. *Bwana Devil*, however, earns him a place in the history of fifties films as the movie that launched the 3-D craze ("A lover in your arms, a lion in your lap!"). Of the six films Oboler directed, *Five* is the one most worthy of attention, respect, and reconsideration.

Plugging into the spirit of the times, Oboler mounted yet another cautionary fable about the much-feared nuclear holocaust everyone believed was right around the corner. Limited to a shoestring budget, Oboler decided to tell the story of "the day after" the world

ends—indeed, the over-acclaimed 1983 TV movie of that name owes a suspiciously large debt to Oboler's long-forgotten film, though that show was widely heralded as a dramatic "breakthrough"—and saved money by doing every aspect of the production himself, producing, writing, and directing the film in and around his own Frank Lloyd Wright house.

The story focuses on the five survivors of the Third World War, who manage to find each other on an unspecified spot of land that certainly appears to be the Southern California coastline. Shortly, we realize they are symbols in an allegory as well as characters in a melodrama: Michael, the innocent young man who appears spiritually in touch with the powers of goodness in the universe; Roseanne, a pregnant girl who represents the earth's potential to restore itself; Charles, a badly used but still honest and courageous black; Eric, a mountain-climber who displays an arrogance that borders on evil; and Mr. Barnstaple, a doomed, dying banker who stands for all the old monetary systems that, like the man himself, are falling by the wayside.

Oboler was able, through the conflict between Eric and Charles, to graft a civil rights theme (the other major concern of the fifties and of fifties films, in addition to nuclear holocaust) onto his message movie about the horrible outcome of an atomic conflict. The madness of racism was never so clear as it is in this vision of a bigot maintaining his hideous prejudices even after all the rest of mankind is gone. But while the animosity between these two grows intense, just as the relationship between Michael and Roseanne mellows into romantic love, the film actually contains less dramatic action than dialogue. This is, essentially, a very talky movie: characters express their views, and do so endlessly—about the result of war, the plight of man, the hope for replenishing the earth, the existence of God, the possibility of peaceful co-existence with one another. In time, the girl loses her baby, while Eric dies after falling into a mass of radioactive material. But Oboler is careful to end the story on a positive (if hesitantly so) note: Michael and Roseanne do march off together, a new Adam and Eve for the post-nuclear world.

If occasionally Oboler slips into purple prose, that can perhaps be forgiven, considering the experimental nature and independent spirit of his project. For while *Five* was released by one of the "majors," Columbia, it is quite obviously a "pick-up" of a non-studio movie. And those who listen too closely to the portentous quality of the dialogue may miss Oboler's radio-inspired use of background noise, which undercuts the talk thanks to its embellished winds set against frightful silences. Or Oboler's neat cinematic eye that oftentimes slips away from the characters he's supposed to be concentrating on in order to study the cloud formations that the people in the story miss but we, thanks to Oboler's careful though seemingly random directing of our line of vision, consider at length. If Oboler was something less than a genius, he was certainly never anything less than original; that term also describes this, his best film.

The Army-McCarthy hearings are still vividly recalled as a memorable blot on the emotional landscape of the fifties, thanks to numerous films (*The Front*, *The Way We Were*) recounting the havoc and hysteria caused by the Red Scare witch-hunting tactics of "Tail Gunner" Joe. But another series of hearings, held at the bequest

The Captive City

An Aspen Picture (1952)

John Forsythe as Jim Austin.

CREDITS:

Produced by Theron Warth; directed by Robert Wise; screenplay by Karl Kamb and Alvin Josephy, Jr., from a story by Mr. Josephy; running time: 90 minutes.

CAST:

John Forsythe *(Jim Austin)*; Joan Camden *(Marge Austin)*; Harold J. Kennedy *(Don Carey)*; Marjorie Crossland *(Mrs. Sirak)*; Victor Sutherland *(Murray Sirak)*; Ray Teal *(Chief Gillette)*; Martin Milner *(Phil Harding)*; Geraldine Hall *(Mrs. Nelson)*; Hal K. Dawson *(Clyde Nelson)*; Ian Wolfe *(Reverend Nash)*; Gladys Hurlbut *(Linda Percy)*; Jess Kirkpatrick *(Anderson)*; Paul Newlan *(Krug)*.

Robert Wise chose to shoot this sequence with Joan Camden and John Forsythe on the steps of a real courthouse in an actual small town.

of a far more respectable if less vividly recalled senator, is all but forgotten, having been portrayed in contemporary movies only once, when Michael Corleone is called before a committee in *The Godfather, Part Two*. In fact, Senator Estes Kefauver's hearings on organized crime, its penetration not only of Big City life but also into our smaller, seemingly innocent communities, was a harrowing reality of the early fifties, leading to a resurgence of the crime film, including such excellent items as Joseph Kane's *Hoodlum Empire* (1952), Fritz Lang's *The Big Heat* (1953), Phil Karlson's *Phenix City Story* (1955), and Nicholas Ray's *Party Girl* (1958). The first, though, was *Captive City*, a trim, taut little drama which even had the blessing of Senator Kefauver himself, lending the film an extra punch of authenticity by proclaiming in an epilogue that this programmer conveyed the essence of what he'd been trying to communicate to the American people.

A straightforward, unassuming combination of late forties film noir somberness and early fifties American neorealist documentation, the film focuses on Jim Austin, an easygoing, youthful newspaperman running a small journalistic endeavor in a typical small town. Jim, happily married and certain he'll never have anything more thrilling to report than a lost cat, is stunned when a private investigator stumbles into his office, informing Jim there's a dark undercurrent to this brightly lit community, a seamy underside to which the white collar Jim remains complacently oblivious. Intrigued and concerned but not yet alarmed, Jim will find his smug self-assurance that his town is above and beyond such things challenged when that private eye turns up dead. The safe thing would be to let the very idea of criminal intrusion into their sacrosanct world die with this man, but haunted by the fellow's words, Jim cannot. When he goes to the police Chief, Gillette, the man refuses to even listen to the possibility that the detective may have been killed by a powerful organization, insisting this was nothing more than a routine mugging and murder. Infuriated by the official insistence that nothing is going on which need concern him, Jim investigates on his own, and finds that an elaborate bookmaking racket has permeated every strata of society, and that the rich, powerful, and apparently respectable folks involved with it will take any step necessary to silence him.

Jim is not so very different, then, from Dr. Stockmann, the hero of Henrik Ibsen's turn-of-the-century *An Enemy of the People*, as he attempts to tell the local population of a horrid scandal he's uncovered, only to realize most of the "good folks" who constitute his decent community want only to cover up the stench to protect their own involvement. Ultimately, there is a confrontation between Jim and Mr. Big, a crime czar

named Murray Sirak. Unable to tell the truth in his paper without being held libel owing to lack of proof, there's finally nothing the ever more isolated Jim can do but meet with Senator Kefauver himself.

John Forsythe lacked the larger-than-life magnetism of a true movie hero, but his quietly effective acting would prove perfect for the emerging medium of television, where he'd enjoy an endless run of successes. Indeed, were *The Captive City* made today, it would probably be a network TV movie of the week. It is worth reviving as a representative example of a significant cycle of films that was to the fifties what the Warner Brothers gangster epics had been to the thirties.

Breaking (Through) The Sound Barrier

A London Film (1952)

CREDITS:

Produced by David Lean; directed by Mr. Lean, with Aerial Unit direction by Anthony Squire; screenplay by Terence Rattigan; running time: 109 minutes.

CAST:

Ralph Richardson *(John Ridgefield)*; Ann Todd *(Susan Garthwaite)*; Nigel Patrick *(Tony Garthwaite)*; John Justin *(Philip Peel)*; Dinah Sheridan *(Jess Peel)*; Joseph Tomelty *(Will Sparks)*; Ralph Michael *(Fletcher)*; Vincent Holman *(A. T. A. Officer)*; Robert Brooks Turner *(Test Bed Operator)*.

Ann Todd (right) as Susan Garthwaite, the devoted daughter and dedicated wife who attempts to work up a suitable interest in the airplanes the two men in her life so dearly love.

For 1952's Best Picture of the Year, Hollywood awarded the Oscar to *The Greatest Show On Earth*, Cecil B. DeMille's glitzy, garish all-star extravaganza; the statuette might have more appropriately gone to *High Noon*, Fred Zinnemann's early, excellent example of the adult-psychological western which, with its effectively brief running time and tense black-and-white photography, neatly displayed the way in which European realism—such a major influence in the postwar years—might be successfully grafted onto a long-standing American movie genre. As previously noted, many of the realist influences came from Italy, whose naturalistic techniques and social-protest themes had created, in America, a trend for on-location shooting and storylines about ordinary people facing everyday problems. But just as significant (though not nearly so well documented) was the influence of British filmmakers, who had long since begun blending fact and fiction in fascinating ways.

Breaking (Through) the Sound Barrier stands tall, even when compared to the long list of superb British films imported into America in 1952: *Tom Brown's Schooldays*, *Bonnie Prince Charlie*, *The Man in the White Suit*, and *The Magic Box* among them. Still, this striking example of what the British like to call "dramatized-documentary" (and what we tend to less correctly refer to as "docu-drama") is nearly impossible to rediscover today. The film reveals, in low-key approach, the experiences of various scientists and test pilots involved in the creation of modern air transport, and the necessity of literally breaking through the sound barrier—flying beyond the sonic speeds—to create the first workable jet plane. Sir Ralph Richardson brought his dignified presence to the role of John Ridgefield, a scientist whose dedication to finding the means by which the challenge can be met and the problems eventually solved is precariously balanced (in this stunning performance) between an impassioned dedication and a fanatical obsession. His daughter Susan, a lovely young woman who cannot understand the lure of conquering the heavens, only wants to live a normal life with her husband. Susan was poignantly played by Ann Todd, a talented British beauty of the time whose work was always respected but who never achieved proper recognition. In the film, her husband, Tony Garthwaite, was played by Nigel Patrick with the proper combination of breezy charm and serious commitment to the cause. It is his death during an attempt to put her father's ideas into action that causes the dramatic conflict between father and daughter.

Playwright Terence Rattigan (*Separate Tables*) based his screenplay on the lives of numerous actual characters, consolidating them and compressing their experiments into a three-cornered drama that would be easy for the mass audience to follow. This left the writer free to emotionally involve the viewers and, once they were hooked on the melodramatic angle, then educate everyone with somewhat simplified but highly valuable information about the current state of flight. Working from this scenario, director David Lean leant the film a hard-edged semblance of reality while also adding a stark visual poetry that combined artistry with actuality.

Lucy dines with the Peels (Dinah Sheridan and John Justin), another husband and wife involved in the flight program.

Like so many other British filmmakers, Lean was influenced by the government's tendency to make dramatic films that were designed to disseminate information. This tendency was instigated by the country's well-meaning Ministry of Propaganda before that term became a dirty word, merely referring to the government's benign sense of a duty to keep their people informed and seizing on the movie medium to do so. Lean would eventually solidify his reputation with such enormous, expensive films as *Bridge on the River Kwai*, *Lawrence of Arabia*, *Dr. Zhivago* and, most recently, *A Passage to India*; in the fifties, he was best known for his superb adaptations of Dickens, including *Oliver Twist* and *Great Expectations*. Despite all his fine work, before and since, his greatest film remains the one that is, unaccountably, most difficult to see today.

The Story of Robin Hood

A Walt Disney Film (1952)

CREDITS:

Produced by Perce Pearce; directed by Ken Annakin; screenplay by Lawrence Edward Watkin; running time: 83 minutes.

CAST:

Richard Todd *(Robin Hood)*; Joan Rice *(Maid Marian)*; Peter Finch *(Sheriff of Nottingham)*; James Hayter *(Friar Tuck)*; James Robertson Justice *(Little John)*; Martita Hunt *(Queen Eleanor)*; Hubert Gregg *(Prince John)*; Bill Owen *(Will Stutley)*; Reginald Tate *(Hugh Fitzooth)*; Elton Hayes *(Allan-a-Dale)*; Antony Eustrel *(Archbishop of Canterbury)*; Patrick Barr *(King Richard)*; Anthony Forwood *(Will Scarlett)*; Hal Osmond *(Midge the Miller)*.

Friar Tuck (James Hayter), Robin (Richard Todd), and Little John (James Robertson Justice) plot against their enemies.

The meeting of Robin and Little John.

The Story of Robin Hood contains a natural and believable image of Robin and Marian as sweet teenagers.

When in 1973 the Disney company released their animated version of *Robin Hood* (with animals taking on all the roles), they quietly removed their live-action film on the same subject from distribution. What a pity! Like most of their later feature-length cartoons (including the equally disappointing versions of *Sword in the Stone* and *The Jungle Book*), their animated Robin Hood is emotionally empty, a harmless, technically polished time-killer, whereas their earlier *Robin Hood* is as fine a film on the subject as one could ask for: less spectacular, admittedly, than the better known versions starring Douglas Fairbanks and Errol Flynn, but every bit as worthy a retelling of the great legend.

Disney, a stickler for authenticity, sent his crew to England for location shooting, picking the personable young British actor Richard Todd to play the lead. Todd would also star in two additional colorful and historically accurate British Disney films, *The Sword and the Rose* (a.k.a. *When Knighthood Was in Flower*) and *Rob Roy, the Highland Rogue*. *Robin Hood* boasts that remarkable blend of entertainment for adults and children that Disney, in his prime, was so brilliant at pulling off. This is a family film, not a kiddie picture, constantly balancing complex political ideas and emotionally adult situations with the spirited action and zestful comedy necessary to sustain the interest of youthful audience members.

It likewise takes a fascinating approach to the myriad Robin Hood legends, neatly reconciling the different sources. Over the centuries, Robin has been variously portrayed as a Saxon Lord (Locksley), a Norman Earl

The future Lord of Locksley meets Queen Eleanor (Martita Hunt).

Adult audiences were impressed with the understated acting styles, so British in nature and so different from the delightfully overblown Hollywood heroics of the famed Warner Brothers version. Merely compare Basil Rathbone's hissably sneaky villain to Peter Finch's quiet Machiavellian official and the distinction is clear. Surprisingly, the Disney version must be tagged more mature in its approach. Children loved the whistling arrows with which Robin and his men signal each other in the forest. Teenagers were able to relate to the film because Robin was played as one himself. Important, too, is the fact that this movie was made before the Disney company banished the idea of death from their films: the sheriff's unhappy demise (he falls into the closing drawbridge) is far more frightful than anything in the "grown-up" versions, as satisfyingly gruesome as the death of the wicked witch in *Snow White*. Obvious also is Disney's eye for the beautiful moment: the nighttime torchlight departure of Richard and the Crusaders is as awesome as the magnificent tableaus in his finest animated films.

Hans Christian Andersen

An RKO Radio Picture (1952)

CREDITS:

Produced by Samuel Goldwyn; directed by Charles Vidor; screenplay by Moss Hart, from a story by Myles Connolly, with words and music by Frank Loesser and choreography by Roland Petit; running time: 120 minutes.

CAST:

Danny Kaye (Hans Christian Andersen); Farley Granger (Niels); Renee Jeanmaire (Doro); Joey Walsh (Peter); Philip Tonge (Otto); Roland Petit (The Hussar, danced by The Prince in 'The Little Mermaid' Ballet); John Brown (Schoolmaster); John Qualen (Burgomaster); Jeanne Lafayette (Celine).

A family film in the finest sense of the term, *Hans Christian Andersen* combined music and dance on the level of a top Broadway show. It was designed with adults in mind but with a series of stories that appealed to children: The Steadfast Tin Soldier, Thumbelina. Perhaps because those episodes were not dramatized in the way one might have expected for a child's film—The Little Mermaid, for instance, is presented in the form of

(Huntingdon), and a commoner (Fitzooth). Rather than deciding on one, Disney chose to combine them all, effectively compressing the entire body of Robin Hood legends (often contradictory) into a single narrative line. In fact, the film might better have been titled *The Song of Robin Hood*, for while it does follow the traditional Disney approach of opening with an image of a storybook, it quickly shifts to Allan-a-Dale, the medieval minstrel who turns into a human Jiminy Cricket, singing the story, ballad-style, directly to us, while wandering in and out of the tale.

Though the most famous events are all here, they're presented in a drama quite different from those previously seen. The arrow splitting incident, for instance, does not form the film's grand finale (as in most other versions) but is featured early, when Robin and his father, Fitzooth, enter a tournament shortly after Richard's departure for the Crusades. Robin is a lovesick swain, quite mad for the highborn Marian Huntingdon his humble family works for. When, after becoming an outlaw during John's reign, he eventually marries her, he automatically takes on the Earlship of Huntingdon, though Richard makes him Lord of Locksley as well.

a sophisticated ballet—the movie, though modestly popular, did not strike the kind of chord with children that a Disney presentation might have (doubtless, Walt would have done the Andersen story in live-action and Andersen's tales as animated interludes). Yet owing to the association of the Andersen stories with children, the movie has never been fully accepted as an entertainment for grown-ups; and owing to the ballet, it's never been marketed as a kid's film. Certainly, it is something of an anomaly: a musical styled for adults with substance for children.

As an opening title admits, this is not an attempt at a film biography but a totally fanciful entertainment, creating a fictional romantic-obsession on the part of Danny Kaye's Hans for a beautiful dancer who does not appreciate him, but who willingly accepts his stories as strong material for her performances. Renee Jeanmaire, introduced here to American audiences, strikingly performed the Little Mermaid ballet opposite Roland Petit (of the Ballet de Paris), who also choreographed the motion picture. The innovative sequence, demonstrating how effective classical-style ballet can be within a totally cinematic conception, has never received the attention and acknowledgement it deserves. Director Charles Vidor did not merely sit back and shoot the dance sequence but carefully suited his camera style to it, resulting in a happy marriage between the art forms of dance and film. For this sequence, musical supervisor Walter Scharf drew material from the work of Franz Liszt; for the remainder of the film, composer Frank Loesser created

"The Little Mermaid Ballet."

pleasant and sometimes memorable songs, including "Inchworm" and "Ugly Duckling."

The score is so strong that it's surprising to learn this was not based on a Broadway show; indeed, in an age when such original musical films as *Seven Brides for Seven Brothers* have been adapted to Broadway, it's amazing no one has thought to do that with *Hans Christian Andersen.*

65

The storyline is a bit sticky, occasionally maudlin: Moss Hart's script gives us a hero who is innocent almost to the point of being a numbskull, though perhaps he and Danny Kaye were aiming for an approximation of the traditional noble fool of literature. Kaye is something of an acquired taste for anyone who did not grow up watching his films. Suffice it to say that back in the fifties, while the lowbrows were enjoying Jerry Lewis and the highbrows were thrilling to Alec Guinness and Alastair Sim, middlebrows had their own comic clown in the carrot-topped Kaye, who mugged (though never as mercilessly as Lewis) and mimed (though never as brilliantly as Guinness or Sim), cavorting in a way that verged on slapstick but never went so far as to turn off his polite audience.

The film featured Farley Granger, always a competent actor if never a forceful one, though certainly among the popular matinee idols of the late forties and early fifties until Robert Wagner came along and replaced him. And there is Joey Walsh, a much-underrated child actor with eyes so sad they could break a viewer's heart. The film is nicely played out on patently artificial sets, which have Copenhagen resembling an earth-bound Oz made up of Gingerbread houses, an approach which seems most appropriate considering the confectionary quality of the plot.

Hans Christian Andersen was considered too formidable and too dense for popular consumption, so was cut by 20 minutes for its TV version, a move which allowed the networks to showcase it, with commercials added, in a two-hour time slot. That cut of the film destroys the movie's charm; hold out for the complete version, and hope it will resurface someday.

In a rare shot, studio technicians ready the dancers for filming.

Where's Charley?

A Warner Brothers Presentation (1952)

CREDITS:

Produced by David Butler; directed by Mr. Butler; screenplay by John Monks, Jr., based on the play *Charley's Aunt* by Brandon Thomas; running time: 97 minutes.

CAST:

Ray Bolger (Charley); Allyn McLerie (Amy); Robert Shackleton (Jack); Mary Germaine (Kitty); Horace Cooper (Spettigue); Margaretta Scott (Dona Lucia); Howard Marion Crawford (Sir Francis); Henry Hewitt (Brassett); H. G. Stoker (Wilkinson); Martin Miller (a photographer).

For millions of moviegoers, the name Ray Bolger is synonomous with the lovable scarecrow from 1939's *The Wizard of Oz.* Sadly, though, his career as a song 'n' dance man—onstage, as well as in Hollywood—has otherwise been largely ignored. Though the scarecrow certainly deserves acclaim as a charming characterization, it's nonetheless a supporting role. Bolger's most representative work remains his interpretation of the intrepid Charley in the tuneful version of a beloved old upscale drag-show that proved a hit first on Broadway, then onscreen.

This is the musicalized version of *Charley's Aunt*, a charming chestnut of a Victorian farce by Brandon Thomas, which sets up a simple but highly workable comic situation, then provides endless variations on its single theme. Charley is a precocious Oxford student who desires to have several attractive young ladies visit him in his rooms. They, being most proper, cannot consider it unless there is a chaperone present; Charley, being a bit (but not too much) of a rake, would like to entertain the girls without any old maids hovering about. So he disguises himself as his own aunt, then finds himself forever having to jump back and forth between his actual self and the fabricated relative.

Naturally, there are more than a few contrivances in such a plot, necessary to keep the humorous bits coming at us in rapid succession; audiences tend to willingly overlook such matters, just so long as the material is funny enough. Here, it is just that, thanks in large part to Bolger's interpretation: his wild wag of a Charley, as set against the mock seriousness of the prim and good aunt, add up to his greatest performance. And with Frank Loesser providing such lovely, lyrical numbers as

Ray Bolger as Charley.

The incomparable Mr. Bolger dances with his beloved "Amy."

Horace Cooper greets "Charley's Aunt" while Robert Shackleton looks on.

"Once in love with Amy," we sense that this was always meant to be a musical. Indeed, it's almost impossible today to go back to the original "straight" version of the play, so associated has that particular song become with this story; we sense something is missing in any production that does not include it.

Charley had all the makings of a classic musical movie, and probably would have been had someone

with a stronger sensibility for that genre than David Butler directed—say, Busby Berkeley, Stanley Donen, or Vincente Minnelli. Butler has serviced the material rather than interpreted it, so his work is mainly of the journeyman variety, capturing a first-class piece of theater on celluloid rather than truly "making a movie" out of it. The benefits are that millions who would never have gotten to see Bolger romping unabashedly as Charley had the opportunity to enjoy the show, and that a great moment of theater has been preserved forever. The deficit is that it's less a film adapted from a play than a filmed play. *Where's Charley?* is more the musical equivalent of *Cyrano de Bergerac* than *Death of a Salesman.*

Once one accepts that, there's much to admire here in addition to Bolger's beautifully bouncy performance. Allyn McLerie combined a graceful ability to dance with an ever dour face as the oh, so desirable Amy; Mary Germaine, as the striking blond Kitty who dashes off with Charley's pal Jack, was not only a looker but a natural singing talent. On-location shooting in England may explain the reason for this cast of virtual unknowns who gave Bolger solid support.

Yet it remains his vehicle from start to finish, a gay, giddy conceit that never fails to charm. Bolger's lanky body and wistful face made him unique among singing/dancing comedy stars of his day; if he lacks the easy accessibility of Danny Kaye or happy earnestness of a Donald O'Connor, then Bolger is the musical's equivalent of Buster Keaton, that subtle and stoic veteran of silent screen comedy. Whenever this film is revived at college campuses or for film societies, novitiates are dazzled to discover that their beloved scarecrow had a life onscreen beyond that in *The Wizard of Oz.* The pity is that *Where's Charley?* is revived so rarely.

Ray Milland as The Thief.

The Thief

A United Artists Release (1952)

CREDITS:

Produced by Clarence Greene; directed by Russell Rouse; screenplay by Mr. Greene and Mr. Rouse; running time: 85 minutes.

CAST:

Ray Milland *(Dr. Allen Fields)*; Martin Gabel *(Mr. Bleek)*; Rita Gam *(The Girl)*; Harry Bronson *(Harris, The FBI Man)*; John McKutcheon *(Dr. Linstrum)*; Rita Vale *(Miss Phillips)*; Rex O'Malley *(Beal)*; Joe Conlin *(Walters)*.

Throughout the late 1930s and early forties, Ray Milland seemed little more than one more studio contract player, a competent actor but a rather bland presence, more a matinee idol than a true movie star and—like Ronald Reagan—a leading actor in B films, a second lead in A movies. Then, just as he was hitting middle age and the eventual winding down of that kind of lucrative career, Milland won the key role in Billy Wilder's stunning study of an alcoholic's hallucinatory experiences, *The Lost Weekend* (1945), picking up an Oscar for his remarkable portrayal.

From that point on, Milland was admirably willing to risk his newfound status with offbeat little projects, and none was quite so intriguing as *The Thief.* Though the storyline itself was a rather routine spy drama, the technique was striking. For at a time when most moviemakers were attempting to add more to the filmgoing experience—advanced color processes, wraparound sound effects, ever wider screens, even a brief fling at three-dimension—Milland and his colleagues Clarence Greene and Russell Rouse went the other route, turning out the first commercial film with no dialogue since that fateful day 25 years earlier when Al Jolson, in *The Jazz Singer,* had announced: "You ain't heard nothin' yet!"

This Cold War melodrama centered on Dr. Allen Fields, employed in Washington as a nuclear physicist (immediately introducing the recurring fifties' theme of our love/hate relationship with atomic weaponry) who turns traitor, photographing some top secret information which he plans to turn over to Bleek, Beal, and Miss

Phillips, representatives of an unnamed foreign power obviously meant to be Russia. The film chronicles, in minute detail, the plan by which they will attempt to smuggle this information out of the country. However, a freak accident takes the life of one of the conspirators, and as a result, the Federal Bureau of Investigation immediately becomes aware of the spy ring's presence. As they close in on the remaining members, the scientist turned thief enters into an elaborate chase as he tries to hide from the encircling agents.

The film focuses on his harried odyssey, including a brief stopover with a beautiful girl (Rita Gam, in her film debut) he meets in a tenement building. By the movie's end, Dr. Fields has slithered his way from the handsome Georgetown district of D. C. to the very top of the Empire State Building in New York. And while the lack of dialogue may seem little more than a gimmick (and, to a degree, that was the case), the filmmakers did prove less can sometimes be more by summoning up memories of movies from an earlier era, when crisp photography and crackerjack editing more than compensated for the lack of voices, which sometimes turn moving pictures into talking pictures. Here, Herschel Gilbert provided a nifty tempo through his musical score that intensified the ever mounting suspense, while Sam Leavitt's cinematography caught all the real settings with a vivid off-kilter camera eye, adding a heightened visual sense.

Though the film does not have any dialogue, it is hardly silent. For in addition to Gilbert's score, there is a striking reliance on natural sounds: we hear the places of Washington and New York as never before, since the noises of the cities are for the first time in a film not competing with talk from the main characters. Though many critics carped that we do not discover the motivation for Milland's betrayal of his country (such a concept is virtually impossible without at least a couple of lines to explain why he did what he did), that did not bother most moviegoers, who simply accepted this as a typical example of a high-level traitor (and, heaven knows, there had been enough of them in the news that the public was hardly surprised to find one dramatized in the film) with fuzzy, tenuous reasons of his own. The audience merely remembered similar faces on the front pages of the newspapers, projecting the motivations they had read about onto Ray Milland's anguished face. Certainly, the depth of his performance (all the more impressive, since he was unable to rely on the vocal inflections ordinarily basic to his characterizations) made this man a convincing portrait of a contemporary type, in a film that proved, so far as actors are concerned, silence can indeed be golden.

Invasion, U.S.A.

A Columbia Pictures Release (1953)

CREDITS:

Produced by Albert Zugsmith and Robert Smith; directed by Alfred E. Green; screenplay by Robert Smith; running time: 74 minutes.

CAST:

Gerald Mohr (Vince); Peggie Castle (Carla); Dan O'Herlihy (Mr. Ohman); Robert Bice (George Sylvester); Tom Kennedy (Bartender); Wade Crosby (Congressman); Erik Blythe (Ed Mulvory).

The Thief sees a potential enemy in everyone he crosses paths with.

Gerald Mohr and Peggie Castle recoil in horror from the parachuting Russians.

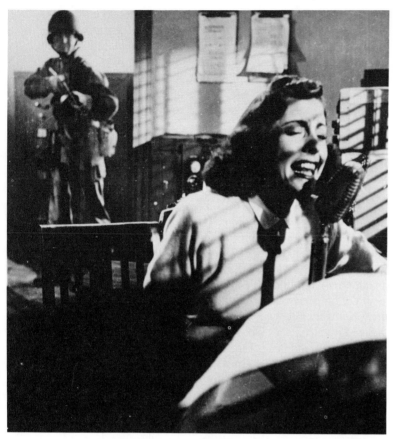

As a radio announcer courageously attempts to warn the populace, a Russian sniper shoots her in the back.

Poverty Row producer Albert Zugsmith's quickie flick about a Russian Invasion of the United States has been unofficially remade (a polite way of saying ripped off) three times in rapid succession: in John Milius's *Red Dawn*, which had The Brat Pack demolishing Soviet invaders after the U.S. Marines proved incapable of the job; *Invasion, U.S.A.*, which swiped even the title for a Chuck Norris cheapie; and *Amerika*, ABC TV's week-long mini-series which opened with a bang and went out with a whimper.

Zugsmith's modest little exploitation flick rates as far superior, though that's not saying a lot. This Right Wing cautionary fable (the warning is that if we don't build up a large arsenal of atomic weapons, we can expect the Russians to come falling out of the sky any day) exemplifies what can be achieved on a virtual shoestring. While the running time is listed as 73 minutes, it's worth noting that nearly an hour of that time is taken up with stock newsreel footage, which Zugsmith assembled (at times, quite effectively) to give his film a certain documentary flavor and an epic scope, despite the fact that most of the new footage for this film was shot with a cast of six.

Zugsmith (who would later desert politics for sex, mounting in the early sixties such irresistibly sleazy items as *Sex Kittens Go to College* with Mamie Van Doren and *Platinum High School* with Terry Moore) got his hands on a great deal of footage left over from World War II, then alternated that material with a series of short takes featuring various actors whose placement in

More Russians come parachuting out of the sky; stock footage padded out well over half of the film.

juxtaposition to the stock shots gave the impression that, rather than German or Italian, we were looking at American cities which had been bombed out. Zugsmith did not name the enemy, but gave his invaders thick Russian accents. An independent producer, Zugsmith then talked Columbia, one of the majors, into releasing the film (a then-novel approach which would become ever more routine) for a fast turnover, as sensationalized advertising created a blitz of interest in a film that purported to warn Americans what might be about to happen.

Like *Invaders From Mars*, a far superior film which has at last achieved the cult status it deserves, *Invasion U.S.A.* ends with the realization it has all been a dream; the main characters, we realize, had fallen under the spell of a hypnotist they were watching on TV in the neighborhood bar. But that conceit works less effectively in this film, for in *Invaders From Mars*, the "twist ending" was hinted at throughout the movie, thanks to the semi-surreal looking sets and garish color schemes. There is no such justification to the resolution here, only a need for the filmmakers to untangle themselves in some way.

Still, if Zugsmith does not prove on reconsideration to be an unappreciated genius, he was at the very least an original. His film is as energetic as it is outrageous, earning him a place of dubious honor somewhere between William Castle and Hugo Haas. That may not be much, but it's more than can be said for any of the filmmakers who ripped him off in the early eighties. Even today, *Invasion, U.S.A.* delivers more punch in a shorter time than any of those limp, longwinded items. This film is still fun to watch, which is more than anyone can say for *Amerika*.

Pick-Up on South Street

A 20th Century-Fox Release (1953)

CREDITS:

Produced by Jules Schermer; directed by Samuel Fuller; screenplay by Mr. Fuller from a story by Dwight Taylor; running time: 80 minutes.

CAST:

Richard Widmark *(Skip McCoy)*; Jean Peters *(Candy)*; Thelma Ritter *(Moe)*; Murvyn Vye *(Capt. Dan Tiger)*; Richard Kiley *(Joey)*;

Love, Sam Fuller style: as Skip McCoy (Richard Widmark) embraces Candy, we're unsure whether he's planning to kiss or kill her—and so is she!

Willis B. Bouchey *(Zara)*; Milburn Stone *(Winoki)*; Henry Slate *(MacGregor)*; Jerry O'Sullivan *(Enyart)*; Harry Carter *(Dietrich)*; George E. Stone *(Police Station Clerk)*.

In the minds of French fans of American films, Sam Fuller ties Nicholas Ray as the director of the fifties who best embodies the notion of total filmmaker: shaping diverse and varied projects from a wide range of genres into personalized expressions of his own unique point-of-view, stamping them with a distinctive signature that serves as a logical visual extension of his themes. Without question, Fuller's most perfectly realized project was this striking suspense film fashioned around a topical issue. *Pickup on South Street* is as quintessentially fifties as it is unmistakably Fuller.

Jean Peters as Candy.

In a way, Fuller's script resembles the kind of hard-boiled story Hitchcock would have told had he deserted the civilized characters of his upscale world to concentrate on lowlife denizens, while retaining his basic premise of how anyone can at anytime slip into a nightmare world which exists just on the edge of everyday life. Skip McCoy, an amoral pickpocket, lifts a purse from a pretty lady on a train. What he could not know is that Candy carried (and he now possesses) a modernized MacGuffin in the form of a pilfered top-secret microfilm strip she was about to deliver to communist agents. To save her own skin, Candy must retrieve it and hand the valuable item over to her boss, Joey, who beats her badly when he learns of the slip-up. We are stunned to see Candy respond positively to the beating; when she rushes off to seduce Skip and he likewise slaps her around, she seems more turned on by his fists than by his occasional kisses. Before long, Skip and Candy resemble gutter precursors of Cary Grant and Eva Marie Saint in 1957's *North by Northwest*, pursued by both enemy agents and our own police, able to trust no one but each other despite each person's fear the other may prove betrayer at any moment.

A *film noir* for the early fifties, this picture maintains the urban jungle of those postwar films but replaces the jaded knights and lone wolf protagonists with something new and remarkable. Fuller exerted a striking influence on the career of Richard Widmark by casting the one-time incarnation of cold-blooded killer who had gleefully sent a wheelchair-bound old lady hurtling down a staircase in *Kiss of Death* as an offbeat, anti-heroic leading man in the emerging tradition of Mickey Spillane's Mike Hammer. Skip McCoy is an unromanticized, unregenerate heel, a slob-as hero whose only saving grace is that he's an American, and the characters he takes on are all communists. Jean Peters, the actress usually cast in decorative roles for harmless cardboard-costume pictures (*Anne of the Indies*, *Lure of the Swamps*) here displayed a sensitivity as the sado-masochistic tramp she never revealed before or after this, her finest hour. Scene-stealing character actress Thelma Ritter, who worked her way into audiences' hearts in films like Hitchcock's *Rear Window*, was uncharacteristically nasty as a stool pigeon who pays dearly for talking out of turn.

The connection with Daryl F. Zanuck and Fox allowed Fuller a slightly larger budget than he enjoyed on his Poverty Row independent projects (*I Shot Jesse James, Verboten!*), though this is still a modest enough affair. Fuller's world is a bleak, brutal, unyielding arena, a morally gray battleground where characters sometimes surprise themselves by rising to heroic proportions they—and we—thought them incapable of. With an attitude that takes its cue from Widmark's cruel, cynical grin, Fuller approaches lurid material with a slam-bang visual sensibility that somehow straddles outright exploitation and crude artistry. He is to the American B action film what Luis Bunuel would soon be to the more prestigious arthouse import: a filmmaker who forces a bleak, unsparing vision of the world as a moral sewer down a viewer's craw and forces us to take the whole shot. *Pickup on South Street* is the *Viridiana* of fifties *film noir*, daring to display the dark underside of the Eisenhower era.

Little Boy Lost

A Paramount Picture (1953)

CREDITS:

Produced by William Perlberg; directed by George Seaton; screenplay by Mr. Seaton, based on a story by Marghanita Laski; running time: 95 minutes.

CAST:

Bing Crosby *(Bill Wainwright)*; Claude Dauphin *(Pierre Fernier)*; Christian Fourcade *(Jean)*; Gabrielle Dorziat *(Mother Superior)*; Nicole Maurey *(Lisa Garret)*; Collete Dereal *(Nelly)*; Georgette Anys *(Mme. Quillebouef)*; Henry Letondal *(Tracing Service Clerk)*; Michael Moore *(Attache)*; Peter Baldwin *(Lt. Walker)*.

In a Fuller film, sex and violence are always the reverse sides of the same coin: here, Candy lets Skip have it shortly after making love to him.

Bill (Bing Crosby) observes the sweet, sad-eyed Jean (Christian Fourcade) and knows that he wants him for his own son.

In a flashback, Bill recalls his final days with the woman he loved (Collete Dereal).

Following the death of Bing Crosby and the release of *The Hollow Man*, a scathing "Daddy Dearest" style biography penned by son Gary, Bing's once majestic image as a great American father as well as a show business legend was considerably tarnished. How ironic, then, to note in retrospect that his best dramatic role (and I'm not forgetting *The Country Girl*) featured him as a man experiencing difficulty in dealing with the institution of fatherhood, but in the end rising gloriously to the occasion.

Little Boy Lost cast Crosby as Bill Wainwright, who returns to France ten years after his service there as a radio reporter during the war. While stationed overseas, Wainwright had an affair with a young Frenchwoman who was later killed while working with the Resistance. Wainwright was aware the woman had become pregnant by him; as the years passed, he'd been haunted by a growing sense of responsibility, as well as a nagging desire to see his son. So he sets out on a desperate search to find the boy, finally narrowing down the child's whereabouts to a single orphanage. One of the boys at that place, he realizes, is his child. But which one?

His old friend Pierre begins a search for documents that will prove precisely which boy is Wainwright's. In the meantime, though, Bill has been befriended by the Mother Superior running the school, a woman who must maintain a serious and seemingly aloof demeanor to maintain order with her passel of sad, lost children, but who loves and cares for them more than she dare show. She lets Wainwright observe the children at their studies and play; he feels instinctually drawn to one, sensing this is his child even before Pierre can track down the documents.

Bill finds himself reawakening to life in the company of Lisa (Nicole Maurey).

This child is the saddest of the lot, a disaster at sports (at one point, Wainwright peers out the window just long enough to see the boy, playing soccer, miss a kick which sends him flying, an action greeted with jeers from the other boys) but otherwise a sweet, sensitive loser whose lonely demeanor tugs at Wainwright's heartstrings. This is the boy who needs him the most (the child is constantly picked on by the school's nasty bully); and Wainwright trusts it will turn out that way on paper, because he anticipates bringing little Jean back to the States, showing his son how special life can be. But the documents prove that Wainwright's son is the school bully, the one who takes pleasure in beating the child he so wants to be a father to.

In the movie's denouement, Wainwright—making plans to bring his blood-son back home—changes his mind, deciding instead to adopt the boy he feels is, on an emotional if not physical level, his own. Their final embrace of reunion is heartbreakingly beautiful, in part because of Crosby's fine, unsentimental playing of the scene, in part because of the fabulous presence of an eight-year-old boy, Christian Fourcade, the most striking screen child since the waif in *The Bicycle Thief*. This touching film combined the best aspects of European realism with the highest form of Hollywood emotionalism.

The message of the movie, if one can apply so grandiose a term to so softspoken a human drama, is that Wainwright finally learns responsibility is greater and broader than he imagined; in a sense every American soldier is responsible for every child born to a European woman out of wedlock. The sense of his moral growth is at the base of the film's beauty. The film is sometimes confused with a movie of the late 1940s called *The Search*, which introduced Montgomery Clift as an American serviceman helping a lost child find his mother.

That Fred Zinneman film, like this one, featured something of a quasi-documentary approach in its relating of a singular story that allowed the filmmakers to comment on the broader scope of a serious problem in postwar Europe. But despite moments of pictorial beauty and a notable sensitivity for its subject, *The Search* never equalled *Little Boy Lost* in poignancy.

In real life, Mr. Crosby may indeed have been something of a washout as a father. But on screen, in this marvelous film that remains as sadly lost as the little boy of its title, he ably represented the father every one would like to have had.

Maggie McNamara as Patty O'Neill.

The Moon Is Blue

A United Artists Release (1953)

CREDITS:

Produced by Otto Preminger; directed by Mr. Preminger; screenplay by F. Hugh Herbert, from his own stage play; running time: 95 minutes.

CAST:

William Holden (*Donald Gresham*); David Niven (*David Slater*); Maggie McNamara (*Patty O'Neill*); Tom Tully (*Michael O'Neill*); Dawn Addams (*Cynthia*); Fortunio Bonnova (*Television Announcer*).

The most remarkable thing about *The Moon is Blue* is that it's so unremarkable—so tepid an attempt at risqué comedy, so stagey and theatrical in its approach to adapting what was obviously a stage play, so uninvolving in its presentation of a romantic situation—that it's almost impossible for anyone happening upon it today to comprehend how this could ever have caused a furor. But it became a runaway box-office hit by being at the center of a noisy scandal. For the Production Code, which had been instituted in Hollywood some thirty

Two types of Playboy—the American (William Holden) and the British (David Niven)—argue while Patty looks on.

Two types of Playboy—the American (William Holden) and the British (David Niven)—argue while Patty looks on.

years earlier by Joseph Breen's self-censoring office for motion pictures, refused to grant this film a passing grade since it contained words deemed unfit for decent folk to hear. In the Jack Nicholson/Eddie Murphy era, when the "F Word" is spoken onscreen with oppressive abandon, it's awesome to realize the offending words in question were "virgin," "seduce," and "pregnant."

Today, *The Moon is Blue* would receive a G rating: the female lead does not surrender her virginity or become pregnant, only discusses such things in the most polite manner possible. Maggie McNamara played the girl, a bit of a free spirit who remains conventional in her actions while enjoying intellectual freedom. She willingly goes to the apartment of a bachelor, Donald Gresham, a risqué decision to begin with; she then confounds matters further by openly talking with him about his previous affairs with pretty women of little virtue. But she does not surrender, or even consider doing any thing of the sort, stunning Donald so that he asks this paradox of progressive attitudes and traditional actions to marry him, which she happily agrees to do. And that, as they say, is that.

Charmingly, Patty flirts with the older man.

The notoriousness comes in what we hear spoken in this tediously talky turkey. The film clearly stands on the side of The Establishment, if it does throw a bone to Women's Lib. Author Herbert wholeheartedly endorses young ladies who speak up with forthrightness and open-mindedness, just so long as they remain chaste. The implication of the ending, certainly, is that only by

This essentially innocent film was once considered too risque for popular consumption; today, it would be rated G.

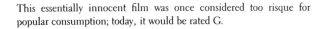

remaining so will a girl get the right guy: Donald has discarded all the women who thought conservatively but acted liberally. It's the other combination that wins him over, which is why—when confronted with Patty, who talks (no pun intended) a blue streak—there's nothing to do but propose.

Maggie McNamara had a short, sad career. Introduced here and in the glossy technicolor soap opera *Three Coins in the Fountain* (which, incidentally, holds up nicely indeed), she looked a great deal like Audrey Hepburn, with a similar slender-as-a-reed shape, long neck and large eyes, winsome appearance and wistful manner. But if Hepburn was the perfect embodiment of

that type, McNamara always seemed an imperfect second choice, the actress you'd hire if you wanted Hepburn but couldn't afford her. NcNamara was to Hepburn what Jayne Mansfield was to Marilyn Monroe. She also suffered from severe mental problems, and was committed to an institution. After her release, she was unable to revive her career, and soon faltered again, her mental health problems aggravated by physical ones which shortly caused her to take her own life.

William Holden, brashly charming as the playboy, continued to assert his appeal as a key leading man of the day; David Niven provided a suave charm as the Brit upstairs who allowed his own daughter a great deal of emancipation. Whether his attitude was healthy and wise or dangerously over-indulgent is never made clear, since the script dances around such issues. The real treat in this film, though, comes in watching Dawn Addams in the role of Niven's precocious and pouty daughter. A ravishing beauty, Addams kicked around American films in the fifties, playing leads in B pictures and supporting roles in A films. Twenty-five years later, she was glimpsed briefly in European imports like *Lust For a Vampire*, looking every bit as gorgeous as she had as an ingenue, if not more so. Her ravishing and underrated appearance makes this otherwise dated, often lumbering movie bearable. *The Moon is Blue* is one of those megahits of one era, the success of which is practically inexplicable to anyone who did not experience it in the original context.

The classic ad, which captured the charm of the film itself.

Lili

A Metro-Goldwyn-Mayer Film (1953)

CREDITS:

Produced by Edwin H. Knopf; directed by Charles Walters; screenplay by Helen Deutsch, from the short story by Paul Gallico; running time: 81 minutes.

CAST:

Leslie Caron *(Lili Daurier)*; Mel Ferrer *(Paul Berthalet)*; Jean Pierre Aumont *(Marc)*; Zsa Zsa Gabor *(Rosalie)*; Kurt Kasznar *(Jacquot)*; Amanda Blake *(Peach Lips)*; Alex Gerry *(Proprietor)*; Ralph Dumke *(M. Corvier)*; Wilton Graff *(M. Tonit)*.

With *An American in Paris*, MGM uncovered a great new star, Leslie Caron. There was only one problem: what to do with her? Despite tremendous talent, Miss Caron proved difficult to cast. Her figure was full and

Mel Ferrer had his finest role as Paul, physically and emotionally crippled puppeteer.

feminine, yet there was something waiflike about this Frenchwoman's appearance; she had a gamin quality, the enchanting ability to seem in some ways a worldly woman, in others an innocent vivacious child. Throughout her career, this would determine her unique screen persona and limit the roles audiences would accept her in. Thankfully, her producers did find one vehicle that called out for this quality: the lilting, lovely *Lili*.

There is much magic to this sweet, sometimes sad, occasionally strange film, less a traditional musical entertainment than a bittersweet romantic drama set to music until it turns into a bizarre mixture of dream, fable, and allegory at the very end. Lili is an orphan girl who runs away with a circus and falls in love with Paul, a crippled puppeteer. Though he likewise loves Lili, Paul—who has been hurt once too often by women—cannot allow himself to become vulnerable again by admitting such emotions to her, face to face. He conveys his feelings through children's plays, where his lifelike puppets serve as his mouthpieces. Otherwise, Paul hides behind a facade of nastiness and cruelty. Lili, hurt, tries to break through that barrier, until the emotional pain becomes so deep she runs from the carnival demimonde. Even on the open road, though, Lili is pursued by mental images of the puppets, in her imagination lifesize, as they trek along with her, the group looking a bit like Dorothy and companions in *The Wizard of Oz*.

That comparison is fair: the allegorical quality, in which the puppets become living embodiments of human strengths and weaknesses, is not unlike that of the Lion, the Tin Man, and the Scarecrow. Caron conveyed the same warm, restless child-woman appeal as the young Judy Garland. *The Wizard of Oz* managed, after a disappointing initial release, to gradually endear itself as a classic; no such status has ever come to surround *Lili*, however deserved.

Carnival, a Broadway show based on the film, featured Anna Maria Alberghetti, semi-successfully subbing for

Caron, exhibiting a pleasant singing voice but none of the radiance. Even Caron might not have been able to make the show click, though, for it lacked the haunting title song by Bronislau Kaper, which people hummed incessantly: "The song of love is a sad song/Hi Lili, Hi Lili, Hi Lo . . ." Indeed, that tune has remained in the public's consciousness long after the movie that contained it has been forgotten.

Perhaps the one thing that distinguishes the movie from *Wizard*—its relatively frank depiction of adult relationships, including not only Paul and Lili but also the seductive magician whom Lili is also drawn to and his breathtaking, scantily clad wife Rosalie—had something to do with the treatment *Lili* received from its distributor. Simply, MGM didn't know what to do with it. Sensing that adults would not take to it owing to the aura of childlike wonderment, they released it as a children's picture, though the intensity of the characters' sexual obsessions make it a rather odd film for matinees. In fact, that's where most of us fifties moviegoers first saw—and fell in love with—*Lili*.

Mel Ferrer projected the proper note of doom and sadness as the tragic artist Paul, though finally it is Caron who makes the bittersweet project click. She is one of the few mature actresses of her time who could make us believe, when she speaks to puppets, that she forgets who is manipulating them behind the scenes. Mary Pickford might have made audiences accept such a conceit, but not many women since could convey the necessary naivete without appearing cloying. Combining the wide-eyed wholesomeness of Doris Day with the Gallic sex appeal of Brigitte Bardot, Leslie Caron offered a unique screen presence. Few films conveyed her special aura as effectively as *Lili*.

Ethel Merman as "Madam."

Call Me Madam

A 20th Century-Fox Film (1953)

CREDITS:

Produced by Sol C. Siegel; directed by Walter Lang; screenplay by Arthur Sheekman, based on the musical comedy by Howard Lindsay and Russel Crouse; running time: 117 minutes.

CAST:

Ethel Merman (Mrs. Sally Adams); Donald O'Connor (Kenneth); Vera-Ellen (Princess Maria); George Sanders (Cosmo Constantine); Billy De Wolfe (Pemberton Maxwell); Helmut Dantine (Prince Hugo); Walter Slezak (Tantinnin); Steven Geray (Sebastian); Ludwig Stossel (Grand Duke); Lilia Skala (Grand Duchess); Charles Dingle (Senator Brockway); Emory Parnell (Senator Gallagher).

Any list of the great stage performers whose theater-magic failed to translate into similar cinematic charisma must be headed by Ethel Merman, certainly one of the great ladies of the American musical theater. Understandably, with the birth of sound—which caused every Hollywood studio to scramble in a mad competition to sign up popular stage stars of the day—Merman had her choice of offers, opting to go with Paramount Pictures, who during the early thirties cast her in such items as

Follow the Leader, We're Not Dressing, and Cole Porter's *Anything Goes,* which had been literally designed as a stage vehicle for the young Merman. But the excitement that Merman generated merely by walking out on a stage (never mind the thrill when she began singing!) did not happen when she was blown up to a larger-than-life image; the camera simply did not love her. So further film vehicles were few—a nice turn in *Alexander's Ragtime Band* (1938), a cameo in *Stage Door Canteen* (1943)—until Fox decided, after her ten-year absence from films, to try once more and turn Merman into a movie star, as they prepared to compete with MGM in turning out glossy Technicolor musicals.

The effort lasted for only two films, and the second—*There's No Business Like Show Business*—is the better remembered, if only because it featured Marilyn Monroe at her height, singing the torrid "Tropical Heat Wave." Most of the *Show Business* cast members were also present, a year earlier, in this forgotten film which rates as the better of the two. For it allowed the public at large to experience what Broadway audiences acclaimed (Merman did the play 644 times) as one of the great showstopping performances of all time. More often, Merman—like Mary Martin, Chita Rivera, and Gwen Verdon—would have to suffer the slings and arrows of outrageous theatrical fortune, as roles designed with her in mind were handed to movie stars who often had someone else's singing voice dubbed in. In the early sixties, Warner Brothers would prove less charitable when (over the howl of theater purists and Merman fans) they gave Rosalind Russell the Merman role in the film version of *Gypsy.* At least in *Call Me Madam* Merman got to play the role written for the purpose of positively exploiting all her talents to the hilt.

With a wide array of Irving Berlin songs to perform,

Merman played Mrs. Sally Adams (a fictionalization of real-life Washington hostess Perle Mesta) who was named Ambassadress to Lichtenburg and unconsciously struck something of a blow for Women's Lib by proving she could handle the chores as effectively as any man. Donald O'Connor—the perfect second lead for everyone from Gene Kelly to Francis the Talking Mule—neatly handled the role of Mrs. Adams' press secretary, while George Sanders—often seen as ultra-civilized villains—here attempted one of his rare forays into the musical genre, and was critically applauded (in the role of the European general Merman fell for) as a performer of such numbers as "Marrying for Love" and (in a duet with Merman) "The Best Thing for You Would Be Me."

Like *Roman Holiday,* Audrey Hepburn's premiere vehicle, *Call Me Madam* contained a Cinderella story in reverse, as Kenneth falls for a princess; but Vera-Ellen, however much she resembled Hepburn in slimness, was not similarly born for movie stardom, despite the lithe young lady's singing/dancing talents; this, *Show Business,* and the seasonal favorite *White Christmas* would prove to be the highlights of her shortlived screen career.

The impact of the film finally rested with Miss Merman, belting out songs with the best of the brazen, brassy ladies who made their mark on Broadway, where critics and audiences alike were astounded by someone able to sing loud enough to reach playgoers in the back of the balcony. Sadly, though, films called for a more subtle delivery, and Merman was never able to constrain her gusto. What seemed charming onstage was, perhaps, a bit much on the big screen. Certainly, *Call Me Madam* is more a filmed play than a true movie musical, yet it still shines as a preservation on celluloid of one of Merman's greatest moments.

A royal portrait: George Sanders, Ethel Merman, Vera-Ellen.

Island in the Sky

A Paramount Picture (1953)

CREDITS:

Produced by Robert Fellows and John Wayne; directed by William A. Wellman; screenplay by Ernest K. Gann, from his novel of the same name; running time: 109 minutes.

CAST:

John Wayne (Dooley); Lloyd Nolan (Stutz); Walter Abel (Col. Fuller); James Arness (McMullen); Andy Devine (Moon); Allyn Joslyn (J. H. Handy); James Lydon (Murray); Harry Carey Jr.

John Wayne as Dooley.

Dooley instructs his fellow crew members how best to survive their perilous situation.

80

The star is John Wayne, the subject a plane about to crash, the director William A. Wellman, the period of release 1953–54. Ask anyone to name the film, and they'll scoff at how easy your trivia question was: *The High and the Mighty*, with The Duke whistling the famed title song in the opening sequence, then helping Bob Stack attempt to keep an airborne *Grand Hotel* from going down. Only that well remembered film, hailed in its time as a classic of suspense and human-interest drama, plays now as a lethargic, overwrought, unnecessarily long soap opera. There's another movie that fits the description nicely, though this one has been lost over the years: *Island in the Sky*, the little movie Wayne and Wellman made the same year, only with a modest budget, a tighter length, a rugged black-and-white look instead of the high-gloss Technicolor of *The High and the Mighty*. Ironically, it's *Island in the Sky* that still plays beautifully.

In *The High and the Mighty*, Wayne and Wellman opted for slickness; here, the approach was starkness. In the opening, Dooley—piloting a transport across Greenland during World War II—finds his motor conking out. Shortly, he and the servicemen on board are stranded in the snow country. The film then details, in near-documentary fashion, the attempts by the men to survive, the various processes by which a group of professionals would calmly go about ensuring their own longest possible survival span in trust that a rescue mission will find them before the last hope is gone; alternated with this is an equally low-key depiction of that rescue mission, allowing us to look through a window at this particular corner of reality and see how the team of solid professionals would doggedly go about trying to track down the position of the plane. In the end, owing to the professionalism of both groups of men (and the leaders of each group, played by Wayne and Walter Abel respectively), the rescue is successfully enacted. The film has allowed us to see the necessity for a level-headed approach to such a problem as the logical route toward its solution, and also to comprehend—from watching what amounts to a "case study" of a typical handling of such a situation—the precise nature of an operation that was previously only sketchily understood by the public at large. In that sense, the movie is highly influenced by those British films, in large part sponsored by their government, which presented a gentle form of propaganda (simply, disseminating information) in the guise of entertainment, holding their audience with interesting

characters but sending the audience home having learned about a fascinating process about which they were previously ignorant.

Naturally, then, there are none of the big scale histrionics that mark *The High and the Mighty*. Even Wayne, generally a larger-than-life actor, appears remarkably restrained, never slipping into the heroic stance that ordinarily defines him. Perhaps that's the reason why the movie has been "lost" for so long: it certainly is an uncharacteristic Wayne performance, but one which remains strong and warm in the memory.

Also in the film are several performers who would figure prominently in the ongoing assemblage of characters-in-repertoire that The Duke would rely ever more heavily on in his sunset years. Andy Devine's bustling comic sidekick dutifully served not only Guy Madison on TV's *Wild Bill Hickock* but also Wayne in *The Man Who Shot Liberty Valance*. Harry Carey Jr., who had joined Wayne for *Red River* and *Three Godfathers*, would become as much a staple of western films as his famous father had been. Several young TV stars, including Mike Connors (*Mannix*) and Darryl Hickman (*The Americans*) received their first exposure here, while Carl Switzer, Alfalfa of the *Our Gang* comedies for Hal Roach, had a nice character part; Wellman would use him again, unrecognizable as an ancient Indian shaman, in *Track of the Cat*. Also on board were James Arness and Fess Parker, a pair of budding cowboy stars in the Wayne mold; before long, they would enjoy considerable success as the stars of TV's *Gunsmoke* and *Davy Crockett*, a pair of parts each calling out for "a young John Wayne."

5,000 Fingers of Dr. T

A Columbia Pictures Release (1953)

CREDITS:

Produced by Stanley Kramer; directed by Roy Rowland; screenplay by Dr. Seuss and Allan Scott, based on the story by Dr. Seuss; running time: 88 minutes.

CAST:

Peter Lind Hayes (Zabladowski); Mary Healy (Mrs. Collins); Hans Conried (Dr. Terwilliker); Tommy Rettig (Bart); John Heasley (Uncle Whitney); Robert Heasley (Uncle Judson); Noel Cravat (Sergeant Lunk); Henry Kulky (Stroogo).

Little orphan Bart (Tommy Rettig) would like handyman Zabladowski (Peter Lind Hayes) for his father-figure.

which serves as the sleeping child's fantasy projection of what he would secretly like to do.

Dr. Seuss's remarkable ability to concoct stories that do not condescend to kids but view the world as they do is in evidence here. Naturally, the child recoils from the terrifying symbol of culture by retreating to a friendship with a blue collar worker who stands as the polar opposite of Terwilliker. That's Zabladowski, the simple, sincere plumber Bart would like to have marry his mother. Peter Lind Hayes nicely played the part, though his oddball appeal—Hayes looked like a cross between Carleton Carpenter and Orson Bean—made him an unlikely candidate for movie stardom. His greatest success—along with that of his wife, Mary Healy, who plays the Mom—came on television, where their combination of down-home charm and softspoken satire made them popular variety show performers throughout the fifties. Hans Conried, he of the ultra-pretentious manner, proved a perfect choice for the villain, while Tommy Rettig parlayed his quiet appeal into a three-year run as Jeff on the original *Lassie* TV show.

Director Roy Rowland effectively lent his film the ambience of the comic strips kids of the fifties devoured, so that it pictorially partakes of a child's point-of-view by studying a high culture he cannot comprehend through the vision of a popular culture that is natural to his

Stanley Kramer labored throughout the fifties to supply the adult audience with a sufficient number of serious cinematic statements, effectively producing *(The Men, High Noon)*, less effectively directing *(Pride and the Passion, Not As a Stranger)* films establishing him as king of the message movies. Once, though, this high-minded filmmaker took time off from his well-intentioned efforts at liberal enlightenment; this bizarre opus—Kramer collaborated with Dr. Seuss (of "Cat in the Hat" fame) to produce a surreal kiddie movie—stands as an ingenious oddity.

Bart is a nice, normal boy with one great problem: his widowed Mom makes him take piano lessons, positive this will offer the child an in-road to "the finer things in life." Bart would rather be watching television or out playing baseball. In his mind, his teacher, Dr. Terwilliker, takes on a monstrous aspect; when Bart is supposed to be practicing, he's more often slipping into grotesque fantasies about Terwilliker. At night, while Bart sleeps, the trap door of his unconscious mind flies open; before long, he's lost in a labyrinthian dream in which the doctor presides over a wicked land, an off-kilter combination of Oz and the Candyland Pinocchio and Lampwick were carted off to. Only here, kidnapped children like Bart are forced to forever practice the piano, until Bart finds the courage to lead the others in a rebellion

But that purveyor of High Culture, Dr. Terwilliker (Hans Conried), has other ideas.

82

As the film progresses, the sets become ever more surreal.

sensibility. It's one of those special movies parents can share with their children, enjoying the undercurrent of sophistication that younger viewers miss. If it is ever revived, film addicts will joyously rediscover a fabulous but forgotten film which combines the best qualities of *Willy Wonka and the Chocolate Factory*, *Invaders from Mars*, and *The Little Shop of Horrors*.

Cease Fire

A Paramount Picture (1953)

CREDITS:

Produced by Hal Wallis; directed by Owen Crump; screenplay by Walter Doniger, from a story by Mr. Crump; running time: 89 minutes.

The child's nightmare grows ever more tense.

No, that's not Sean Penn in the center but a real-life GI playing himself.

CAST:

Capt. Roy Thompson Jr. *(Lieut. Thompson)*; Cpl. Henry Goszkowski *(Patrol Sgt. Goszkowski)*; Sgt. Richard Karl Elliott *(Elliott)*; Sfc. Albert Bernard Cook *(One Ton)*; Pvt. Johnnie L. Mayes *(Mayes)*; Cheong Yul Bak *(Kim)*; Sfc. Howard E. Strait *(Strait)*; Pfc. Gilbert L. Gazaille *(Bad News)*; Pfc. Harry L. Hofelich *(Hofelich)*; Cpl. Charlie W. Owen *(Owen)*; Cpl. Harold D. English *(English)*; Pfc. Edmund J. Pruchniewski *(Pruchniewski)*; Pvt. Otis Wright *(Wright)*; Pfc. Ricardo Carrasco *(Carrasco)*.

The new realism in the postwar cinema reached an apex with *Cease Fire*, the film which—between Roberto Rossellini's *Open City* (1946) and Haskell Wexler's *Medium Cool* (1969)—must be counted as the most significant experiment at combining fact and fiction. In our own age, when the docudrama has emerged as an important if controversial form of entertainment, *Cease Fire* deserves to be revived and closely studied as a landmark in moviemaking history. Yet this is a film that's almost never mentioned, even among diehard film buffs.

Co-writer/director Owen Crump had an idea for a motion picture about the Korean conflict, conceiving of a film which would fall halfway between Sam Fuller's dramatic account of the action in *The Steel Helmet* and the documentary version offered in the 1951 film *This Is Korea*. After receiving sanction from producer Hal Wallis and official permission (as well as a promise of future cooperation) from the Department of Defense, Crump

journeyed with a minuscule film crew to the front lines. Once there, he closely studied the situation, then hurriedly penned a script about a day in the life of an ordinary infantry company attempting to fight in this undeclared and confusing war.

Word spread that a cease fire might begin any moment. Crump was intrigued by the irony: all around him, men were dying, though they knew the cessation of hostilities was near. The filmmaker decided to give his story extra punch by having the mission that would serve as the plot-line take place on the day when that cease fire began, though this had not yet happened when he shot the film.

Assigned to work with the Seventh Division, Crump picked his cast from among the soldiers. He chose several before completing the script, in such cases making the names of the characters identical with the names of the men who would play them, and to a degree writing the characters as facsimiles, or dramatized representations, of those men. This does not mean, though, that the men were playing themselves: the focal character of the story is the young lieutenant leading the reconnaissance mission, but he is played by a captain. A number of the men die in the film, but in real life, they were not killed on this mission, since this mission did not actually exist, but was invented for the purpose of the story. Yet the mission was closely based on a number of actual and similar ones, and a number of the men who took part in the film were killed in action shortly after their brief hiatus to "act" in a movie, including one who had "died" in the story.

The shooting of the film in an area where a different kind of "shooting" was going on lends this movie a bleak, stark authenticity no war movie before or since has ever boasted, other than outright documentaries like John Huston's famed *Battle of San Pietro*. Incredibly, though, it was shot and released in the 3-D process, apparently to increase the sense of reality even further, though that gimmick only proved distracting and put the film in the same league as *Bwana Devil* and *House of Wax*. But what is this: a drama, a documentary, a dramatized documentary or a docudrama? No one could decide then, and it isn't much easier to do so now. Certainly, this is a one of a kind film, but it also makes clear how incredibly important "reality filmmaking" became to the American cinema during the fifties, with such grim quasi-actualizations of life all but replacing the old notion of tinseltown.

Among those great films which deal honestly with the ordeal of the ordinary fighting man in a twentieth century war—*All Quiet on the Western Front, A Walk in the Sun, The Story of G. I. Joe, Platoon*—*Cease Fire* ought to hold a place of special honor. Among the great

Today, no one can identify the soldiers who appeared briefly in the movie.

A brief respite from war.

documentary/drama experiments—the aforementioned *Open City* and *Medium Cool*, the likewise acclaimed *Salt of the Earth* and *Four Days of Naples*—*Cease Fire* should be considered and reconsidered. Inexplicably, it is almost unknown, despite the fact that it's quite remarkable on both counts.

Split Second

An RKO Picture (1953)

CREDITS:

Produced by Edmund Grainger; directed by Dick Powell; screenplay by William Bowers and Irving Wallace; running time: 85 minutes.

CAST:

Stephen McNally *(Sam Hurley)*; Alexis Smith *(Kay Garven)*; Jan Sterling *(Dottie)*; Keith Andes *(Larry Fleming)*; Paul Kelly *(Bart Moore)*; Arthur Hunnicutt *(Asa)*; Robert Paige *(Arthur Ashton)*; Richard Egan *(Dr. Garven)*; Frank de Kova *(Dummy)*.

Split Second takes one of the great melodramas of the 1930s, *The Petrified Forest*, and effectively updates it for the atomic era. In the 1936 film version of that Robert Sherwood play, the desert in which a gang of killers hold assorted wayfarers captive symbolizes the Depression itself. Here, a similar situation unfolds, only with a neat twist for an early fifties audience with an insatiable appetite for tales featuring nuclear orientation. In this version, the desert where criminals and civilians stand-off turns out to be an H-bomb test site, as they discover they're sitting near a detonator about to go off.

As Sam, titular leader of the gang, Stephen McNally displayed the kind of scruffiness associated with Bogart's Duke Mantee, if none of that earlier actor's implicit skill. More interesting is Alexis Smith, one of the truly underrated glamour girls of the era. She plays, with just the right jittery touch of nervous intensity, a woman who will do anything to survive, egging her current lover (Robert Paige) into a fight with the gangster that the poor sap can't possibly win, seducing the criminal in hopes he'll take her with him when the gang deserts the other poor folks, even luring the husband (Richard Egan) she planned to desert out to the ghost town hideaway to care for the gangster's wounded companion (Paul Kelly). In the end, she tricks herself, literally leaping into the gangster's car when the test time is moved up and they have several minutes, rather than two hours, to make a

Sam Hurley (Stephen McNally) keeps oldtime desert rat Asa (Arthur Hunnicutt) covered, while Larry (Keith Andes) and Dottie (Jan Sterling) look on.

frantic getaway. In their desperation, they drive closer to the launch site, run off the road and get stuck in the sand, staring helplessly and hopelessly at the bomb tower as it blasts off. The others, meanwhile, have rushed into a cave the old prospector Asa (the incomparable Arthur Hunnicutt, among other roles the best Pa Kettle ever) told them about, and survive the blast. Among them: Jan Sterling, usually cast as an unregenerate slut but here quite sympathetic, and Keith Andes, a forgotten leading man of B movies.

Of course, knowing what we do today about the after-effects of the Nevada desert testing, it seems sadly safe to say when they emerge from the cave an hour later, the people exposed themselves to deadly radiation. After all, the entire cast and crew of the film *The Conqueror* died from cancer after shooting that spectacle in the desert not far from where the atomic tests had been held. Incredibly enough, Dick Powell directed that John Wayne/Susan Hayward vehicle, and also this film, which blithely suggested that radiation after-effects were not a problem. Powell died in the early sixties of a cancer that appears to have begun around 1954, the time when he was shooting *The Conqueror*.

On a more positive note, it's worth mentioning Powell's career as well as his ironic association with the two films. Typed as a light-leading man in thirties musicals, Powell survived in the forties by changing his image and taking on tough guy roles in downbeat *film noirs*. In the fifties, rather than drift into B movies as friends Ronald Reagan and Robert Taylor were doing, he again made a transition, to the character roles he now seemed suited

for in films like *The Bad and the Beautiful*, and to directing. In addition, Powell was one of the first movie people to understand that television could be an asset. Powell produced, as well as starred in, such TV projects as *Four Star Playhouse*, an anthology alternating Powell and fellow aging movie stars Charles Boyer, David Niven, and Ida Lupino; this allowed them the steady work of an ongoing show without the permanent grind (or tiresome association with a single character) of a weekly series. Friends Reagan and Taylor likewise hosted shows, but they picked up paychecks for their work, while producer Powell signed paychecks and became far wealthier than he had in his salad days as a superstar.

As a film director, his work is sometimes blithely written off as nondescript, but that's not the case with this, his premiere picture behind the cameras. Tense and taut, with a brooding mood of bleakness and a crackling sense of suspense, *Split Second* was surefire entertainment that could only have been created at this specific moment in time, revealing how traditional and ongoing story forms can, when approached by clever writers, be given a topical twist.

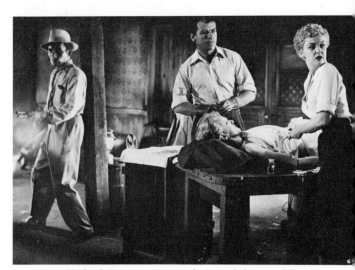

Dr. Garven (Richard Egan) operates on the wounded criminal Bart (Paul Kelly) even as sirens warn of the impending bomb test.

The Atomic Kid

A Republic Picture (1954)

CREDITS:

Produced by Mickey Rooney; directed by Leslie H. Martinson; screenplay by Benedict Freedman and John Fenton Murray, from a story by Blake Edwards; running time: 86 minutes.

CAST:

Mickey Rooney *(Blix Waterberry)*; Robert Strauss *(Stan Cooper)*; Elaine Davis *(Audrey Nelson)*; Bill Goodwin *(Dr. Rodell)*; Whit Bissell *(Dr. Pangborn)*; Robert E. Keane *(Mr. Reynolds)*.

In recent interviews, Mickey Rooney has chosen to recall his career as the child-star of MGM in the 1930s and adolescent screen hero of early forties who, when he passed beyond his teen years, couldn't get a job. His memory, though, is cloudy on this subject. If by "couldn't get a job" he means in the kind of high-class project to which he'd become accustomed in his earlier years, there's validity to his claim. In fact, though, Rooney worked regularly throughout the fifties, starring in a TV show called *Hey, Mulligan!* while taking on character roles in big pictures and leads in little ones. He even jumped into the actor-as-producer gambit the big boys—John Wayne, Kirk Douglas, Burt Lancaster—were becoming involved with, though on a more modest scale. One of his B pictures stands in many ways as the representative comedy film of its era.

The Atomic Kid begins as the humorous counterpart to the topical-drama *Split Second*. Once again, the subject is the then frequent nuclear bomb testing on our southwest deserts. The film begins with an effective pseudo-documentary approach (so very characteristic of American moviemaking in the postwar era), as a somber voice-over narrator intones about the government and military cooperation during a test, while we see what appears to be actual news footage of the careful minute-

Blix (Mickey Rooney) and Stan (Robert Strauss) can't understand what all the weird mannequins are doing in a house on the desert.

by-minute preparations. Today, such sequences seem an effective satire on the oppressively widespread use of documentary techniques in fiction films at the time.

Meanwhile, wandering around the desert, oblivious to the test, are two lovable losers, Blix and Stan. Lost and discouraged, the uranium miners happen upon an isolated house, at which point Stan goes for help, leaving the exhausted Blix to rest up. The film cuts back and

The survivor, holding his "toasted" sandwich.

87

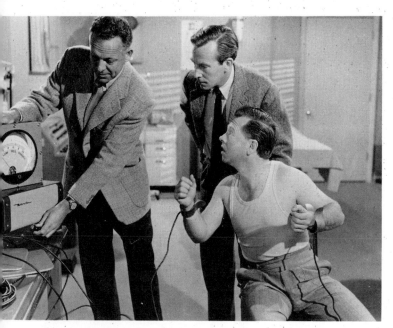

How did he survive? Bill Goodwin and Whit Bissell are the scientists testing him for radioactivity.

Blake Edwards, who in the seventies would, with *Victor/Victoria* and *"10,"* emerge as a writer-director comic auteur in the Capra/Sturges/Wilder tradition, here first proved his potential. From our vantage point, *The Atomic Kid* displays an embarrassing naivete about the after-effects of such testing; there's no hint that, in a few years time, Blix would develop cancer as a result of the exposure, despite surviving the initial blast. For that, one has to go to a more recent film, like the brilliant *Desert Bloom* (1986), with its hindsight understanding that the government's reassurances of absolutely no long-range repercussions were irresponsible. Though *The Atomic Kid* lacks such insight, it nonetheless stands as an effective if forgotten attempt to present several key topical issues in the context of a comedy programmer.

Carmen Jones

A 20th Century-Fox Film (1954)

CREDITS:

Produced by Otto Preminger; directed by Mr. Preminger; screenplay by Harry Kleiner, adapted from the book and lyrics to the stage show of the same name by Oscar Hammerstein 2nd, inspired by Bizet's opera that in turn had been taken from a previous story by Prosper Merimee; running time: 105 minutes.

CAST:

Dorothy Dandridge (Carmen); Harry Belafonte (Joe); Olga James (Cindy Lou); Pearl Bailey (Frankie); Diahann Carroll (Myrt); Roy Glenn (Rum); Nick Stewart (Dink); Joe Adams (Husky); and featuring the voices of Le Vern Hutcherson (Joe), Marilyn Horn (Carmen), and Marvin Hayes (Husky).

forth between the accurately portrayed ultra-serious images of servicemen making final arrangements for the blast (they are stunned when, only moments before the bomb is to go off, Stan wanders into their encampment), and Blix, who trudges about the house, helping himself to food and drink, initially confused as to the lifelike mannequins positioned at tables, gradually coming to understand precisely what's happening. Rooney's clever playing of Blix's growing awareness is marvelous; his helpless hysteria when the truth finally dawns on him is a classic comedy performance given a topical context.

Up to this point, the film sets up, then sustains a comic suspense. What happens afterwards is something of a letdown, replacing much of the initial satire with sheer silliness. Blix somehow survives the bomb blast, causing the government to engage in all sorts of testing in hopes of learning how and why he lived. There's an overly conventional romance with his nurse, played by pretty Elaine Davis (Mrs. Mickey Rooney at the time). And some deft comic playing as his old pal Stan (Robert Strauss was then between his memorable roles for Billy Wilder, as Animal in *Stalag 17* and as the lecherous handyman in *The Seven Year Itch*) makes clear he's very much a man of the 1950s by characteristically trying to exploit his buddy's situation, using the mass media (especially the new, significant force of television) to turn Blix into an instant celebrity. Finally, there's the ever-prevalent fifties fear of an unseen Russian takeover, as some seemingly friendly fellows turn out to be Red agents.

When *Carmen Jones* was presented on the New York stage in 1943, it seemed the very sort of entertainment that could only be mounted for the sophisticated New York theater crowd. The idea of such a show ever being adapted to film was unthinkable: how could the little old lady in Dubuque that *The New Yorker* is not written for be expected to relate to a musical about Negroes when it played at her suburban movie theater? Then came the Civil Rights movement of the early fifties, and all that changed. As black Americans captured the headlines, Hollywood sensed a trend. Understandably, then, *Carmen Jones* reached the screen, but not for a full eleven years after it had first played New York.

Dorothy Dandridge as Carmen Jones.

Carmen—as in Merimee's novel and Bizet's opera—is a fabulous wanton, a lowerclass femme fatale who inspires lust in aristocratic men and takes a terrible pleasure in inciting such hapless fellows to acts of near madness. Now, though, she is a black, living in the deep South. Betraying the World War II origins of this latest incarnation of the legend, the story is set at a parachute plant, where Carmen works. The seduced, then abandoned hero of the piece is a soldier named Joe, the Negro example of the typical American "GI Joe" of the war years. When Carmen drops him for the prizefighter Husky (sitting in for the Spanish toreador who in the original stole the cigarette maker from the cavalryman Don Jose), the romantic triangle swiftly erupts into violence.

Why is this fascinating if flawed film so rarely revived? In its time, blacks were proud that so many fine Negro performers had the chance to work in the context of a film—shot in color and in the CinemaScope process—clearly not intended only for black audiences. *Carmen Jones* was, then, a breakthrough. From the vantage point not only of the late eighties but even a mere five years after the film's initial release, certain problematic areas became evident. First, the black performers did not sing songs of their own culture, but a white's beautifully composed though ethnically inaccurate approximations of such things, as the music of Bizet's arias were married to lyrics intended to approximate Negro slang as Ham-

merstein (mis)understood it. Second, the black performers were not allowed to sing for themselves, perhaps not so surprising in the case of Miss Dandridge (always better known as an actress than a singer) but unforgivable with Harry Belafonte, one of the great song stylists of his time. Third, the film was directed by a white artist, admirable in 1954 but almost offensive a short time later, when the Civil Rights Movement made enough strides that black artists came to rightly feel films which purported to communicate their culture ought to be made by them. Like Steven Spielberg's recent *The Color Purple, Carmen Jones* seems flawed in its depiction of black males as prisoners of their own insatiable sexuality, a view that might be acceptable coming from a black director, less so from a white, however noble his purpose.

One thing is undeniable: this was Dorothy Dandridge's greatest moment in movies. Though her career has been tragically forgotten—an ironic fate, considering how truly tragic was this beautiful, talented woman's life—she was in fact the female equivalent of Sidney Poitier, the first black actress to be accepted as a mainstream sex symbol of American movies. Her handful of films—*Island in the Sun, Porgy and Bess*—reveal both her artistry and her sensuality. While her sultry but sensitive screen presence gave new pride to black women who saw in her an exciting, emerging identity for themselves, Miss Dandridge could not psychologically deal with being a black, however light skinned, and therefore denied full acceptance (through marriage to a white) into Hollywood's dominant culture. Her demise at her

Carmen appears to enjoy inciting fights between Joe and her new boyfriend, Husky (Joe Adams).

One of the quieter moments for Carmen and Joe.

own hand brought about an end to her emotional anguish. A sad final irony, though: in the cast of this, Dandridge's starring vehicle, was Diahann Carroll, the very woman who in time would win the kind of total acceptance Dandridge died believing would always be denied her, and women like her.

Adventures of Robinson Crusoe

A United Artists Release (1954)

CREDITS:

Produced by Oscar Dancigers and Henry Ehrlich; directed by Luis Bunuel; screenplay by Phillip Roll and Mr. Bunuel, adapted from the novel by Daniel Defoe; running time: 90 minutes.

CAST:

Dan O'Herlihy (Robinson Crusoe); James Fernandez (Friday); Felipe De Alba (Captain Oberzo); Chel Lopez (Bos'n); Jose Chevez, Emilio Garibay (Leaders of the Mutiny).

The general rule of thumb is that great novels never make for great films, if only because the very thing that made them so great to begin with—the way they were written—is automatically lost in the process of adaptation. But some great novels seem even less suited to

movies than others, and Defoe's *Robinson Crusoe* is one, owing to a plot that seemingly leaves little room for the interaction of actors, which is so crucial in the film medium. Most of the story concerns one man, alone on a deserted island for some 20 years, and his mental ruminations. Yet that material made for one of the best book-to-film adaptations ever, even though it is shamefully overlooked in almost all studies of the relationship between literature and the cinema.

Dan O'Herlihy won a much deserved Oscar nomination for his portrayal of Crusoe, who in the mid-sixteen hundreds manages to survive a shipwreck that claims the lives of all his comrades, only to find himself attempting to survive an even greater adversary than the sea. He is face to face with nature in the raw, and attempts to recreate the kind of civilization he left behind. The battle is not easily won, but if Defoe conceived of the tale as a kind of pre-Darwin vision of survival of the fittest, then he gave us a Crusoe who is fit indeed. The hero does prove victorious over nature: the land is tamed, the jungle converted into a garden, rough nature giving way to a proper, civilized (if solitary) home. As Crusoe strolls about his little world, carrying an umbrella to

Dan O'Herlihy, as the young Robinson Crusoe, transports valuable items from the ruined ship to his new island home.

protect himself from the glaring sun, he appears almost a caricature of the English gentleman, though his clothes are made from hides rather than fine cloth. And when a native happens to come into his possession, Crusoe likewise succeeds in completely civilizing this example of natural man.

Bunuel remained remarkably faithful to the letter of Defoe's book, while at the same time converting the ancient tale into the kind of contemporary fable of interest to this ultra-modern filmmaker. Bunuel is, after all, the writer-director who would six years later create *Viridiana*, the first classic of the ever-more radical sixties; in that film, his solipsistic nun begins to question the existence of God. That sort of cinematic existentialism-bordering-on-nihilism is also found in Bunuel's interpretation of Crusoe. For the most memorable scene in the movie has no parallel in the book, expressing Bunuel rather than Defoe: following the death of his beloved dog (and before the arrival of his man Friday), Crusoe—wielding a torch—rushes out into the raging surf, screaming up into the heavens for God to show him some sign that He exists and that life has meaning beyond the primitive growth of the jungle.

Crusoe, having lived alone so long that he doubts his own existence, shouts up into the heavens, challenging God to speak to him.

The movie achieves a balance between Bunuel and Defoe, an aesthetic and intellectual tension between the great literary artist who supplied the story and the great cinematic artist who brought it to vivid visual life. The great moments are all there: Crusoe, struggling against the sea in the opening; Crusoe, as a near-senile old fool, dancing about his makeshift castle; Crusoe, having given up hope of ever seeing another soul, dumbfounded at the sight of a single footprint on the beach. O'Herlihy, in his only significant movie lead, made a marvelous Crusoe, capturing the man's ever changing moods—his courage, his loneliness, his sadness, his triumph—in a role that demanded he be onscreen in nearly every shot and, for more than three-fifths of the running time, do so alone; James Fernandez made a fine, unstereotypical Friday, awed by Robinson's gadgets, quick to learn and adjust to white ways.

For the sake of some action, there's an extended version of Crusoe's fight with the cannibals from whom he rescues Friday and also a battle with some mutineers in the last reels; likewise, much of the idiosyncratic exposition has been cut away. What remains intact is the essence of the tale, here strikingly conveyed in the film's luscious color photography. But United Artists, not knowing how in the blazes to sell this one, released it as

At last, a companion: Crusoe rescues Friday (James Fernandez) from cannibals.

Then must teach him how a "civilized" man lives; first, there's a haircut.

a kiddie matinee feature, making the most of the pirates, who lavishly adorned the posters and lobby cards. Though the movie deserved better, it did nonetheless leave an indelible impression on some children of the fifties who caught it one rainy Saturday afternoon, your author included.

Red Garters

A Paramount Picture (1954)

CREDITS:

Produced by Pat Duggan; directed by George Marshall; screenplay by Michael Fessier, with songs by Jay Livingston and Ray Evans; running time: 91 minutes.

CAST:

Rosemary Clooney (Calaveras Kate); Jack Carson (Jason Carberry); Guy Mitchell (Reb Randall); Pat Crowley (Susana Mar-

tinez); Joanne Gilbert *(Sheila Winthrop);* Gene Barry *(Rafael Moreno);* Cass Daley *(Minnie Redwing);* Frank Faylen *(Billy Buckett);* Reginald Owen *(Judge Winthrop);* Buddy Ebsen *(Ginger Pete);* Richard Hale *(Dr. J. Pott Troy).*

Alain Bernardin, proprietor-producer of Paris's famous Crazy Horse Saloon (immortalized in Woody Allen's *What's New, Pussycat?*) always insists he based the conception for his striptease/cabaret on the Wild West dancehall seen in some Yvonne De Carlo western he caught in the late forties, then filtered through his Frenchman's naughtier sensibility. However, it's hard to believe he did not on some level, however unconscious, have *Red Garters* in mind. For the world's most successful nude show bears striking resemblance to Hollywood's least successful (commercially speaking) western musical spoof. This is a wild cut-up in the tradition of *Destry Rides Again* (which preceded it) and *Cat Ballou* (which followed). A curio—and a clever, charming one at that—*Red Garters* rates as Paramount's most offbeat original book musical, and one of the commercial American cinema's more outlandish exercises in outright surrealism.

But "surrealism" can be a pretentious term, so most reviewers of the time preferred to call this "stylized" instead. That it was, with suggestive sets consisting only of the frames for buildings, weird skies of hallucinogenically bright yellows and reds, looking so bizarre that at the time mainstream audiences didn't have any conception what it was up to (the film seemed too silly for middlebrows, too sophisticated for rubes). The purpose, though, was to present a purposefully exaggerated distillation of previous western stereotypes. Untold numbers of oaters depicted the supposed "code of the west," calling for a fair fight in which good defeats evil at the end. *Red Garters* shamelessly debunked such notions, as the cartoonish incarnations of goodguy and badguy strut their stuff—in song and ballet—then reveal the absurdity of such stereotypes when they fail to follow up on what's expected. This may be the only western where the cavalry arrives too late and the hero loses the last gunfight.

Rosemary Clooney claims to have been positive, while

Rosemary Clooney struts her stuff. Hoofer Buddy Ebsen is confined behind the bar, to the far right.

Another of the provocative dance numbers begins with Clooney fully clothed.

filming, that this movie would be hailed as a break-through, and was stunned when *Red Garters* died at the box-office. Despite her grand voice, Miss Clooney never quite clicked in films—the seasonal favorite *White Christmas* with Bing Crosby and Danny Kaye remains her only major screen success—and the box-office fail-ure of this innovative and energetic picture pretty much spelled an end to any hopes for Hollywood musical stardom. Her career as a pop singer continued to flourish until rock 'n' roll came along and changed the American musical scene forever, wiping out the careers of most performers with a Big Band (rather than Big Beat) orien-tation. Guy Mitchell, cast here as the handsome hero, likewise never made the jump from recording star ("The Rovin' Kind") to movie musical star, though Jack Car-son—as the corrupt boss of the Red Dog Saloon—added another clever characterization to his long list of credits. Gene Barry, playing the Mexican bandido, would soon be seen as a dandified western hero on TV's *Bat Master-son*. Only Buddy Ebsen was shortchanged here by a script that left scant time for his unique hoofing.

Red Garters is the kind of American film that usually appeals more to the French, since they appreciate our most outlandishly artificial items in a way we rarely do

until they proceed to explain such films to us. But even they appear to have overlooked this one. *Red Garters* ought to be one of the cult items forever running at some revival house just off the Champs-Elysees, but it isn't—unless one counts the unconscious impression it must have made on Mr. Bernardin, for surely the Crazy Horse Saloon had its germination here.

The Littlest Kidnappers

A J. Arthur Rank Organization Presentation (1954)

CREDITS:

Produced by Sergei Nolbandov and Leslie Parkyn; directed by Philip Leacock; screenplay by Neil Paterson; running time: 95 minutes.

CAST:

Duncan Macrae *(Grandaddy)*; Jean Anderson *(Grandma)*; Adrienne Corri *(Kirsty)*; Theodore Bikel *(Willem Bloem)*; Jon Whiteley *(Harry)*; Vincent Winter *(Davy)*; Francis De Wolf *(Jan Hooft Sr.)*; James Sutherland *(McNab)*; John Rae *(McCleod)*; Jack Stewart *(Dominie)*; Jameson Clark *(Cameron)*; Eric Woodburn *(Sam Howie)*; Christopher Beeny *(Jan Hooft Jr.)*; Howard Connell *(Jenkins)*.

Only a few movies effectively convey on film the way the world looks to a child: among them, Rene Clement's *Forbidden Games* and the independently made American shoestring-budget feature *The Littlest Fugitive* stand out, along with this gem. *The Little Kidnappers* was the first film set in Nova Scotia (in fact, the on-location shooting was done in Scotland) to ever receive wide acceptance in the United States. Emerging as the sleeper of its year, *Little Kidnappers* broke out of its initial arthouse release, finding its way into neighborhood theaters where it charmed mainstream moviegoers every bit as much as it had the small coterie that usually applauds such non-Hollywood offbeat items. The following spring, special Oscars went to the film's two young stars, for their unstereotypical and unsentimental portrayal of youth.

The year is 1900, and Harry and Davy are orphans, growing up in an isolated area where conditions are harsh. Their Grandaddy believes he must not under any circumstances spoil the children, so he denies them even the one precious item of luxury most of the other boys and girls in this essentially impoverished neighborhood of Scottish immigrants possess: a dog to love and care for. The boys beg, when they dare, but to no avail. And they receive little help from their grandma, who quietly submits to grandaddy's attitude even when the withered old woman's sad eyes reveal she knows he is too extreme and unsparing. For to give the nine-year-old Davy and the five-year-old Harry a dog would not be to spoil them, but only to allow them the natural outlet for the love they so hunger to express. When the boys come upon what they perceive as an abandoned baby, they take it, hide it, and diligently care for it. As far as they are concerned, the baby has no one else. What they cannot know is that they need this baby far more than it needs them.

Much of the film is spent chronicling the ever more intricate ways in which the children hide the baby from the adult population, and how they go about feeding it with goat's milk. But the inventive plot by Neil Paterson is always augmented by Philip Leacock's masterfully unpretentious direction. He closes in on the boys' faces as they relish the baby's consumption of its nourishment,

allows their expressions to visually make all the movie's statements about the wonderful things that can be accomplished by merely having an object for the most decent and human affections.

The film is broadened a bit by subplots, including the difficult romance between Kirsty and Willem that leads to the infant's need for foster parents. Yet what one recalls from this film is the remarkable combination of

Jon Whiteley, "The Baby," and Vincent Winter.

Early in the film, the boys Harry and Davy follow their ancient grandfather to their new home in Nova Scotia.

95

unaffected humor and believable horror that result from the "kidnapping": the striking little gags, both visual and verbal (the way little Vincent Winter pronounces the word "baby" in the thickest Scottish accent had audiences in the mid-fifties enthralled) and the growing sense of melancholy that settles in as we realize—as disturbed as we are delighted—that these boys, so starved for the chance to love, will eventually lose what they have found.

The starkness of the backgrounds adds immensely to the sharp, unsparing portrayal of vulnerable, impressionable little people living in the sternest of situations, but unable to repress their youthful instincts. Likewise, the bleak black-and-white photography heightens that effect immensely; one groans at the thought of this particular item being colorized in order to lend it a new lease on life. Yet it certainly is overripe for rediscovery. Indeed, at a time when there are several cable TV networks (Nickelodeon, The Disney Channel) specializing in full-family fare and presumably starved for proper product, it's remarkable to think that at the time of this writing, neither has unearthed this magnificent little movie. After all, too many movies about children mistake sentimentality for sensitivity; this film realistically depicts the sadder side of being young, doing so with a poignancy that is always mellow but never maudlin.

Destry

A Universal-International Release (1954)

CREDITS:

Produced by Stanley Rubin; directed by George Marshall; screenplay by Edward H. North and D. I. Beauchamp, from the novel by Max Brand; running time: 95 minutes.

CAST:

Audie Murphy (Tom Destry); Mari Blanchard (Brandy); Lori Nelson (Miss Phillips); Thomas Mitchell ("Rags" Barnaby); Lyle Bettger (Decker); Edgar Buchanan (Mayor); Wally Ford (Curtis); Mary Wickes (Bessie Mae); Lee Aaker (Child); Alan Hale, Jr. (Jack Larson); Morgan Woodward (Sheriff Joe Bailey).

In 1939, George Marshall fashioned a film that, along with John Ford's *Stagecoach*, helped create a renaissance for the western. *Destry Rides Again*, an affectionate spoof of the oater, allowed James Stewart his introduction to the genre in the role of a mild-mannered sheriff,

while helping Marlene Dietrich salvage a sagging career by working without benefit of her usual Svengali, Josef von Sternberg. Few directors would consider remaking a movie widely considered a classic, so it was up to Marshall himself to tell the story once again, when Universal-International decided to haul out the tale fifteen years later as a vehicle for war hero turned B movie actor Audie Murphy. While the result may not quite be a cinematic diamond on the order of the Stewart-Dietrich version, this is at the very least an unheralded gemstone, easily the best B western of the decade.

Decker, a smiling dudeish villain who runs a crooked gambling den and saloon, shoots honest Sheriff Joe Bailey in the back; the corrupt mayor then appoints a drunken former deputy, "Rags" Barnaby, as the new

Audie Murphy as Tom Destry.

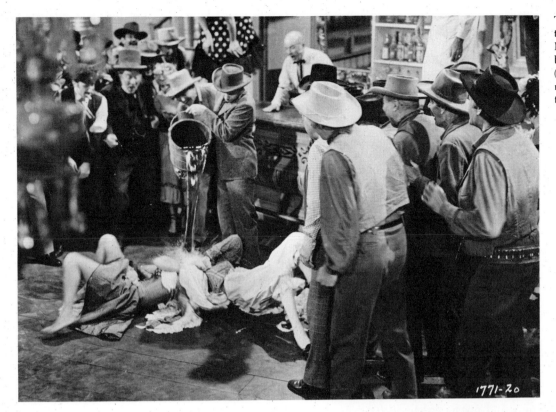

The famous "cat fight" between Mari Blanchard and Mary Wickes as the town busybody; as Edgar Buchanan (third from Audie Murphy's right) looks on, Destry cools the girls off.

lawman. But their plan appears to backfire, when Rags sends for Tom Destry, son of the legendary lawman Rags once worked for. When the stage arrives, the outlaws briefly laugh; instead of a larger-than-life fellow, Destry is short and softspoken, and doesn't carry a gun.

Destry is a disappointment for Rags, but his presence proves disarming. A kind of cowboy precursor to Columbo, Destry's apparent naivete throws the baddies off guard, allowing Tom to learn the truth about the killing. When he finally cannot settle things with words, Destry straps on his Dad's guns and proves himself the fastest man alive. By that time, he's romanced two beautiful women: the blond homesteader Miss Phillips and the brunette hussy Brandy. It's Brandy who finally saves Destry during the climactic gun duel by shifting allegiances and catching a bullet meant for him, dying in Destry's arms with a kiss after wiping away the lipstick he always felt covered, rather than enhanced, her innate beauty.

Max Brand's sentimental potboiler has proven something of a popular classic: an earlier 1922 version starred Tom Mix; and in 1950, a slightly revamped version, *Frenchie*, starred Shelley Winters and Joel McCrea; in the late fifties, a popular Broadway musical version featured Gene Barry, though a 1966 TV series with John Gavin failed to click, heralding the end of the trail for *Destry* remakes.

Destry proves that, when words fail, he can be surprisingly fast on the draw.

In fact, *Destry* might have provided a nifty TV vehicle for Murphy, and considering the success of his film version, it's surprising no one thought of turning it into a series for him. (Murphy did star in an ill-fated 1960 TV series version of an old Alan Ladd western, *Whisper-*

97

ing Smith). As a rediscovered film, *Destry* serves as a fine showcase for Murphy's genial screen personality. Though he's been written off as one more newsworthy celebrity who used his notoriety to break into movies, and often openly stated that he believed he had no talent at all, such comments seem an unfair understatement of his worth. If his Texas twang mostly confined him to B westerns (*Kansas Raiders, Tumbleweed, Guns of Fort Petticoat*) Murphy was at the very least as legitimate a star of that déclassé genre as, say, Roy Rogers or Gene Autry. Besides, Murphy attracted some serious attention those perennial drugstore cowboys did not, winning leads in John Huston's prestigious *Red Badge of Courage* (1951) and *The Unforgiven* (1960), in both cases delivering fine performances. Likewise, he held his own against James Stewart in the A western *Night Passage* (1957), and was strong in Joe Mankiewicz's adaptation of Graham Greene's *The Quiet American* (1958), the first major film about CIA involvement in Viet Nam. An underrated movie performer whose natural grace allowed him a 20-year screen career (celebrity notoriety in and of itself usually leads to two or three films at most), in retrospect it seems safe to say had Murphy gone to Hollywood without his record as a war hero, his career would have been pretty much the same. In that case, the only picture he would not have done would have been *To Hell and Back* (1955), in which Audie Murphy played Audie Murphy.

Suddenly

A United Artists Release (1954)

CREDITS:

Produced by Robert Bassler; directed by Lewis Allen; screenplay by Richard Sale; running time: 77 minutes.

CAST:

Frank Sinatra (*John Baron*); Sterling Hayden (*Tod Shaw*); James Gleason (*Pop Benson*); Nancy Gates (*Ellen Benson*); Kim Charney (*Pidge*); Paul Frees (*Benny Conklin*); Christopher Dark (*Bart Wheeler*); Willis Bouchey (*Dan Carney*); Paul Wexler (*Slim Adams*); Jim Lilburn (*Jud Hobson*).

Frank Sinatra won an Oscar for his energetic performance as Angelo Maggio, a jive-talking, lovable, doomed soldier in the 1953 classic *From Here to Eternity*. To his credit, Sinatra did not initially employ his newfound

prestige to coast, but sought out the most interesting vehicles available. Often, the character he would play was anything but "sympathetic," the operative word for most stars. No more perfect example exists than the psychologically complex and multi-dimensional characterization of a thoroughly despicable man he offers in *Suddenly*.

The film begins in a small, sleepy California town where the likeable local sheriff, Tod Shaw, prepares for a top secret transfer of the President of the United States from train to car. Shaw stops by the home where his fiancée Ellen, her elderly father, and her little boy live. He is stunned to find a group of gunmen there; led by John Baron, they've taken over this strategically placed house and set up a high powered rifle. From here, these paid assassins plan to kill the president for some group they know nothing about but which has met their fee. As the next hour slowly ticks by, Shaw—at first quite helpless—gradually realizes the bizarre mental make-up of the group's leader may allow the sheriff to subvert the terrible plan.

Most of the movie's running time takes place in the living room of the Benson home; in a tautness that rivals *High Noon*, Johnny Baron taunts the helpless sheriff,

Frank Sinatra as Johnny Baron.

makes advances to the pretty Ellen, attempts to befriend the little boy Pidge, tries to win respect from the elderly Pop. Baron is a psychopath, absolutely desperate for respect and admiration, attempting to attain what he needs by gaining total power over the middleclass people, the agents of law and order, even the number one man in the country; this will (in his own twisted mind) justify the existence of this sick, sleazy man who has always been shoved onto the edges of everyday life by "good people" who want nothing to do with him. He desires most of all to be thought of as a man of fierce courage, so relentlessly reminding everyone he was awarded a silver star in Korea that we eventually come to doubt its truth. Baron's vision of himself, the sheriff in time realizes, will prove his fatal flaw, the single chink in this swaggering but insecure man's thin shield of emotional ice that distances him from the world around him.

Sinatra might likewise have "distanced" himself from the character, playing Baron in such a way that we're always aware of the superstar effectively portraying this monstrous man. Instead, Sinatra totally merged with the hideous character, a dangerous but courageous move for an actor of his status, since there is the possibility he will be so convincing in the role that the public may forever

The moment of truth: Sheriff Shaw (Sterling Hayden) stops the assassination just in time.

identify him with it. Here, all our sympathy goes out to Sterling Hayden's character, whose effective amateur psychology so disarms the already distraught hit man that he grows ever more vulnerable, as his ravenous hunger for respect allows him to be overpowered at the last possible moment. In a marvelously ironic ending, after the president has passed through the town without incident, the sheriff then encounters a travelling salesman asking for directions; before driving away, the man laughingly comments on the name of this quiet town—Suddenly—and how inappropriate he considers it for so sleepy a crossroads. Though the sheriff says nothing, the sardonic look on Hayden's face conveys a twist-ending worthy of Hitchcock.

For years, Suddenly was unavailable for viewing, as was The Manchurian Candidate, a later Sinatra vehicle which also dealt with a presidential assassination. One explanation holds that Sinatra, a close friend of President Kennedy, was so distraught by the actual assassination his films had predicted that Sinatra used his influence to keep them from being seen for more than ten years after the incident in Dallas. Recently, Suddenly has resurfaced, though not without a new problem to surmount: many prints of the film now circulating on cable TV and home video have been colorized, which totally destroys the effectiveness of this superb little suspense film by replacing its appropriately bleak black-and-white images with garish, glossy colors.

99

The Egyptian

A 20th Century-Fox Film (1954)

CREDITS:

Produced by Darryl F. Zanuck; directed by Michael Curtiz; screenplay by Phillip Dunne and Casey Robinson, adapted from the novel by Mika Waltari; running time: 140 minutes.

CAST:

Edmund Purdom *(Sinuhe)*; Jean Simmons *(Merit)*; Victor Mature *(Horemheb)*; Gene Tierney *(Baketamon)*; Michael Wilding *(Akhnaton)*; Bella Darvi *(Nefer)*; Peter Ustinov *(Kaptah)*; Judith Evelyn *(Taia)*; Henry Daniell *(Mikere)*; John Carradine *(Grave Robber)*; Carl Benton Reid *(Senmut)*; Tommy Rettig *(Thoth)*; Anitra Stevens *(Nefertiti)*.

The fifties was the decade in which Hollywood had to meet the challenge of television, and one of the many ways filmmakers attempted to lure the public away from the box in their living rooms and back into the theaters was the creation of the Biblical-era superspectacle: in living color on an ever-larger widescreen, featuring wrap-around sound and extraordinarily extended running times, as well as a cast of thousands, filmmakers promised the public something they couldn't get on TV. The ruse worked; people packed the theaters to see, in the first half of the decade, the cardboard spectacle of *The Ten Commandments*, as designed by the fading director Cecil B. DeMille, and in the second half, William Wyler's less artificial, more impressive *Ben-Hur*, which had little in common with DeMille's papier-mâché product other than the ancient world setting and the presence of Charlton Heston.

But Heston was not the only star of such films. At that time, Edmund Purdom became as closely associated with this genre as Heston, though he proved unable to sustain his career. Not that Purdom was perceived by Fox as the perfect choice to bring to life the hero of the bestselling book, which used its religious preachments to justify its sexual frankness, a guise that harkens back beyond DeMille to Griffith. Both Marlon Brando and Paul Newman passed on the role of Sinuhe, so Purdom—a contract player who saw this as his bid for stardom—took it on, along with a similar role opposite Lana Turner in *The Prodigal* one year later. But when he found himself standing in for an overweight Mario Lanza in *The Student Prince*, Purdom begged out of his studio contract, only to find himself in a little-seen syndicated TV series called *Sword of Freedom*, then travelling to Rome where failed Hollywood hopefuls eked out a living doing sword-and-sandal mini-epics.

The Egyptian isn't four hours long; it only seems that way. To be fair, it does feature an elaborate and handsomely constructed vision of the pyramids and their environs, but employs them far less effectively than, say, Howard Hawks's much maligned though quite lively *Land of the Pharoahs*. *The Egyptian* is thuddingly dull as it chronicles a confused doctor, alternating from dedication to duty and enjoyment of the good life. The film laboriously details the hero's early years, to no discernible purpose, then concentrates on an ordinary, familiar tale of an innocent man's seduction by a femme fatale (the long forgotten Bella Darvi).

Victor Mature, whose career had begun to slip since playing Samson in a DeMille epic, had recently enjoyed a resurgence of success in such quasi-religious fare. His broad-shouldered build made him a natural for this genre, and he had performed admirably in Fox's *The*

Robe. Jean Simmons, also a veteran of *The Robe*, was featured here as a serving wench, so it seemed clear Fox hoped lightning would strike twice. No such luck. *The Robe* had enjoyed the distinction of being the first CinemaScope release, and part of the reason audiences went in droves was to experience the newest sensation. *The Egyptian* was clearly just more of the same, only not done nearly so well or written half so pungently. If *The Robe* seems a tad cold and aloof today, it at least offered an intriguing mix of fact and fiction. *The Egyptian* is a story barely worth telling, much less at such inordinate length.

Amazingly, this was directed by Michael Curtiz, the man behind not only such spiffy topical classics as *Yankee Doodle Dandy* and *Casablanca*, but who enjoyed great success with costume films, too: *Captain Blood*, *Charge of the Light Brigade*, *Adventures of Robin Hood*. But that had been during the heyday of Warner Brothers, during the 1930s, when Curtiz was a contract director for that studio and a key member of a team known for turning out hits. Even he couldn't save *The Egyptian*, though several crowd scenes evidence his sincere attempt to do so.

Today, *The Egyptian* stands as one of the films of the fifties that could only have been produced during that particular time, revealing the misguided belief that bigger would necessarily be better and scantily costumed dancing girls would always bring out an audience.

Edmund Purdom as The Egyptian, with friend (Victor Mature).

The once idealistic young man surrenders to pleasures of the flesh.

The Pharoah's grand parade.

By safely setting their stories in ancient times, filmmakers could get away with more graphic depictions of lust (citing "historical accuracy") than they could in contemporary settings.

102

The Adventures of Haji Baba

A 20th Century-Fox Film (1954)

CREDITS:

Produced by Walter Wanger; directed by Don Weiss; screenplay by Richard Collins, based on the nineteenth century novel by James Justinian Morier; running time: 94 minutes.

CAST:

John Derek (Haji Baba); Elaine Stewart (Fakzia); Thomas Gomez (Osman Aga); Amanda Blake (Banah); Paul Picerni (Nurel-Din); Rosemarie Bowe (Ayesha); Donald Randolph (Caliph); Melinda Markey (Touareg); Peter Mamakos (Executioner); Kurt Katch (Caoush).

Like *The Egyptian*, *Haji Baba* was made during the mid-fifties, when producers were mad for spectacles that allowed for widescreen, color, and wraparound sound. But whereas *The Egyptian* made the mistake of boring its audience with a longwinded and listlessly humorless tale, *Haji* is from start to finish characterized by an undercurrent of tongue-in-cheek naughtiness. The film

John Derek seduces yet another of the film's lovelies.

constantly kids itself, sending itself up in a saucy and surprisingly sexy style. The costumes on the girls are unbelievably daring; the tone of the entire romp is not so different from what we'd see and hear in a Feydeau bedroom farce, only here transplanted to a mythic fairy-tale-for-adults image of a never never land Baghdad. Even by today's standards, the girls are gorgeous, their costumes daringly scanty, the mood of satiric sexiness sustained throughout, the production values first rate. This film never slows down long enough to let a viewer consider how silly it all is; *The Adventures of Haji Baba* rates as a delightful rediscovery.

The mood is clearly established in the opening sequence, as we hear the velvet voice of Nat King Cole sing the title song while the camera lingeringly passes over a bevy of harem girls, who are revealed almost as completely as the original *Playboy* Playmates of the Month that were being unveiled at about the same time the film appeared. In fact, this film would have served well as the subject for a "Girls of *Haji Baba*" pictorial, if *Playboy* had only come up with that format then, for every lady in sight is a looker, precisely the sort of wholesome though vixenish fleshpot *Playboy* preferred to photograph in the fifties.

And for the women, there's John Derek. Throughout the fifties, Derek competed with Rock Hudson for the title of the era's prize hunk. But the kind of dramatic and comic roles that turn a contract player into a superstar—*Giant, Pillow Talk*—never came Derek's way. So despite the fact that he was always a better performer

John Derek as Haji Baba.

The beautiful Amazons capture men in combat.

than Hudson—Derek's twinkling eyes communicated a masculinity that was clearly not faked—he dropped out of acting to photograph and direct the beautiful women who were drawn to him: Ursula Andress, Linda Evans, Bo Derek. In Haji, he found a role that fit him well, as the Persian barber who escorts the runaway Princess (in true comic/romantic picaresque fashion, the beautiful girl disguises herself as a boy) from oasis to oasis. They have nothing in common but their arrogance: Haji has wagered a friend that in six months, he can win the hand of the caliph's daughter; she has just refused her father's dictate that she marry a man he has chosen for her. The spoiled lady—who at first takes a dislike to Haji and scorns him constantly—gradually comes to realize she's in love with the common man, and becomes a better person for it. Along the way, they are kidnapped by a tribe of bandits, then taken from those bandits by a group of beautiful Amazons who hide in the hills and prey on the passing caravans.

Despite the constant disrobing of the women and the camera's relentless concentration on their impressive torsos, the film has something of a feminist slant. As the leader of the Amazons, fiery redhead Amanda Blake (just before she took on the role of Miss Kitty in TV's *Gunsmoke*) explains she and her warriors (the implication is that half the girls are lesbians, the other half nymphomaniacs) are fugitives from the harems, now returning some of the pain men perpetrated on them during their bondage. When a man is captured he is sexually exploited until exhausted, then slowly tortured. A woman is given the choice of joining the Amazons or sold into slavery, the idea being any woman who does not want to join the liberated band had better admit her retrograde role by living it to the extreme.

Banah appears ready to make an exception in the case of Haji, who's only too willing to flatter her with his favors, exploiting the Amazon's lust to gain her confidence and flee once more with Fakzia. Their adventures involve enough sadism and sensuality to make this seem like a blueprint for an X feature, though everything is suggested rather than graphically depicted, so *Haji* somehow qualifies as a family film. Today, anyone wanting to see where Derek's vision of women began need only catch *Haji Baba*.

Donovan's Brain

A United Artists Release (1954)

CREDITS:

Produced by Tom Gries; directed by Felix Feist; screenplay by Mr. Feist, adapted from the novel by Curt Siodmak; running time: 83 minutes.

CAST:

Lew Ayres *(Dr. Patrick J. Cory)*; Gene Evans *(Dr. Frank Schratt)*; Nancy Davis *(Janice Cory)*; Steve Brodie *(Herbie Yocum)*; Lisa K. Howard *(Chloe Donovan)*; Tom Powers *(Adviser)*; Michael Colgan *(Tom Donovan)*; Kyle James *(Ranger Chief Tuttle)*; Stapleton Kent *(W. J. Higgins)*; Peter Adams *(Mr. Webster)*; Victor Sutherland *(Nathaniel Fuller)*.

Watching *Donovan's Brain* today, it's hard to believe that the film was released as late as 1954. For with its modest production values and downbeat black-and-white approach to a combination of science-fiction and horror, any knowledgeable film lover who takes a casual glance would guess this was a 1950 or 1951 release, judging from the look and ambience of the piece. Even more

than tone, though, *Donovan's Brain* is so basic to the notion of fantastic cinema in the fifties that it's hard to conceive the film could have arrived as late as mid-decade, but that's in fact the case.

The significance of the film rests in its combining the usually distinct sci-fi and horror genres in a way that seems quite unique to the fifties, though in truth the storyline does date back further than that. An earlier film version, *The Lady and the Monster*, was indeed shot a decade previous by George Sherman. In the fifties adaptation, Patrick J. Cory is a brilliant young research scientist, working at an isolated lab on the feasibility of keeping a human brain alive after the body has expired. By chance (some would uncharitably say contrivance!), a plane crashes nearby, claiming the life of a multi-millionaire, Tom Donovan. Over the objections of both his wife Janice and his assistant, Frank Schratt, Cory decides to try and keep Donovan's brain alive in a saline solution. What he doesn't know is that Donovan was a monster of a man, and his cruel, calculating brain—now intent on making sure his will is executed precisely as he wants—uses a form of hypnosis-telepathy to overcome the personality of the scientist, reducing him to a virtual slave who will do Donovan's bidding. Before the eyes of his wife and assistant, Cory gradually begins to take on the physical appearance, the speech patterns, and the personality and values of the deceased Donovan.

Before World War II, such notions were considered pretty fantastic; after the atomic bombing of Hiroshima

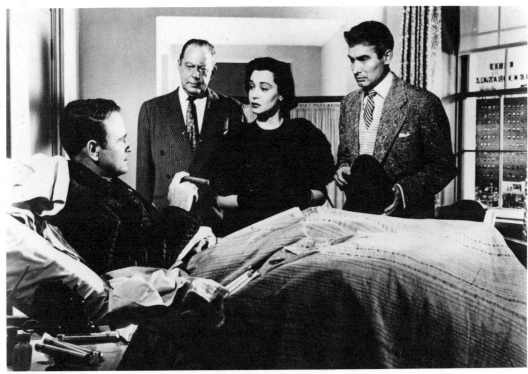
From his bed, Dr. Cory explains his problem to his wife Janice (Nancy Davis) and colleagues.

105

Hoping for the best, Dr. Cory proceeds with his plan: Lew Ayres, Tom Powers, and Nancy Davis.

brought that conflict to a close, the general population soon came to believe just about anything was possible from our scientists, meanwhile suspecting that things developed with the best of intentions might well turn out to be quite horrific.

Donovan's Brain can be considered a mid-twentieth century equivalent of the Frankenstein myth or Dr. Jekyll and Mr. Hyde, with its decent scientist turned into something of a raving lunatic owing to the awful results of his experimentation. He is, like Victor Frankenstein and Henry Jekyll, a man of much knowledge but little wisdom, so overcome by his own narrow brilliance in his field that he fails to consider the moral ramifications of his work.

The film, though, is almost never revived, and there are people professing to be fans of horror and sci-fi who freely admit to not knowing of it. Perhaps that's because Felix Feist's direction is often labored and ponderous, though that can be said of many films of the period which nonetheless are known and regarded, if not often watched. *Donovan's Brain* remains a prototype of its genre, though one that receives far less attention than many of the lesser films descended from its premise.

106

Riot in Cell Block 11

An Allied Artists Release (1954)

CREDITS:

Produced by Walter Wanger; directed by Don Siegel; screenplay by Richard Collins; running time: 80 minutes.

CAST:

Neville Brand *(Dunn)*; Emile Meyer *(Warden)*; Frank Faylen *(Haskell)*; Leo Gordon *(Carnie)*; Robert Osterloh *(Colonel)*; Paul Frees *(Monroe)*; Alvy Moore *(Gator)*; Dabbs Greer *(Schuyler)*; Whit Bissell *(Snader)*; James Anderson *(Action)*; Carleton Young *(Barrett)*; Dan Keefer, Harold J. Kennedy, William Schallert *(Reporters)*.

Anyone who came to *Riot* expecting an update of the Warner Brothers prison pictures so popular in the thirties and early forties was in for something of a surprise, perhaps even a shock. For this was not about an attempt to break out of The Big House, but rather concerned a decision by prisoners to riot in hope their action would allow them to express dissatisfaction with living conditions. No one had ever made a prison picture like that before, but then again, no producer was in quite the same position as Walter Wanger: He had, after maiming a man he'd discovered in an adulterous relationship with his wife Joan Bennett, done time.

The movie pits two men of iron will against each other: Dunn, a prisoner who feels he and the other men should not have to suffer dehumanizing conditions of awful food and enforced idleness; and the unnamed warden, who believes that only by a firm, cold application of such conditions can he maintain order. The prison takeover is organized around a strategy of drawing in the media, sharing with them their problems, then surrendering immediately. The focus is on the mass media, and the manner in which an event is planned around the "event-mentality" contemporary reporting has for better or worse (and, as clearly shown here, it's for the worse) drifted into. Like better known films as diverse as Jose Ferrer's *The Great Man* and Elia Kazan's *A Face in the Crowd*, *Riot in Cell Block 11* concerns a world in which the media actually creates the events it is supposedly only reporting.

This is also a fifties film in terms of its documentary approach to the subject. Wanger filmed this in California's Folsom State Prison, using actual inmates for sup-

Dunn (Neville Brand) and his followers get the good word that their demands have been met.

Director Don Siegel captured the lacerating intensity of the prisoners' anger.

porting roles, whereas previous prison pictures had been done in mock-up fabrications. Not only what's in front of the camera, but the way in which the camera is employed, heightens the realism, for Don Siegel furthered his reputation as a strikingly innovative director of small projects with his news-camera approach.

Riot proves how valuable low budget pictures can be in terms of communicating filmmakers' ideas without compromise. At the movie's end, the warden—sensing what it is Dunn hopes to accomplish—allows the prisoner to believe he will be given an audience with reporters, at which he can air his grievances so they'll be conveyed to the public. Dunn meets with the newsmen, then immediately calls off the riot, feeling he's accomplished his aim. What he's then told by the warden is that the meeting was a sham; the reporters were actually the warden's stooges. Stunned, Dunn listens as the warden explains the riot accomplished absolutely nothing, though the prisoners will of course have their sentences extended. He also tells Dunn that, some day, his hopes for a more decent life for prisoners will be realized, though his actions will not immediately bring that about, as his sacrifice was in vain. Dunn is then led back to his cell.

108

A rare mellow moment, as the prisoners are briefly reunited with their loved ones.

That ending can absolutely anger an audience, which is precisely what everyone concerned wanted: viewers left the theater frustrated, wanting to do something about the situation. Compare this with the ending of Elia Kazan's prestigious *On The Waterfront*, released the same year. *Waterfront* initially devastated the audience with its depiction of atrocities suffered by the longshoremen, then copped out completely by insisting Marlon Brando's Terry Malloy had singlehandedly cleaned up the docks, so there was no need for us to worry—or do anything further about it. Budd Schulberg had originally written a tougher ending in which Terry is killed by the mobster bosses, so nothing has been accomplished—an ending that was directly comparable to the one here and which would have likewise sent the audience home angry and upset. But that was a big budget movie, so for box-office safety's sake, it was necessary to soft soap the ending. That was not the case with a little film like this, since there was much less riding on it. The honesty and integrity does not, in the case of this film, come crashing to a halt just before the final scene.

109

Another example of Siegel's famous ability to make the viewer an active participant in the film rather than a passive observer.

The Indian Fighter

A Brynaprod Film (1955)

CREDITS:

Produced by William Schorr; directed by Andre de Toth; screenplay by Frank Davis and Ben Hecht, from an original story by Ben Kadish; running time: 88 minutes.

CAST:

Kirk Douglas *(Johnny Hawk)*; Elsa Martinelli *(Onahti)*; Walter Abel *(Captain Trask)*; Walter Matthau *(Wes Todd)*; Diana Douglas *(Susan Rogers)*; Eduard Franz *(Red Cloud)*; Lon Chaney, Jr. *(Chivington)*; Alan Hale, Jr. *(Will Crabtree)*; Elisha Cook *(Briggs)*; Michael Winkelman *(Tommy Rogers)*; Harry Landers *(Gray Wolf)*; William Phipps *(Lt. Blake)*; Ray Teal *(Morgan)*; Hank Worden *(Crazy Bear)*.

In the fifties, Kirk Douglas succeeded in doing what Bette Davis had tried (and failed) to do twenty years earlier: break the stranglehold of the studios by refusing to remain under contract to Warner Brothers. Bridling at the idea that he had to do whatever some movie mogul wanted, Douglas bought out of his contract, and became the first of the independent producers. He collected projects that intrigued him, then shopped them, striking deals in which the highest bidding studio would distribute a film he produced and starred in. Though Douglas isn't officially listed as the producer of *The Indian Fighter*, this was the first project produced under his own banner, Bryna Productions, named for his mother. Before long, John Wayne would have Batjac, Burt Lancaster his Hecht/Hill/Lancaster company. But it was Douglas who broke the ice, and in so doing, changed the future of Hollywood and the nature of the movie business.

At first glance, *The Indian Fighter* might not seem worth the effort. After all, the title sounds like the kind of traditional western Douglas had previously been forced to do: *Across the Great Divide* and *The Big Trees*. Likewise, the basic plot—a seasoned frontiersman guiding a wagon through hostile country—appears pretty conventional. But the sensibility of the script, like the production arrangements for the picture, is something else entirely. The opening sequence, in which Johnny Hawk spots the beautiful Indian girl Onahti bathing, was

Kirk Douglas as Johnny Hawk.

In this retouched studio-publicity-still, the initial tryst between Kirk and Elsa Martinelli is made to appear a romantic seduction.

The controversial rape scene, in which the Indian woman is overpowered by a good guy who often acts worse than the bad guys do.

The "hero" takes obvious pleasure from the fact that the woman he has dominated and enjoyed at his whim would like to kill him.

hero behave like this before, and the western film would never again be quite the same.

Douglas's character is truly a rugged individualist, not in the common romanticized misconception of that term as a strong and iconoclastic chap, but in the political sense as first espoused by the Coolidge and Hoover Administrations—a man who has no loyalty to anyone but himself and his own success, operating strictly out of self-interest and the belief that what's best for him will in the long run be best for society at large. "I'm beginning to wonder what side you're on," Captain Trask says to Hawk, with good reason; Hawk is such a double-dealer that we likewise wonder if he will indeed prove to be a good guy when, near the film's end, the wagon train is menaced by some angry braves. He does, but only because saving the caravan suits his own purpose. Frank Davis and Ben Hecht infused the film not only with some surprisingly racy sexual situations but also a modernist 1950s sense of wry humor, which laughs at the western clichés, while Andre de Toth captured the Oregon locations with the kind of striking color scheme (in the obligatory CinemaScope mode) audiences of the fifties demanded. Ultimately, though, this is Mr. Douglas's film; while playing an individualistically inclined pioneer of the old west, he proved himself to be one for the New Hollywood.

itself a knockout, for she is very clearly nude, though this is somewhat hidden by the foliage, creating a peek-a-boo effect for viewers. What follows is more shocking still: Hawk then proceeds to rape her in the water. And he is, mind you, the ostensible hero of the tale.

He is, then, anything but your routine movie westerner, the stern protector of womankind. Onahti (played by the breathtaking Italian actress Elsa Martinelli, here introduced to American audiences) initially scratches and bites him, though Hawk apparently enjoys this immensely; after resisting, she then gives in to his advances, enjoys being forced to make love. After having conquered her, Hawk is blasé in his treatment of the woman owing to her eventual sweet-surrender, though at this point she, having submitted, turns into a virtual love slave. The situation is not so very different from the distinctly sado-masochistic portrayal of sexuality as a cruel power struggle rather than a gentle expression of love as seen in some of the early Sean Connery James Bond films. Douglas would further explore this in two other strange, baroque westerns: *Man Without a Star* and *The Last Sunset*. One can imagine what feminists would say today about such a sequence! In the fifties, it was startling; simply, no one had ever seen a cowboy

Unchained

A Warner Brothers Release (1955)

CREDITS:

Produced by Hall Bartlett; directed by Mr. Bartlett; screenplay by Mr. Bartlett; running time: 75 minutes.

CAST:

Elroy Hirsch (Steve Davitt); Chester Morris (Kenyon J. Scudder); Todd Duncan (Bill Howard); Barbara Hale (Mary Davitt); Johnny Johnston (Garrity); Jerry Paris (Ravens); John Qualen (Haskins); Peggy Knudsen (Elaine); Tim Considine (Win Davitt).

Sometimes, a song outlives the motion picture for which it was composed, turning into a standard that becomes a part of our pop-culture consciousness. Few people realize that the haunting "Mona Lisa" was from a routine thriller with Alan Ladd called *Captain Carey, U.S.A.*, or that "Nature Boy" had been contained in an

Steve (Elroy Hirsch, *second from left*), and Warden Scudder (Chester Morris, *second from right*) meet with the advisory board; otherwise, the assembled cast members were mainly actual inmates of Chino.

offbeat anti-war item featuring Dean Stockwell, *The Boy With the Green Hair*. Likewise, "The Unchained Melody" remains one of the most popular ballads to come out of the fifties, but how many people who hear the wistful message of that lonely love song realize it was originally performed in a study of life in a minimum security prison?

Kenyon J. Scudder's book *Prisoners Are People* served as the starting point for a script that was eventually shot entirely on-location at The California Institute for Men, featuring inmates, guards, and staff as themselves in all but the key roles. Chino was the first great experiment at a "wall-less" prison, and the project allowed filmmaker Hall Bartlett ample opportunity to realistically portray the daily living conditions there, where Warden Scudder—a striking contrast to the warden in *Riot*—insisted on operating from the theory that his prisoners were human beings; though they'd been convicted of crimes, they were either in jail for first offenses or less serious crimes and should not be systematically stripped of their individuality and dignity. His idea was to create a prison that would prove to inmates that society had faith that they could, in time, live normal and meaningful lives on the outside. The way in which his staff was trained to work with the men formed the basis of the "docu-" portion of this docudrama.

The "-drama" portion—considered necessary to hook an audience emotionally so they could then be intellec-

Steve is comforted by his visiting wife (Barbara Hale).

tually turned around in terms of their possible prejudices about such an institution—concerned a single (fictional) prisoner, Steve Davitt. A relatively young man, he has been imprisoned for manslaughter, following an argument which spilled over into a fight and resulted in an

113

unintentional death. Steve is terribly bitter, and considers running away, in hopes of rejoining his wife Mary and his little boy Win. Fortunately, Bill Howard, a black prisoner who has befriended Steve, manages to stop this, for such a move would cause Steve (when recaptured) to be sent to a maximum security prison, and furthermore would endanger the entire Chino experiment, convincing officials that Scudder is wrong, that such men can't be trusted to obey an honor system.

Many critics felt this human interest melodrama was written in a routine and clichéd manner, failing as dramatic entertainment to adequately support the educational documentary surrounding it. But the film did fit in perfectly with the Civil Rights theme so prevalent in the fifties by casting a black actor as the white hero's ostensible conscience (in some respects, their relationship seems a precursor of *The Defiant Ones*, but with the convicts in prison rather than on the outside), allowing Duncan an opportunity to sing the title song: "Oh, my love, my darling, I hunger for your touch; are you still mine?"

In the film's powerful finale, Steve decides to run, but Bill blocks his way, trying to talk him out of it, then fighting him to keep Steve from ruining his own life and

Kenyon's idealistic experiment. Following a brutal fistfight, Steve defeats Bill and, leaving him lying on the ground, begins to climb the simple chain-link fence that's the only thing keeping the prisoners from the outside. But as he's about to go over, Steve thinks better of it. Bill's action has caused him to consider the consequences of what he is about to do, so he stops and climbs back down. The part of Steve called for a Burt Lancaster style star, and football great Elroy "Crazylegs" Hirsch fit the bill nicely, though this and his screen biography, *Crazylegs*, rate as his only two starring vehicles. Perhaps *Unchained* appeared too late in the decade to rate as a smash hit; the public had already tired of the docudrama form, opting to attend ever more lavish spectacles instead, while critics were likewise no longer impressed by a style that had seemed a breath of fresh air only five years earlier. But if *Unchained* was the last such film, it was by no means the least, and ought to be remembered for more than just its song.

The Last Frontier

A Columbia Release (1955)

CREDITS:

Produced by William Fadiman; directed by Anthony Mann; screenplay by Philip Yordan and Russell S. Hughes, from a novel by Richard Roberts; running time: 98 minutes.

CAST:

Victor Mature (Jed); Guy Madison (Capt. Riordan); Robert Preston (Col. Frank Marston); James Whitmore (Gus); Anne Bancroft (Corinna); Russell Collins (Capt. Clarke); Peter Whitney (Sgt. Maj. Decker); Pat Hogan (Mungo); Manuel Donde (Red Cloud); Guy Williams (Lt. Benton); Mickey Kuhn (Luke); William Calles (Spotted Elk).

Most film historians credit *High Noon* (1952) for the renaissance of the western; a few backtrack further, noting that *The Gunfighter* of one year earlier actually introduced many of the nuances that would characterize the psychological westerns of the 1950s. Revisionist studies prove, though, that it was actually *Winchester '73* in 1950 that began the western revival. That film neatly balanced familiar formulas (the hero who wants revenge for his father's death) with innovative psychological shadings (the man he's after turns out to be his own brother), also establishing James Stewart as a classic cowboy star

The Natural Man and the Representative of Civilization: Victor Mature and Robert Preston as "Jed" and Col. Marston.

The three mountain men at odds with the native Americans.

in the Gary Cooper mold. Throughout the fifties, Stewart would appear in a succession of superb westerns—*Bend of the River, Man From Laramie, The Far Country, Naked Spur*—for Anthony Mann, who was also responsible for the best known late fifties western vehicles of Henry Fonda *(The Tin Star)*, Gary Cooper *(Man of the West)*, even Barbara Stanwyck *(The Furies)*, which like the Stewart films balance a sense of the west's natural beauty rivaling John Ford's and a bleak vision of the struggle to survive quite beyond anything in the more sentimental Ford's work.

The Last Frontier is Mann's least known western, lacking the superstar casting of those other pictures. Another reason for its failure to stir much interest at the time is that, unlike his pictures about traditional cowboy heroes, *The Last Frontier* concerns the mountain men who have been sadly overlooked as national folk heroes.

Like the other Mann westerns, though, *Last Frontier* boasts his bitter, pessimistic, fatalistic (though never superficially cynical) sensibility; it is, if anything, even more characteristic of the filmmaker's unique vision than his better known works.

The story takes place during the Red Cloud War, a little known conflict which the army was unable to win; it was the Indians who eventually dictated the terms of the peace treaty signed at Fort Laramie. Understandably, few filmmakers had previously approached this material, but following the Korean Conflict, which did not end with a spectacular victory as did World War II, American audiences were more able to deal with a film which portrayed (safely positioned within a western setting) the contemporary and complex attitude of ambiguousness about a war which we couldn't win and didn't understand.

Three fur trappers are warned by the Sioux and Cheyenne to stay off their ground, and wander to the army fort, where they attempt to start a new life; civilization has caught up with them and ruined their near-savage trade, so they try and go to work for civilization as scouts. But they quickly prove as out of place in the cavalry as they were on the open prairies. In particular, Jed is caught halfway between civilization and nature, at once at odds with his unpleasant commanding officer, Colonel Marston, but also in love with the officer's wife, Corinna. He vacillates between the two worlds until the colonel proves himself something less than the fittest, getting killed (along with most of his men) in a tragic battle. Then, Jed—the natural man who perseveres, wins, survives—ironically ends up running the army, with the colonel's widow on his arm.

Mature, nurtured as a star in the Henry Wilcoxen tradition by Cecil B. DeMille in the late forties, struggled valiantly to establish himself as a Kirk Douglas/Burt Lancaster style leading man throughout the fifties, though he remained in the second-string line-up that included Sterling Hayden and Richard Egan. Guy Madison, here seen as a sympathetic officer, enjoyed his greatest fame as TV's *Wild Bill Hickock*, where the unsavory real-life desperado was portrayed as Superman in a buckskin leotard. Madison was never able to move beyond the typecasting engendered by that kiddie show. Fans of Anne Bancroft, who often incorrectly consider her a stage actress (*Two For the Seesaw, The Miracle Worker*) who then made the transition to A movies like *The Graduate*, are often stunned to realize she began her career as a blond Hollywood starlet in films like this and *Gorilla at Large*.

Good Morning, Miss Dove

A 20th Century-Fox Film (1955)

CREDITS:

Produced by Samuel G. Engel; directed by Henry Koster; screenplay by Eleanore Griffin, adapted from the novel by Francis Gray Patton; running time: 107 minutes.

CAST:

Jennifer Jones *(Miss Dove)*; Robert Stack *(Tom Baker)*; Kipp Hamilton *(Jincey Baker)*; Robert Douglas *(Porter)*; Peggy Knudsen *(Billie Jean)*; Marshall Thompson *(Pendleton)*; Chuck Connors *(Bill Holloway)*; Biff Elliott *(Rev. Burnham)*; Jerry Paris *(Maurice)*; Leslie Bradley *(Alonso Dove)*; Eddie Firestone *(Makepeace)*; Richard Deacon *(Mr. Spivey)*; Mary Wickes *(Miss Ellwood)*.

Every era of Hollywood produces its sentimental classic, a melodramatic three handkerchief movie that has matrons exiting tearfully. For the fifties, *Good Morning, Miss Dove* was unquestionably that film. This unabashed wallow portrayed the life of a self-sacrificing spinster teacher, who has dedicated her career to educating and uplifting several generations of children in a small town, and now lies helpless in a hospital. The movie, incomparable in terms of audience manipulation, effectively balances chuckles and tears. It's what used to be called a women's picture and today probably would not get made except as a TV movie of the week. It handsomely represents a genre that is pretty much bygone, and rediscovering it today is like coming upon a faded scrapbook in Grandmother's attic; we can be charmed, amused, touched by the antiquated vision of the world it enshrines, perhaps saddened by the fact that such honest sentiment does not seem appropriate in our contemporary world. If we have to conclude that *Good Morning, Miss Dove* is "a bit much," there is nonetheless much to enjoy about it.

Like the heroine of *The Prime of Miss Jean Brodie*, the prim, Victorian Miss Dove is a strict disciplinarian, a loved, respected, and feared teacher. The key difference is that, in *Miss Jean Brodie*, the film took a decidedly ironic approach; toward the end, Miss Brodie is betrayed by the very students she dedicated herself to; at the same time, she realizes that her life has been a sham, her values quite ridiculous, perhaps even odious. In teaching her British girls to love and admire the early Mussolini and his fascist approach, she has inadvertently done more harm than good. That's what makes *Brodie* a true tragedy, but *Miss Dove* is, in comparison, a soap opera. There's no critical cutting edge, since we are asked to take her at face value. Considering the charm and craftsmanship with which this sweet if essentially superficial film was mounted, that's not so hard to do.

The students remember Miss Dove as a stiff woman who never smiled; but when they—now grown-ups, making their way in the world—learn she's apparently dying, they realize their success is due to her, and the values this stern, aloof, seemingly cold but in fact deeply dedicated lady instilled in them. So the graduates of Cedar Grove School in Liberty Hill rally around: Holloway, whom she turned from a tough street hoodlum into a respected cop; Maurice, the Jewish boy she defended from anti-Semitic attacks and turned into a playwright; Porter, the banker on whose institution she helped stop

Jennifer Jones as "Miss Dove."

Miss Dove at work, dedicating her life to teaching the children of one small town.

119

a run; Baker, the brilliant young surgeon who must perform the difficult operation on his former teacher. Will the discipline she instilled in him so long ago allow Baker to pull her through now?

If many of the situations seem maudlin in the summation, they appear less so while watching, simply because the film was made with such grand style. Everything about this movie clicks, but the centerpiece—the key to its appeal—is Jennifer Jones. She typifies the kind of star (Joan Fontaine, Greer Garson, and Jean Simmons are others) who are considered overwhelmingly important for a period of time (great actresses as well as great lookers), then gradually slip out of sight in a way the true superstars—Bette Davis, Barbara Stanwyck, Joan Crawford, Katharine Hepburn—absolutely refuse to do. After a few early B pictures under her real name, Phyllis Isley, Jennifer Jones won an Oscar in 1943 for her first lead, the inspirational *Song of Bernadette*; there followed a long string of impressive A pictures including *Since You Went Away*, *Duel in the Sun*, *Portrait of Jennie*, *Madame Bovary*, and the great romantic movie of the fifties, *Love Is a Many Splendored Thing*, opposite William Holden. After that impressive string of much-admired A movies, she began to recede in the public's interest; beautiful and talented, she simply did not have the kind of staying power that makes a superstar out of someone like Elizabeth Taylor, who to a large degree usurped Jones's roles and proved to have a lasting impact that Jennifer did not.

Tom Baker (Robert Stack) helps carry the sickly Miss Dove to the hospital.

Moonfleet

A Metro-Goldwyn-Mayer Film (1955)

CREDITS:

Produced by John Houseman; directed by Fritz Lang; screenplay by Jan Lustig and Margaret Fitts, based on the novel by J. Meade Falkner; running time: 89 minutes.

CAST:

Stewart Granger *(Jeremy Fox)*; George Sanders *(Lord Ashwood)*; Joan Greenwood *(Lady Ashwood)*; Viveca Lindfors *(Mrs. Minton)*; Jon Whiteley *(John Mohune)*; Lilliane Montevecchi *(Gypsy Woman)*; Melville Cooper *(Felix Ratsey)*; Sean McClory *(Elzevir Block)*; Alan Napier *(Parson Glennie)*; John Hoyt *(Magistrate Maskew)*; Donna Corcoran *(Grace)*; Jack Elam *(Damen)*; Dan Seymour *(Hull)*.

In 1955, Fritz Lang created a masterpiece that Hollywood had no idea how to go about selling. Owing to *Moonfleet*'s assumption of a child's point of view and the ostensible appearance of several pirates, the film was in many areas double-billed with Walt Disney's *Davy Crockett* for Saturday matinee consumption by kids. But a film about children is not necessarily a film for children, and those of us who caught *Moonfleet* at an early, impressionable age experienced an outlandish, demanding movie that would haunt our memories for the rest of our lives.

Young John Mohune, suddenly finding himself a penniless orphan, journeys across the English countryside to the forbidding coast, where he arrives at a crumbling mansion. His dying mother had told him that the man living there, Jeremy Fox, would care for him. But the boy interrupts one of Fox's orgies of sex and drink; the semi-delirious brigande laughs at the idea that he might become foster father to a child, though the unstated implication is that he may well be the boy's father. Still, young John stays on, gradually changing the man, who in time comes to want nothing more than to protect this still innocent lad from the ugliness of the world around them.

In Fox, Stewart Granger found his most taxing role, and magnificently rose to the occasion. Throughout the fifties, he starred in MGM's handsome series of Technicolor costume pictures (*King Solomon's Mines*, *Scaramouche*, *The Prisoner of Zenda*), but while *Moonfleet* shares with them a strong evocation of period, it operates on a level of moral complexity those other films did not

Stewart Granger as Jeremy Fox, in action.

As the corrupt Lord Ashwood (George Sanders) looks on, young John Mohune (John Whiteley, of *The Little Kidnappers*) meets Fox for the first time while the Gypsy (Lilliane Montevecchi) looks on.

Though Fox is intrigued with the child, he's seduced again by the wanton gypsy, among other women.

approach. Fox is something of a smuggler, leading a secret band on midnight forays that the local magistrates would like to stop. He and the boy do discover a fabulous diamond, which will serve as the child's eventual fortune, the means by which Fox can create a happy future for the lad who comes to mean everything to him. But there are betrayals and adventures along the way, including adult relationships that John manages to remain oblivious to: Fox's tawdry relationships with both Lady Ashwood, the wife of a corrupt Lord, and Mrs. Minton, the beautiful woman who was seduced by Fox, left her husband to pursue a sordid sexual life with him, then is casually deserted by the adventurer. But the most memorable sequence involves the child's midnight shortcut through a supposedly haunted graveyard, where he trips

and falls deep under the ground, as if swallowed up; no film has ever more frightfully captured a child's nightmare vision of what it means to be buried alive.

Combine the costume-drama plotting of Robert Louis Stevenson, the eerie atmosphere of seaside terror from Daphne Du Maurier, and the philosophic sensibility of Albert Camus, and you have the vision Fritz Lang offered in this mesmerizing mood piece. The film is at once baroque in its striking visual design and existential in its psychological portrait of a decadent man trying to redeem himself by performing a moral action in a ruined, amoral world. Much of the film's poignancy derives from the way Fox desperately attempts to live up to the boy's impossibly heroic vision of him, and the bittersweet note on which the story ends. Though Fox

Fox confronts his band of cut-throats.

123

Fox finally stops Lord Ashwood's coach in order to defend the boy, who may indeed be his own son.

has been mortally wounded in a duel during which he protected John, he will not let the child see him die; like Shane transformed from gunfighter to swashbuckler, Fox insists he will be back, then sets out to sea in a small craft, a realistic incarnation of the symbolic Flying Dutchman. Little John, now dressed in finery and cared for by gentle folk, is last seen confidently assuring his good new guardians that he'll be happy to stay with them until Fox returns for him. The guardians look at each other askance, but will not tell the boy the terrible truth of what Fox was really like in the eyes of everyone but this boy, or that by now the man has succumbed: they, like Fox, cannot bring themselves to destroy John's extreme state of radical innocence. Which is why the boy's final line regarding Fox, as he wistfully looks out to sea, can still bring a tear to a viewer's eye: "He was my friend."

124

Field (Sister Mary Theresa); Tim Hovey (Cadet Thomas "Tiger" Flaherty); Edward C. Platt (Msgr. Collins); David Janssen (Soldier); Milburn Stone (Doc).

The Private War of Major Benson

A Universal-International Film (1955)

CREDITS:

Produced by Howard Pine; directed by Jerry Hopper; screenplay by William Roberts and Richard Alan Simmons, from a story by Joe Connelly and Bob Mosher; running time: 100 minutes.

CAST:

Charlton Heston (Maj. Bernard R. "Barney" Benson); Julie Adams (Dr. Kay Lambert); William Demarest (John); Tim Considine (Cadet Sgt. Hibler); Sal Mineo (Cadet Col. Sylvester Dusik); Nana Bryant (Mother Redempta); Kay Stewart (Mrs. Flaherty); Mary

Too often, Charlton Heston earned his nickname Old Granite Jaw by coming off as a kind of Burt Lancaster clone without the warmth or humor. If one of those pods from *Invasion of the Body Snatchers* that reproduce precise but soulless duplicates of people had been hidden in Lancaster's cellar, it would have probably created Charlton Heston. In fact, Heston only got the role in the film that won him an Oscar—*Ben Hur*—when Lancaster stormed off the set, laughing at how ridiculous he felt he looked in the costumes. Since then, audiences have associated Heston with costume films, though earlier in his career he did a variety of roles in diverse pictures, from a garishly colorful western called *Pony Express* to the dark, somber black-and-white of Orson Welles's *Touch of Evil*. The single type of picture Heston seems least likely for is a gentle comedy, though he did perform admirably in one called *The Private War of Major Benson*.

Major Benson (Charlton Heston) inspects the "men," while Cadet Dusik (Sal Mineo) backs him up.

The Major and the Doctor learn to like one another, while Mother Redempta (Nana Bryant) looks on.

The Major and "Tiger" (Tim Hovey) "take lunch."

126

Tim Hovey was a complete scene stealer.

To paraphrase Orson Welles, any man who hates kids and nuns can't be all bad; if that's true, then Major Benson isn't all bad, at least when we first meet him. A controversial military man, he's removed from his unit by the Pentagon and, as a disciplinary measure, put (temporarily) in charge of a Catholic boarding-school academy for youngsters, presided over by some good sisters. He gives the kids the strong helping of discipline they sorely need, and after a period of resisting him (to give the film its necessary dramatic conflict), they come to appreciate what he's done for them; they, meanwhile, humanize Benson (with a little help from the nuns). The major also falls in love with the gorgeous lady doctor, Kay Lambert, who just happens to be on the premises and conveniently single (also, conveniently,

not a nun), finding himself developing fatherly emotions for an irresistible six-year-old with the saddest eyes and silliest smile in movie history.

The child was played by Tim Hovey, who so wowed audiences as "Tiger" that, less than a year later, Universal reunited him with director Jerry Hopper for a similar (though less successful) comedy vehicle called *Toy Tiger*, with Jeff Chandler and Laraine Day. In addition to that adorable child star, *Private War* also gave early exposure to a number of other young performers: Tim Considine would soon be seen on the "Spin and Marty" and "Hardy Boys" segments of Disney's *Mickey Mouse Club*, then later on *My Three Sons*; Sal Mineo would show up later that year in *Rebel Without a Cause*, for which he received an Oscar nomination.

127

Then there's Julie (or was it Julia?) Adams as the liberated lady doctor. For some reason, she kept changing her first name back and forth in the billing of her films for Universal, where she was a contract player. Her career was most difficult to comprehend, for one moment she'd be on view in an A feature like *Bend of the River*, opposite a star of James Stewart's stature, only to show up shortly thereafter as the female lead in a B monster flick such as *Creature from the Black Lagoon*. But as Julie or Julia, and in big movies or little ones, she always managed to project a nifty combination of ladylike enlightenment and no-nonsense sexuality; she gracefully and easily emerged as the star Joanne Dru had struggled unsuccessfully to become. As Major Benson, Heston displayed a most effective ability to play comedy, a genre he returned to less often than he might have liked.

The Private War of Major Benson was a great hit with kids, who took to its brazen spirit of good-natured fun and sentimental drama. It still plays effectively today; as is often the case with such modest little gems, this film does not date the way some of the more prestigious items of its time do. This remains a delight; young Tim Hovey still speaks to kids who see the film and, in his screen persona, project their worst fears about their own possible incompetence.

Underwater

An RKO Radio Picture (1955)

CREDITS:

Produced by Harry Tatelman; directed by John Sturges; screenplay by Walter Newman, from a story by Hugh King and Robert B. Bailey; running time: 99 minutes.

CAST:

Jane Russell *(Theresa)*; Gilbert Roland *(Dominic)*; Richard Egan *(Johnny)*; Lori Nelson *(Gloria)*; Robert Keith *(Father Cannon)*; Joseph Calleia *(Rico)*; Eugene Iglesias *(Miguel)*; Jayne Mansfield *(Blonde)*.

If ever an actress was ahead of her time, it was Jane Russell. A full decade before Hollywood and the country gave way to what film historian Marjorie Rosen later tagged "Mammary Madness," Russell was introduced by Howard Hughes as the first of the female stars whose drawing power at the box-office correlated directly to the size of her breasts. Though *The Outlaw*, made in 1943, wasn't released until three years later, still photos of Russell revealing much cleavage had already made her a sex symbol, and the first of a new breed. In the fifties, there would be blondes (Monroe, Mansfield) and Italian brunette bombshells (Sophia, Gina), all with statuesque builds, but the woman who kicked off Bosomania was Russell; she was the pioneer. In a marvelous casting coup, she was eventually cast opposite Monroe in *Gentleman Prefer Blondes* (1953), though most of Russell's films are B-budget potboilers: *His Kind of Woman,*

Jane Russell as Theresa.

Theresa explores the undersea kingdom.

Double Dynamite, Macao, The Revolt of Mamie Stover, Hot Blood.

Underwater! was easily the most popular of all the vehicles designed to show her off during the fifties. Filmmakers, growing ever more daring, had wised up to the delights of the wet look: *Boy on a Dolphin* was a bonanza, despite a waterlogged script, because of the way Sophia looked when she emerged from the water, her scanty costume dripping provocatively; *Beneath the 12 Mile Reef* turned the tables and gave girls something to stare at by keeping Robert Wagner in a brief swim suit. Gilbert Roland had co-starred with him in that one, and became something of a fixture for this briefly popular genre when hired to play a similar role as a salty ship's captain in *Underwater!*

Beware any film that has an exclamation mark in its title: that's always an indication the film itself is dull, and someone in the publicity department added the appendage out of desperation. Mostly, this film is just ordinary action-adventure, with the mild novelty of some decent underwater photography. Richard Egan, the Kirk Douglas of second features, played the male lead, a searcher after sunken treasure; with Roland to help him, he hopes to excavate a sunken ship and get his hands on the chest full of gold doubloons that still lay buried there. As Father Cannon, Robert Keith portrayed an aged priest who knows enough about the Caribbean to be brought along, while Russell was cast as Theresa, the wife of Johnny, who does not believe the treasure can be saved. Her presence creates an understandable sexual tension between the men, as they endlessly argue. But they dare not spare too much time or energy on squabbles, for there are sharks all about. The

Theresa climbs on board the boat, unsure which of her two underwater companions has had her.

Theresa grows progressively more testy with the boys.

time Russell made her grand entrance, all the photographers' film had been used up. It was Mansfield who dominated the next day's headlines, and who would shortly supplant Russell as the girl with America's most admired torso.

The Shrike

A Universal-International Release (1955)

CREDITS:

Produced by Aaron Rosenberg; directed by Jose Ferrer; screenplay by Ketti Frings, based on the Pulitzer Prize winning stage play by Joseph Kramm; running time: 88 minutes.

CAST:

Jose Ferrer (Jim Downs); June Allyson (Ann Downs); Joy Page (Charlotte Moore); Kendall Clark (Dr. Bellman); Isabel Bonner (Dr. Barrow); Jay Barney (Dr. Kramer); Somer Alberg (Dr. Schlesinger); Ed Platt (Harry Downs); Dick Benedict (Gregory); Herbie Faye (Tager); Will Kuluva (Ankoritis); Martin Newman (O'Brien); Billy Greene (Schloss); Mary Bell (Miss Wingate).

most dangerous are of the human order, like a local fisherman, Rico, who senses what they are up to.

Despite all the tedious talk, there is one sequence which, in retrospect, helps us understand the film's popularity. After Russell has donned a bathing suit and gone underwater, the men begin sporting with her. In fact, "the underwater seduction" is pretty tame by today's standards, tame even in comparison with the posters used to exploit the movie's most memorable moment by showing Egan and Russell involved in a wild underwater tryst. Onscreen, they appear slowed down by the need to fight the currents as well as each other, and the thrill just isn't there. Certainly a far more striking (if suspiciously similar) scene was featured in one of the best James Bond films of the sixties, Thunderball. But in the fifties, as filmmakers grasped at any straw that might sell a film, the come-on of an underwater coupling proved too much for viewers to pass up. Underwater! was a hit, and a solid one, at the box-office.

One intriguing note: lost in the cast was another shapely bombshell, Jayne Mansfield. Though she entered the movie an unknown, she used her appearance in it to become a star. On the eve of the film's release, the press was invited to photograph top-billed Jane Russell for the obligatory cheesecake photos. Mansfield "happened" to get there first, "fell" in the pool, and "accidentally" lost the top of her bathing suit. By the

Beginning with Best Foot Forward in 1943, then in Girl Crazy and Little Women, June Allyson quickly established her screen image as the wholesome blonde next door, the sweet-faced, wide-eyed all-American flesh-and-blood angel, an incarnation of innocence and purity. As she reached early middle age, Miss Allyson made an easy transition to roles as dutiful, understanding wife to James Stewart in various film biographies: The Stratton Story (1949), The Glenn Miller Story (1954), and Strategic Air Command (1955). They seemed the perfect embodiment of the idealized American couple, circa the fifties, a big-screen Ozzie and Harriett, representing the good, simple life, the couple we all ought to aspire to be. Only once did Miss Allyson dare offer a characterization that cut against the grain of her firmly entrenched image. As is so often the case with reverse typecasting, it presented her with her greatest stretch as an actress; her least typical work is also her best.

After attempting suicide, Jim Downs is spirited off to a hospital emergency ward, then transferred to its psychiatric division. Immediately, his faithful wife is by his side, tearfully holding his hand even as Jim calls out for a woman named Charlotte. Jim is in something of a Catch-22 situation: according to mental health regulations, this talented but presumably self-destructive theater director can only be released (and return to work) if his wife agrees to take him back into their home, though living with her is what drove Jim to despair and into another woman's arms. In flashbacks, we see how their relationship ruined his career, as Ann (an unsuccessful actress) constantly attempted to use his power and prestige in the New York theater community to find roles and, when that did not work, to unofficially co-direct his productions. But her suggestions were wrongheaded, decimating his artistic reputation. Jim knows his only chance to salvage his life is to live with the unaffected, unassuming Charlotte. Jim gradually realizes he'll never be released from the snake pit he's in unless he abandons Charlotte and returns to Ann. When, in desperation, he finally agrees, the doctors look at Ann's long-suffering face and see great nobility there; we see something else, the female monster who purposefully remains oblivious to her own manipulativeness, emotional cruelty, and self-serving instincts, and who—in not only getting Jim back, but now enjoying total power over him—enjoys a terrible triumph.

Though for the film version, the return of Jim to Ann was given a phony hopeful note (this was a Hollywoodization which had to play in Peoria), Jose Ferrer—who had both directed and starred on Broadway, and was here making his film directorial debut—managed to hint at

Jose Ferrer and June Allyson.

In therapy, Jim Downs realizes he can only be released if he returns to his wife Ann.

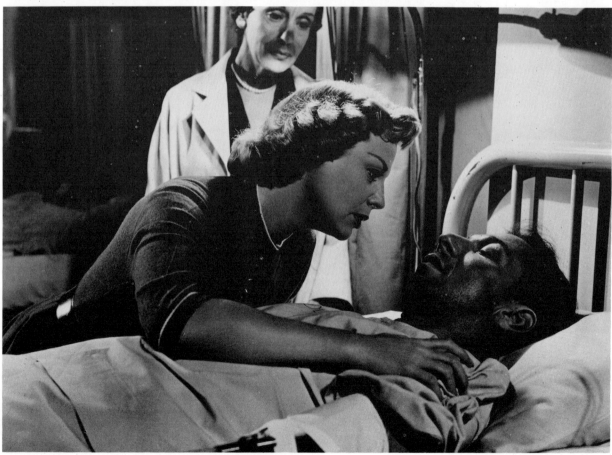

Ever the dutiful wife, Ann rushes to her husband's side, though he calls out another woman's name.

the play's tragic vision of Jim's final decision. At the time, many critics carped about the casting of Allyson, insisting she was all wrong for the role, that (as A. H. Weiler of *The New York Times* put it) the lady "Unfortunately conveys the impression she would not hurt a fly." But as Jim Downs makes clear, a shrike is "an innocent-looking bird who likes to impale her victims on a thorn." Only by casting an actress who in two dozen films over the past dozen years had portrayed innocence incarnate onscreen could the point properly be conveyed. If Ann in the movie is an unconscious manipulator rather than the self-consciously calculating woman in the play, that only adds another fascinating dimension to her psychological make-up.

Today, the value system at work seems debatable. Ann can be seen as a kind of feminist victim of a male oriented society: an aspiring, talented actress expected to quit her career as soon as she marries a successful man, afterwards understandably trying to find some outlet for her own creative instincts in his work. Jim could be considered the arch male-chauvinist who runs to another woman's arms the moment his wife tries to be a full creative partner. But take her as heroine or villainess, Ann remains Miss Allyson's most complex and intriguing characterization, the role which should have won her an Academy Award, or at the very least a nomination.

My Sister Eileen

A Columbia Picture (1955)

CREDITS:

Produced by Fred Kohlmar; directed by Richard Quine; screenplay by Blake Edwards and Richard Quine, based on the play by Jerome Chodorov; running time: 108 minutes.

CAST:

Janet Leigh *(Eileen Sherwood)*; Betty Garrett *(Ruth Sherwood)*; Jack Lemmon *(Bob Baker)*; Robert "Bob" Fosse *(Frank Lippencott)*; Kurt Kasznar *(Appopolous)*; Richard York *(Wreck)*; Lucy Marlow *(Helen)*; Tommy Rall *(Chick Clark)*; Barbara Brown *(Helen's Mother)*; Horace McMahon *(Lonigan)*; Henry Slate, Hal March *(Drunks)*; Queenie Smith *(Alice)*; Richard Deacon *(George)*.

Certain thinly disguised autobiographical stories have such a basic appeal that they prove durable beyond almost anyone's wildest dreams. Christopher Isherwood's

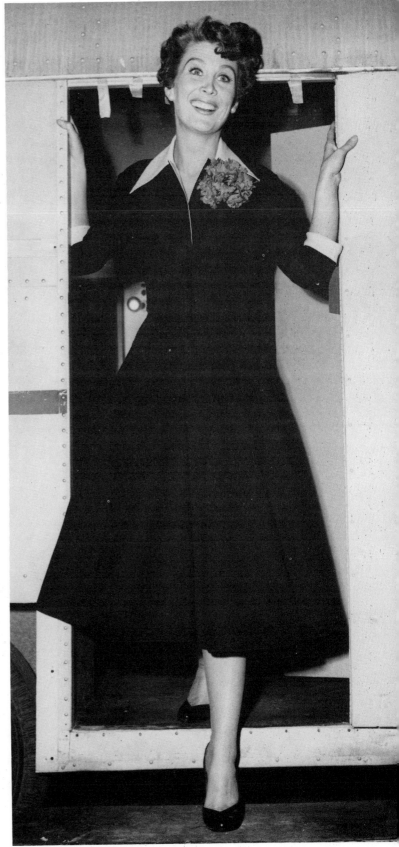

Betty Garrett, leaving her trailer for the first day of shooting on *My Sister Eileen.*

Two innocents arrive in New York: Betty Garrett as Ruth, Janet Leigh as Eileen.

Berlin Stories, which were the basis for the play *I Am a Camera*, the film of it, the subsequent Broadway musical *Cabaret*, and the film of that, provides one striking example. Even more modifications were in store for Ruth McKenney's enchanting *New Yorker* sketches, detailing the high times she and her beautiful but flakey sister had as innocent girls from Ohio, attempting to "make it" in The Big Apple while surviving in a Greenwich Village basement apartment.

Joseph Fields and Jerome Chodorov used those stories as the basis for a 1940 Broadway play, which was then promptly (though less than remarkably) filmed with Rosalind Russell and Janet Blair. The material still seemed potent enough that Betty Comden and Adolph Green wrote a Broadway musical version, *Wonderful Town*, also featuring Miss Russell. For some inexplicable reason, *Wonderful Town* never did make it to the screen, though in 1955 came this musical movie, boasting new songs by Julie Styne and Leo Rubin. It's the very best of all possible versions, though not the last (a disappointing TV sitcom version, starring Elaine Stritch as Ruth and Shirley Bonne as Eileen, ran on CBS from October, 1960 through April, 1961). Since then, this fabulous story has been overlooked. *Wonderful Town* has gone too long unproduced; summer stock companies and regional theaters, take note! And the 1955 film is long overdue for revival; cable movie services could certainly do worse than to fill their late night or mid-afternoon hours with this delectable bit of froth.

The film features some sweet and poignant moments,

The girls dance as they dream of a possible glorious future.

135

In their Greenwich Village basement apartment, the girls realize they can be spied on by passing men.

most notably the first scary, lonely night in their still dreary abode, when the sisters bravely bolster each other's failing resolve with the lilting "There's Nothing Like Love." Mostly, though, this is a song 'n' dance festival, featuring lively numbers that nicely convey the various romances. Though Wreck is around as a self-appointed guardian of the girls' innocence, the gorgeous, naive Eileen still manages to slip away so she can be courted by the drug store clerk Frank and the reporter Chick. Bob Fosse not only played a role but also choreographed, showing early signs of the distinctive hip-oriented style of movement that would develop into his singular signature. Jack Lemmon, as the lecherous publisher with designs on the practical Ruth, got to deliver a rare song, proving himself surprisingly adept.

The tragedy associated with this delightfully frivolous film is that instead of marking the beginning of great things for its top-billed star, *My Sister Eileen* stands as one of her few vehicles. Bosley Crowther, in his *New York Times* review, lauded Betty Garrett this way: "Miss Garrett is okay in shining letters. (She) has the proper skepticism and the right desperation for the role. Her way with a line is homicidal. What's more, she can sing and dance." Boy, could she! And unlike certain other stage stars—Ethel Merman, Julie Harris—whose appeal

did not effectively transfer to film, Garrett seemed a natural in front of the camera. What went wrong? This was, let's recall, the fifties; not the fabled "Happy Days" of rock 'n' roll, but the bleak period of McCarthy madness, when the expression "guilt by association" took on a terrible new meaning. Owing to her husband's mildly liberal politics, Garrett found herself blacklisted; overnight, she disappeared from the public consciousness, not to be seen again until, in 1973, Norman Lear courageously offered the lady a supporting role as Archie Bunker's new neighbor in *All in the Family*. As immense as Miss Garrett's loss was, considering the level of performances we might have been treated to over that 20-year-period, the greatest loss was the one suffered by the moviegoing public, denied the chance to see this musical star that might have been. *My Sister Eileen* is a lighthearted film with a heavy burden, standing as a sweet, sad scrap of celluloid evidence of what might have been a world-class career.

Girl In the Red Velvet Swing

A 20th Century-Fox Film (1955)

CREDITS:

Produced by Charles Brackett; directed by Richard Fleischer; screenplay by Walter Reisch and Mr. Brackett; running time: 109 minutes.

CAST:

Joan Collins (*Evelyn Nesbit Thaw*); Ray Milland (*Stanford White*); Farley Granger (*Harry K. Thaw*); Luther Adler (*Delphin Delmas*); Glenda Farrell (*Mrs. Nesbit*); Frances Fuller (*Mrs. White*); Cornelia Otis Skinner (*Mrs. Thaw*); Philip Reed (*Robert Collier*); Gale Robbins (*Gwen Arden*); James Lorimer (*McCaleb*); John Hoyt (*William Travers Jerome*).

The new freedom of the screen (after the words "virgin" and "pregnant" were spoken in *The Moon Is Blue*, absolutely anything seemed possible) allowed moviemakers an opportunity to tangle with one of the greatest sex scandals of our century: the irresistibly lurid romantic triangle that developed between the aging but still attractive architect Stanford White, the unstable rich boy Harry K. Thaw, and the shapely social-climbing show-

Joan Collins as Evelyn Nesbit Thaw.

Evelyn experiences a hangover.

Appearing a perfect gentleman but actually quite deranged, Harry (Farley Granger) proposes.

girl Evelyn Nesbit. The material clearly begged for screen treatment, so ripe is it with sleazy sex among the upperclass, while Nesbit—the poor little girl from the wrong side of the tracks who worms her way into the haunts of the rich, only to be fatalistically returned to her humble origins—couldn't have been better had she been created by Harold Robbins. With the rigid dictates of the Production Code crumbling, filmmakers could finally dramatize this naturally garish business, and the Fox studio did so in as glossy a manner as possible.

But one thing stood in the way of making the great movie this might have been—the fact that Evelyn Nesbit Thaw was still living at the time. Screenwriters Walter Reisch and Charles Brackett sensed early on in the production that if they told the story truthfully, they and their studio would shortly have a tremendous lawsuit on their hands. So in order to get the movie made, they compromised, simplifying the scandal and the people involved, turning out a portrait of Evelyn that has to be considered the very sort of whitewash job this lady would have herself conducted. In the movie version, Evelyn becomes a naïf, ambitious only in the nicest sense of the term as she tries to use her natural talents and obvious beauty to escape her sordid surroundings. She falls deeply in love with Mr. White, who likewise perceives her as his true love, failing to marry her only because unfortunate circumstances prevent it. Evidence suggests Nesbitt was his mistress, and was clinically used by him as a sex object, just as she calculatedly used him to get what she wanted.

In this reduced version of the tale, Thaw is cast as the villain, a smooth operator who marries the beautiful woman he's obsessed with only to possess for himself someone who means so much to his archrival White. Then the cruel Thaw emotionally brutalizes Evelyn; in a fit of unmotivated jealousy, he publicly murders White and thanks to his prestige and power gets away with it. The novel *Ragtime* and the subsequent film, with their revisionist approach, seem more correct in suggesting the cool operator was Evelyn—clever but not quite as clever as she considered herself. Nesbit tried to use both

men, playing one against the other and creating the mood of violence in the insecure Thaw by constantly comparing her current husband to her former lover. In this sense, Thaw's "not guilty" verdict seems less a miscarriage of justice, in which the super-rich are unfairly judged by different standards than the rest of us, than it was a fair call. He was driven temporarily insane owing to his sexy shrew of a wife's incessant insults and what may have been a post-marital revival of the affair with White.

Here, though, the film became a tearjerker from the woman's point of view, the sort of story Sidney Sheldon would become fabulously rich writing again and again. The final sequence, in which Evelyn—having gone from the bottom to the top and back down to the bottom again—is forced to eke out a living by posing in the red velvet swing in which White had originally discovered her provided the perfect full-cycle conclusion to this three handkerchief weeper. Director Richard Fleischer certainly did mount the film with much flair and vivid color, and if we only see a superficial approach to the

In jail, Harry shows his true colors.

141

In the high country, Evelyn begins to feel threatened by her handsome young husband.

story, it's certainly dazzling to behold. So sad, though, that Joan Collins—who had already proven her mettle at playing bitches in *Land of the Pharoahs* and *The Opposite Sex*—did not get a chance to pull out all the stops as Evelyn. If she had, that character might have been as memorable a monster as her Alexis on *Dynasty*, and Collins's career might have taken off much earlier than it did.

The Last Command

A Republic Picture (1955)

CREDITS:

Produced by Herbert J. Yates; directed by Frank Lloyd; screenplay by Warren Duff, from a story by Sy Bartlett; running time: 110 minutes.

CAST:

Sterling Hayden *(Jim Bowie)*; Anna Maria Alberghetti *(Consuelo)*; Richard Carlson *(Will Travis)*; Arthur Hunnicutt *(Davy Crockett)*; Ernest Borgnine *(Mike Ragan)*; J. Carrol Naish *(Santa Anna)*; Ben Cooper *(Jeb Lacey)*; John Russell *(Capt. Dickinson)*; Virginia Grey *(Mrs. Dickinson)*; Jim Davis *(Ben)*; Eduard Franz *(Senor de Casada)*; Otto Kruger *(Steve Austin)*; Russell Simpson *(Parson)*; Roy Roberts *(Doc Summerfield)*; Slim Pickens *(A Texan)*.

The Last Command was "lost" even in its time: this is the only Hollywood A-budget film ever to be overlooked by the *New York Times* reviewers, though they diligently covered numerous B movies from Republic. As a release from that studio, this represents an aborted attempt to survive (Republic went under shortly thereafter) by moving away from the smaller westerns and serials that had been their staple (TV now supplied viewers with such fare for free), instead mounting large-scale films. But their own stable of contract players didn't have the allure to pull off a box-office coup (though a year earlier, these same actors had appeared in the hit *Johnny Guitar,* that film boasted a rare Republic appearance by superstar Joan Crawford). So when *The Last Command,* filmed as an A-movie extravaganza but released as part of a B-movie double bill, died, it took Republic down with it. Ironically enough, this film about American history's most famous last stand also provided the last stand for its studio.

Shot midway between Walt Disney's *Davy Crockett* in 1953 and John Wayne's *The Alamo* in 1960, this retelling of the birth of Texas freedom takes a somewhat different and intriguing approach. It's the only film on the subject to trace the roots of the conflict back to early misunderstandings between white settlers in Texas and the Mexican governing forces, rather than leaping, as other films do, directly into the fray. To achieve this, *Last Command* focuses on Jim Bowie and his little known friendship with Santa Anna, chronicling Bowie's early efforts

Sterling Hayden as Jim Bowie.

143

Bowie proves his mettle in a knife fight with Mike Ragan (Ernest Borgnine).

to resist violent revolution at all costs, as well as his gradual, hesitant conversion to the cause of Texas independence. Though Santa Anna's tragic arrogance as a leader is made abundantly clear, he's nonetheless humanized in the scene that has him comforting Bowie after Jim's wife (Santa Anna's cousin) and children die of the plague. Though the film simplifies and is less than totally sympathetic to the Mexican's side, it at least depicts that aspect in more detail than any other film. The Mexicans are, if nothing more, people we've come to understand rather than mere moving targets for the white heroes to mow down.

The battle sequences, while not quite on a scale with those in the John Wayne film, are extremely impressive, enough so that when NBC presented an "all new" TV movie on the subject to commemorate the 150th anniversary of the fall of the Alamo in 1986, they in fact liberally lifted almost all the long-shots of the final fight from this film to give their movie a sense of spectacle it would otherwise have lacked. To make *Last Command* appealing as melodrama, the writers added a fictional subplot, involving a beautiful Mexican girl (played by Italian singing star Anna Maria Alberghetti, who did get to perform one number), her crush on Bowie, and the

deep love for her harbored by a young Texan (Ben Cooper) who eventually serves as the doomed fort's messenger. Part of the problem is that these leads are less than dynamic, though worst of all is Richard Carlson, who is bland as the fort's flamboyant commander, Travis, especially compared with Laurence Harvey's quirky performance in this role in the Wayne movie. The great actors in *Last Command* are found in small supporting roles: Jim Davis, Slim Pickens, J. Carroll Naish as Santa Anna, and especially Arthur Hunnicutt as Davy Crockett, perhaps the most accurate screen portrait ever of this authentic American hero.

The script's noble intentions are basic to the film's box-office failure: so much time is given over to political discussions between the various characters that audiences found the slow (if historically accurate) build-up to the battle terribly tedious. At the center of the talk and the action is Sterling Hayden: the John Wayne of the Left, the Burt Lancaster of B movies, he is convincing portraying Bowie's larger-than-life heroic stature, less so in playing the romantic scenes. With the box-office failure of this film, his career—like Republic Studio itself—shortly went into decline.

Santa Anna leads his army towards the Alamo.

The Battle of the Alamo, staged on a grand scale by Frank Lloyd.

Bowie's Last Stand.

This Island Earth

A Universal-International Picture (1955)

CREDITS:

Produced by William Alland; directed by Joseph Newman; screenplay by Franklin Coen and Edward G. O'Callaghan, based on the novel by Raymond F. Jones; running time: 86 minutes.

CAST:

Rex Reason (*Cal Meacham*); Faith Domergue (*Ruth Adams*); Jeff Morrow (*Exeter*); Lance Fuller (*Brack*); Russell Johnson (*Steve Carlson*); Douglas Spencer (*Man*).

"Our planet is dying!"

That remains the best remembered line of dialogue from any of the multitude of science-fiction films produced during the 1950s, an age which saw a renaissance of that form owing to the serious escalation of the space race and the concurrent barrage of reported UFO sightings. Amazingly, though, the film containing that line is all but forgotten, despite its extraordinarily high quality, including every aspect from special effects to storyline. *This Island Earth* is easily the most elaborate sci-fi tale to be mounted in the fifties by someone other than George Pal, and while its message has been mainlined—the nearly nihilistic point of view featured in Raymond F. Jones' novel having been toned down to make this tamer, and more accessible, for a mass audience—it remains provocative and thought-provoking, as well as emotionally satisfying. The characters are flesh-and-blood people of the type that usually inhabit non-

The classic ad.

147

Ruth (Faith Domergue) struggles with one of Metaluna's creatures.

Cal (Rex Reason) and Ruth confront the laboratory of Exeter (Jeff Morrow).

The film begins in Georgia, where a man named Exeter has called together a wide variety of the earth's greatest scientists to develop with their cooperation a workable plan for world peace, as well as a future that might include a positive exploration of the universe. Despite Exeter's claims of altruism, there's something strange, if not quite cryptic, about him; physically, we

fantastic films, only in this case they find themselves sucked into the vortex of an extra-terrestrial experience. The film avoids histrionics and heightened approaches at all times, building slowly but surely to a strong suspenseful conclusion. This is less a typical sci-fi film with bug-eyed monsters (though there certainly are some unpleasant creatures on view) than it is a low-key story that makes its more outrageous moments appear believable and timely.

The survivors make a hasty escape from the doomed planet.

can't help but note his extremely high forehead, which makes him appear more intelligent than any of the others gathered here, while also lending him an otherworldly appearance. Two of the scientists, Cal and Ruth, become convinced Exeter is in fact a scout for some race from another planet, having come to earth to check out the possibilities of an invasion. As things grow ever more tense at the mansion, we sense they are right; having uncovered Exeter's plot, the two try and make a getaway to warn the world, but are pursued by an incredible ray that blasts everything in its path. Eventually, Cal and Ruth are sucked up into Exeter's flying saucer, then whisked through outer space to his faraway planet, Metaluna.

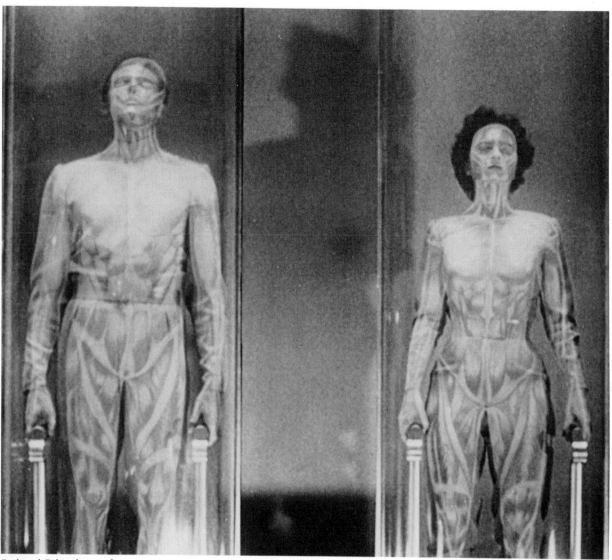

Ruth and Cal in the transformer.

There, they discover the reason for the planned invasion. For years, Metaluna has been involved in an interplanetary war with an enemy world, remaining safe from the enemy's missiles thanks to an impenetrable, invisible shield, but that is even now beginning to give way, so they see their only hope as a desertion to another planet. The one that comes closest to their own, in terms of living conditions, is our earth. But before their embarkation can begin, the enemy breaks through. Cal and Ruth—having battled their way through the Metaluna slave creatures—are just barely able to escape in Exeter's craft (with the dying Exeter's help and blessing) and return to earth to tell the tale.

Like so many of the sci-fi films from the early years of the decade, this is essentially a cautionary fable: we can't help noticing that the purpose of the story is to make us aware of the ridiculousness of Cold War enmities going on at home. But *This Island Earth* rates as quite unique, in that while many other films dealt either with an invasion from space or a trip into space, this film balanced its running time between those two possible plots.

This Island Earth was Universal-International's first foray into full-color sci-fi, and they pulled out all the stops; the color schemes are absolutely breathtaking, the special effects for the creatures are dazzling, rather than the usual man-in-the-monster-suit-with-a-zipper-up-his-back type of stuff. Yet they are always subservient to the tale being told. The panoramic vision of Metaluna, besieged by bombs that tear through its protective lining, is the equal of Disney's excursions into other worlds. *This Island Earth* ought to be remembered for much more than just its single classic line of dialogue.

150

Battle Cry

A Warner Brothers Film (1955)

CREDITS:

Produced by Raoul Walsh; directed by Mr. Walsh; screenplay by Leon M. Uris, adapted from his novel of the same name: running time: 149 minutes.

CAST:

Van Heflin *(Maj. Huxley)*; Aldo Ray *(Andy)*; Mona Freeman *(Kathy)*; Nancy Olson *(Pat)*; James Whitmore *(Sgt. Mac)*; Raymond Massey *(Gen. Snipes)*; Tab Hunter *(Danny)*; Dorothy Malone *(Elaine)*; Anne Francis *(Rae)*; William Campbell *(Ski)*; John Lupton *(Marion)*; Perry Lopez *(Joe Gomez)*; Fess Parker *(Speedy)*; Jonas Applegarth *(Lighttower)*.

Ask anyone to name the biggest box-office hit among 1950s movies about World War II, and they'll guess one of the obvious classics of their kind: *From Here to Eternity, The Caine Mutiny, The Young Lions*. In fact, though, the film that had audiences lining up was *Battle Cry*, considered a bit of an embarrassment in every respect excepting only the financial rewards it reaped.

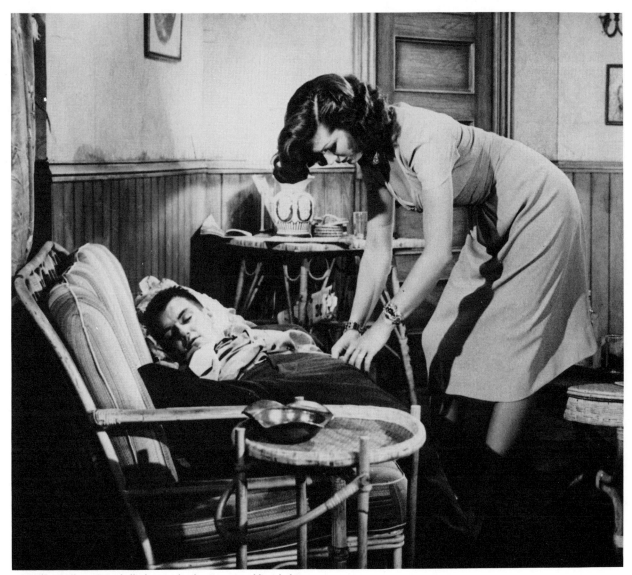

While Ski (William Campbell) sleeps, a hooker (Joan Arnold) picks his pocket.

An immense popular success in its time, *Battle Cry* offers reductive views of man-woman relationships, sloppy performances of tired stereotypes in place of the hoped-for incisive characters, and blatant rah-rah sentimentality ("Sound off," the marines sing as they march in the opening sequence) in place of any perceptive study of battle. Occasionally, you may have the opportunity to catch *Battle Cry* on cable TV some Sunday afternoon, when a ball game is rained out and the programmers need to slip in a long film at the last moment to fill the vacuum.

Battle Cry begins at boot camp, as a new group of marine volunteers get the usual treatment: the ultra-short haircuts, the weeks of grueling training in the field, the romances with the girls these leathernecks meet while in town on weekend pass. Overseeing them throughout such experiences is their tough sergeant with a proverbial heart of gold, Mac. In time, they enter into fierce combat with the Japanese. Before the film's 2½ hr. running time has spent itself, every cliché situation

James Whitmore as Sgt. Mac and Van Heflin as Maj. Huxley provided the film's strongest performances.

Danny (Tab Hunter) goes skinny dipping with wholesome girlfriend Kathy (Mona Freeman).

imaginable has been explored in an obvious (if rousing) way.

Hard to believe, but one reason why the film enjoyed such popularity in its time was what were then considered extraordinarily "frank" situations. In particular, teenage girls enamored of Tab Hunter (this being the brief period when he'd displaced Sonny Tufts as wholesome heartthrob, a status he'd soon relinquish to Troy Donahue) couldn't wait to see Tab seduced by an ultra sexy and married older woman (Dorothy Malone) before he returned to his girl back home (Mona Freeman), a perfect embodiment of what the girls in the audience imagined themselves to be like. The casual handling of this affair, within the context of glossy entertainment, made clear how far the screen had come in terms of achieving a new freedom in the two years since *From Here to Eternity* became embroiled in controversy for

depicting just such a situation, though that film did so with an artistry *Battle Cry* seldom aspired to and never achieved.

For this was sensationalism, if done on a slick level and in an expensive manner. No wonder, then, that Paul Newman—just emerging as the prince of method actors to challenge Marlon Brando's still-reigning king—turned down the part of Danny, certain it would identify him with the kind of schlock he wanted to avoid. Other actors were happy for the exposure, including a pair of TV cowboys: John Lupton, as an intellectual hoping to write a great book about the war, would shortly be playing Indian agent Tom Jeffords in the weekly series version of *Broken Arrow*, while Fess Parker, the dimwitted Speedy, had already become *Davy Crockett* to millions of kids.

But the most engaging performance was offered by an incorrigible scene stealer named Justus E. McQueen, making his film debut as a weird, wary Southerner, L. Q. Jones. Though McQueen enjoyed widespread fame for the role, his agents had trouble finding him more work; mention of his name drew a blank, though all they had to do was allude to his character and producers were happy to hire him. In time, the actor tired of the confusion, and legally changed his name to L. Q. Jones.

Anne Francis was fine as a shady lady the intellectual falls for, Van Heflin his usual underrated self as the doomed Colonel, James Whitmore solid as the Spencer Tracyish sergeant. Aldo Ray, best when playing a threatening type, missed the mark as the easygoing Andy, in

Tab Hunter is suitably gentle with "good girl" Mona Freeman.

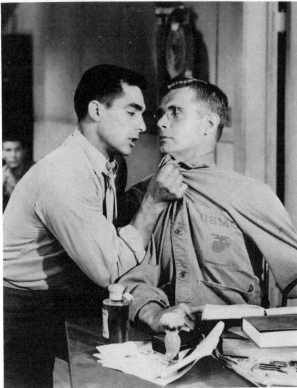

The intellectual Marion (John Lupton) is terrorized by the street fighter Gomez (Perry Lopez).

Andy (Aldo Ray) covers for his friends.

love with a girl (Nancy Olson) he meets in New Zealand. Raoul Walsh, who'd been directing bigscale war actions films ever since the original *What Price Glory?* in 1926, served this superficial concoction up with proper zest. Critics drubbed the film, though audiences made it a hit of the year. Then *Battle Cry* rapidly receded in our collective consciousness.

A Man Called Peter

A 20th Century-Fox Film (1955)

CREDITS:

Produced by Samuel G. Engel; directed by Henry Koster; screenplay by Eleanor Griffin, adapted from the book by Catherine Marshall; running time: 119 minutes.

CAST:

Richard Todd *(Peter Marshall)*; Jean Peters *(Catherine Marshall)*; Marjorie Rambeau *(Miss Fowler)*; Jill Esmond *(Mrs. Findlay)*; Les Tremayne *(Senator Harvey)*; Robert Burton *(Mr. Peyton)*; Gladys Hurlbut *(Mrs. Peyton)*; Richard Garrick *(Colonel Whiting)*; Gloria Gordon *(Barbara)*; Billy Chapin *(Peter John Marshall)*; Sally Corner *(Mrs. Whiting)*; Voltaire Perkins *(Senator Wiley)*; Marietta Canty *(Emma)*.

Even the bookish hero (John Lupton) is seduced by a tart (Ann Francis).

Richard Todd as Peter Marshall.

Peter and his wife Catherine (Jean Peters) in a sad mood.

The special couple at home.

The easiest way to turn off an audience eager for ever more sensational movie fare—as the audience of the fifties clearly was—is to tell them a new film is "inspirational" in nature. That usually signifies a wholesome and boring movie, the kind of film you know you're supposed to see because it's good for you, though it will undoubtedly suffer from a dullness practically unavoidable in a film designed to preach to the converted. Besides, a smug self-righteousness—a holier-than-thou attitude—can often be detected in such works, and that's a turn-off to all but the most ardent born-again viewer. Yet *A Man Called Peter* is the exception to all those rules. This film version of the biography of a man whose most spectacular feat was to be named chaplain of the United States briefly before he died in 1949 featured a simple but irresistible eloquence. As a result, the film transcended its genre. *A Man Called Peter* is, quite possibly, the most moving inspirational movie ever made by a commercial Hollywood studio.

Richard Todd—a fine British actor who worked regularly throughout the fifties, but whose career paradoxically began to fade just when English actors like Richard Burton, Peter O'Toole, and Richard Harris were coming into vogue in the early sixties—was cast as Peter Marshall. This long but never longwinded movie, episodically depicting the routine events of his unspectacular life, managed to do so with such non-sentimental admiration for the man's absolute faith that a viewer was left far more touched than by many films that try to bring major miracles to life but end up looking like nothing more than special effects festivals. Jean Peters, finally working her way up from decorative roles in cardboard costume films into the big leagues at Fox, did just fine by the part of Catherine Marshall, who as Peter's widow had written the book this film was based on.

The movie begins with Peter's great inspiration as a boy, when the young Scot is seized by the notion he must carry his Presbyterian ministry to America, through his experiences at the New York Avenue Church in Washington, D.C., where he is sometimes in conflict with the rather stuffy Miss Fowler, who at first doesn't altogether approve of Peter's intense evangelical zeal or his tendency to use the pulpit for his crusades. In time, though, he wins everyone over through the sheer breathtaking quality of his sermons.

An amazing amount of this movie's running time was given over to Peter's sermons, but if that sounds like a less than exciting prospect for a movie, think again. Marshall's sermons were so fascinating in terms of what they (however unintentionally) revealed about the man who wrote them (they are, taken as a body, a kind of unofficial soul-searching autobiography, disguised as a

Peter "wows" 'em with a kilt.

Mother and son console themselves following the loss of their beloved Peter.

series of weekly sermons for others) that they can spellbind an audience as well as Shakespeare's soliloquies. In Todd, Hollywood found precisely the right person to play Peter, for he creates a man who is formidable if never flashy, so sincerely excited about the Lord that he can't

157

Ambitious but sensitive Fred Staples (Van Heflin) confronts the alcoholic wreck that William Briggs (Ed Begley) has become.

help but excite others. The sermons are the film's big set-pieces, and they are something to hear.

One doesn't have to share Marshall's generalized faith or specific orientation to marvel at what happens when he begins speaking on Sunday mornings; we are immediately aware of being in the presence of a special man, and Todd effectively conveyed that quality so the movie-going audience would understand why people had been so captivated by the man called Peter. Though he would never win superstardom, Todd was a most appealing import from England. Most critics agreed that the great moment in the movie came on Pearl Harbor Sunday, when Peter delivered an interpretation of St. James's views on death to the Naval Academy's midshipmen just minutes before word reached them of the bombing. More often, *Peter* concentrated on the quiet home life of the Marshalls and the little problems of his pastorate. Out of these worthy but seemingly undramatic realities, the filmmakers fashioned a classic inspirational movie.

Patterns

A United Artists Release (1956)

CREDITS:

Produced by Michael Myerberg; directed by Fielder Cook; screenplay by Rod Serling, adapted from his teleplay; running time: 83 minutes.

CAST:

Van Heflin *(Fred Staples)*; Everett Sloane *(Walter Ramsey)*; Ed Begley *(William Briggs)*; Beatrice Straight *(Nancy Staples)*; Elizabeth Wilson *(Margo Fleming)*; Joanna Roos *(Miss Lanier)*; Elene Klamos *(Sylvia Trammel)*; Shirley Standlee *(Miss Hill)*; Ronnie

Welsh, Jr. *(Paul Briggs);* Sally Gracie *(Ann);* Michael Dreyfuss *(Billy);* Adrienne Moore, Elaine Kaye *(Secretaries).*

Patterns is a morality play, though one particularly in tune with the corporate mentality that emerged during this decade. At New York's super-conglomerate, Ramsey and Co., Walter Ramsey exists as a kind of twentieth century monarch, a cold fish of a person and a ruthless chairman of the board of directors. His chief executive officer, William Briggs, tries to temper concern for profits with a care for the human element. Fred Staples, an industrial engineer, is Ramsey's hand-chosen man to replace Briggs. Like Briggs, he's a decent fellow, and much admires the man he is expected to succeed; Briggs likewise thinks highly of the younger man. But as a Machiavellian, Ramsey chooses not to fire Briggs, allowing him to continue working for as long as he lives. Ramsey manipulates situations calculated to create friction between his two underlings, knowing that Briggs suffers from a severe heart condition and the strain will in due time kill him. The question is: will Staples, a

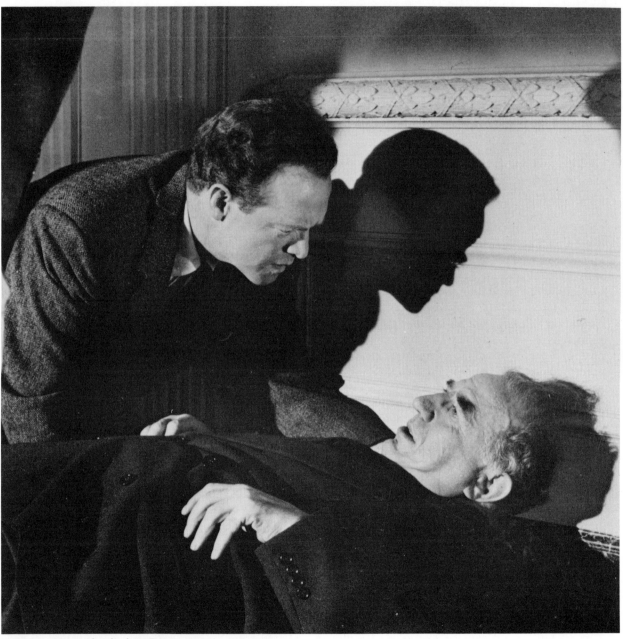

Fred attempts to comfort the dying Briggs.

159

Fred shares his emotional horror with wife Nancy (Beatrice Straight).

good man yet ambitious to climb the corporate ladder, allow himself to be used as Ramsey's pawn in the planned destruction of Bill Briggs?

In addition to its extraordinary high quality, *Patterns* deserves attention on a number of counts. First, it was based on a TV play, and is a further representation of a unique syndrome of the fifties, which saw dozens of plays given a kind of "out-of-town" tryout thanks to inexpensive mountings on live TV. The very best of them—*Marty, Days of Wine and Roses, Judgment at Nuremburg, Requiem for a Heavyweight*—were then given full movie treatment. This has resulted in the myth of a golden age of television, when great dramas were unfolded every evening; in fact, more than 90 percent of the TV plays were awful.

But there were the few gems, and *Patterns* is certainly one of them. A second notable point is that *Patterns* was written by Rod Serling, who would shortly become forever associated with the fantastic genre due to the remarkable success of *The Twilight Zone*. Owing to the ongoing and deserved cult status of that show, the late Mr. Serling has always been thought of as a science-fiction writer, a label he did not appreciate. Though this gentle, generous man was far too polite to ever insult his legion of fans by downgrading sci-fi/fantasy—and too sincerely appreciative of the financial success the show had earned him—he always perceived *Zone* as merely one of many routes he wanted to explore as a writer; in fact, he was far more interested in realistic human melodrama than in such "way-out" material.

The truth is, some of the best remembered *Zone* episodes deal with the problems of 1950s style executives

suffering under the extreme pressure of their chosen careers, and dreaming themselves into the good old days of turn-of-the-century settings. Despite the movement through time and/or dimensions—obligatory for a *Zone* episode—Serling was in those shows writing about the executive as an emerging tragic hero for the fifties. In *Patterns*, he did precisely that, but without the fantasy trappings. Which put his work in line with such key films of the decade as *Man in the Gray Flannel Suit, Executive Suite,* and *Woman's World.*

The Executive Suite, 1950s style: Walter Ramsey (Everett Sloane, standing) presides over his hand-picked coterie of postwar corporate executives.

Though less well remembered than any of those, *Patterns* is perhaps the best of the lot, an incisive, authentic portrait of power struggles in the emerging corporate jungle of the fifties, where a kind of ruthless social Darwinism existed beneath the civilized facade of Brooks Brothers suits. Fielder Cook, who directed the show for TV (in fact, *Patterns* had such remarkable impact when aired in January, 1955, that by popular demand it was brought back a month later, though in this pre-video tape period it had to be fully restaged), was retained for the film; he was one of the first TV directors to win a Hollywood contract as a result of his live television work. Most of the original cast remained intact. At this time, television was not yet so widespread, and even though the show had been seen twice, most of the country—still without TV—was understandably eager to see for themselves what all the shouting had been about.

The Solid Gold Cadillac

A Columbia Release (1956)

CREDITS:

Produced by Fred Kohlmar; directed by Richard Quine; screenplay by Abe Burrows, based on the play by George S. Kaufman and Howard Teichman; running time: 99 minutes.

CAST:

Judy Holliday *(Laura Partridge)*; Paul Douglas *(Edward L. Mc-Keever)*; Fred Clark *(Clifford Snell)*; John Williams *(John T. Bles-* *sington)*; Hiram Sherman *(Harkness)*; Neva Patterson *(Amelia)*; Ralph Dumke *(Warren)*; Ray Collins *(Metcalfe)*; Arthur O'Connell *(Jenkins)*; Richard Deacon *(Williams)*; Marilyn Hanold *(Miss L'Arriere)*; and the voice of George Burns.

If the fifties was the era of the dumb blonde, then Judy Holliday was the class act of that déclassé type. While most of the famous dumb blonde stars, from Marie Wilson to Jayne Mansfield, very often had critics wondering if perhaps the actresses were as dumb as the characters they played, that was never the case here. For Holliday was a gifted comedienne and a closet intellectual, always managing to create just enough distance between herself and her characters to make us realize how much smarter she was than they, without ever making the mistake of becoming aloof from her roles and condescending to her characters—and, with them, the audience. To be fair, though, Holliday's characters were, in one sense, not dumb blondes at all, but smart

cookies without benefit of education. In her best films, like the supporting performance in the Tracy-Hepburn vehicle *Adam's Rib* (1949) that shot her to movie stardom, or her first lead, in *Born Yesterday* (1950), which won her an Oscar, Judy was most often cast as a woman whose street smarts and common sense stun the more sophisticated men around her. She shows up their pseudo-attitudes with what can best be described as her radically innocent approach to life. To a degree, Judy was the actress Betty Hutton was always trying to become, but Judy's genius came in communicating a gentleness under the coarse surface which kept her from becoming, like Hutton, grating.

The Solid Gold Cadillac was one of her best films, completed just three years before Judy retired owing to cancer, which would claim her life in 1965. This was not, like *Born Yesterday*, a case of Holliday portraying a role she'd already made famous onstage; in the original Broadway production, Laura Partridge had been played by Josephine Hull, best known for her *Arsenic and Old Lace* role as one of the two dotty spinsters. For the film version, *Cadillac* was redesigned with Judy in mind, and a romantic plot (so important to the box-office of a film) could be added for the younger, attractive variation of the character without diminishing the play's power.

Laura Partridge is a small stockholder in a major corporation, owning ten shares. Idealistically, she stands up to a corrupt board of directors who would like to bilk the small stockholders out of their 10 percent annual earnings and, in time, wins out over them. It's the kind of role Goldie Hawn would neatly play today, and Judy Holliday can easily be seen as a precursor to Goldie, with her electrifying grin and remarkable charm, a touch whacky perhaps but always wonderful and winning. The best word to describe her delivery may be ingenuous: the incomparable moment here happens when she stands up at a stockholders' meeting and, without hesitation or guile, bluntly (but softly and sweetly) asks the Chairman of the Board: "Just what is it you do to earn your salary?" The beauty of it is, he doesn't have an answer.

Paul Douglas, Judy Holliday, and that car which lent the film its title.

163

Laura Partridge (Judy Holliday), a small stockholder, confronts the corrupt 1950s executives and demands her say.

McKeever, the Washington man with whom (in the film version) Laura becomes romantically involved, was played by Paul Douglas; in many ways, he appeared a kind of upscale version of Broderick Crawford, Miss Holliday's leading man in *Born Yesterday*. The comic approach to corporate life made this very much a film of the fifties, which offered such dramatic variations on the same theme as *Executive Suite* and *Woman's World*. Director Richard Quine managed to keep things moving at such a pace that moviegoing audiences rarely realized the stage origins of the piece.

Also helping to diminish the theatricality was a neat decision to shoot the entire movie in black and white, then do the final scene in color, a cinematic device if ever there was one. When, in the final sequence, Laura is awarded the title object for having cleaned up the company, the scene shifts to full-color to emphasize the beauty of the car; in truth, had the entire film been shot in color, the effect could not possibly be so stunning as it is here, when the sudden leap allows the solid gold cadillac to momentarily steal the scene even from Judy Holliday.

A radical innocent invades the executive suite.

Slightly Scarlet

An RKO Radio Pictures Release (1956)

CREDITS:

Produced by Benedict Bogeaus; directed by Allan Dwan; screenplay by Robert Blees, from the novel by James M. Cain; running time: 99 minutes.

CAST:

John Payne *(Ben Grace)*; Arlene Dahl *(Dorothy Lyons)*; Rhonda Fleming *(June Lyons)*; Kent Taylor *(Frank Jansen)*; Ted de Corsia *(Sol Caspar)*; Lance Fuller *(Gauss)*; Frank Gerstle *(Dave Dietz)*; Buddy Baer *(Lenhardt)*; George E. Stone *(Roos)*; Ellen Corby *(Martha)*; Roy Gordon *(Norman B. Marlowe)*.

In the late forties, no other company turned out *film noirs* quite so effectively as RKO. In dark, cynical stories about lone wolves passing through urban jungles, this studio wrote the book on a unique postwar form of filmmaking; their masterpieces of the genre—*Crossfire, Out of the Past*—still stand as the benchmark examples of this style. By the mid-fifties, though, black and white gradually gave way to the use of color, even for tales of gangsterism and the seedy nightworld. Splashy colors in florid patterns would mark this second generation of *film noir*. At mid-decade, RKO turned out one of the very best, *Slightly Scarlet*, which maintains the sexy, sordid ambience of corruption so essential to the earlier *noirs*. It was present in the dazzling color scheme that would become characteristic of Douglas Sirk, Nicholas Ray, Richard Fleischer, and Edward Dmytryk as each director adjusted to a filmmaking era when even the bleakest of stories has to be told with the brightest of color palettes.

Allan Dwan had been knocking out routine if visually astute programmers for various studios since the earliest days of Hollywood (though he guided Doug Fairbanks through the classic 1922 *Robin Hood, Getting Gertie's Garter* and *Sands of Iwo Jima* seem more typical of the unimposing, unpretentious Dwan's work). He enjoyed his greatest success with this strange James Cain story which took on almost surreal qualities in his heightened telling. Like the better known (and later) *Vertigo, Slightly Scarlet* is organized around reds and greens, here as in the Hitchcock film deftly employed to suggest passion and frigidity in two women who exist in a *doppelgänger* relationship, emerging as the positive and negative poles of a single perverted sex drive.

Rhonda Fleming as June Lyons.

165

Ben Grace (John Payne) finds himself obsessed with both the beautiful redheads, the seemingly nice shady lady June (Rhonda Fleming) and her psychologically twisted sister Dorothy (Arlene Dahl).

The 1950s film version barely dared hint at the lesbian relationship of the two sisters, keeping their physical encounters confined to moments when they were physically threatened.

In the movie's impressive opening sequence, we see Dorothy Lyons released from a woman's prison. Waiting to pick her up is her softspoken, ladylike sister, June, who attempts to care for the psychologically unpredictable Dorothy and rehabilitate the girl. But June is not quite as perfect a lady as she appears. For some time, she has been the secretary-mistress of the city's ultra-honest mayor. Meanwhile, the big boys of crime want to take over this area, and a slick, sleazy lawyer, Ben Grace—a once promising attorney who had idealistic ambitions but has long since sold his soul to the mob—

has the job of overseeing the gradual corruption of an otherwise honest man and his decent city.

To do this, he must seduce June and use the information that she has at her fingertips to destroy the mayor. In the meantime, though, Ben must deal with the kleptomaniac Dorothy, a maneater who wants Ben for herself. Complicating the matter is the fact that it's almost impossible to tell the two women apart. In the movie's most memorable scene, Ben entertains Dorothy at a beachhouse; the bikini-clad beauty (wearing a suit that's appropriately ornamented with a leopardskin mo-

The Production Code insisted they sleep in separate beds.

June muses about Ben.

tif) playfully fools around with a speargun, pointing it at the distraught Ben as part of her sexually tantalizing play; when the gun goes off and nearly castrates him, we see the extent to which this femme fatale is incapable of comprehending her own deadly qualities.

The only flaw in the film also exists with other, better known Production Code versions of Cain's novels, including *Double Indemnity* and *The Postman Always Rings Twice*: the twisted sexual relations the author candidly deals with could only be hinted at by studio-era Hollywood. In fact, throughout the 1970s, rumors persisted that a French remake of *Slightly Scarlet* would star Catherine Deneuve and Brigitte Bardot, in a film which would detail the originally downplayed notion that the women are both incestuous lesbians and repressed nymphomaniacs, who when not sleeping with each other are in bed with Ben, either singly or as a pair. Sadly, that intriguing film never got made. But Hollywood's *Slightly Scarlet* does include plenty of implications along those lines, co-starring two stunning redheads who were born to play sisters, and showing John Payne's quiet, underrated talent at portraying Dick Powell-ish tough guys. Grim in theme but gorgeous to look at, *Slightly Scarlet* is ripe for revival.

Rock, Pretty Baby

A Universal Release (1956)

CREDITS:

Produced by Edmond Chevie; directed by Richard Bartlett; screenplay by Herbert Margolis and William Raynor; running time: 89 minutes.

CAST:

Sal Mineo (Angelo Barrato); John Saxon (Jimmy Daley); Luana Patten (Joan Wright); Edward C. Platt (Dr. Daley); Fay Wray (Mrs. Daley); Rod McKuen ("Ox" Bentley); John Wilder ("Fingers" Porter); Alan Reed Jr. ("Sax" Lewis); Douglas Fowley ("Pop" Wright); Bob Courtney ("Half Note" Harris); Shelley Fabares (Twinky); Susan Volkmann and Carol Volkmann (The Saunders Sisters); April Kent (Kay Norton); Sue George (Lori Parker); Tommy (George Winslow).

When Bill Haley and the Comets hit the airwaves with "Rock Around the Clock," a new era in popular music was born; parents may have scorned rock 'n' roll, comforting themselves with the belief it was only a passing fad, but rock would slowly, gradually win acceptance as a legitimate, even overriding musical idiom. The new sound, which caught in its Big Beat the spirit of those times, allowed an entire generation of teenagers to define themselves: overnight, that holdover from the forties, the Be Bop Baby, gave way to the Dungaree Doll. Leather jackets, the ducktail haircuts, the entire sensibility of the fifties hit popular culture overnight. And while the major movie companies approached all this warily, the small independents sensed they could quickly capitalize with exploitation pictures. Most were hurried, sloppy affairs; *Rock, Rock, Rock* and *Shake, Rattle and Rock* offered lame excuses for stringing together popular acts. *Rock, Pretty Baby* stands as an exception: an attempt to analyze the teenagers of the fifties and the music by which they defined themselves.

Only a year earlier, Sal Mineo played a supporting role in *Rebel*, made just before the rock 'n' roll explosion

The Boys in the Band: that's Rod McKuen on the far left, John Saxon out front, Luana Patten to the right.

Sal Mineo as Angelo Barrato.

and today seeming somewhat incomplete without it. But *Rock*, as the title suggests, is suffused with the sound: 17 separate numbers, performed by Mineo (who enjoyed twin careers, as a rock 'n' roll singer and also as an Oscar-nominated actor for *Rebel*) and friends. Here, he plays Angelo, an ethnic kid hoping music will be his ticket to a better life but not altogether sure he wants to join the Establishment. As the rich boy who, conversely, would like to get himself some street smarts, John Saxon looked like a junior league Brando; a fine actor, he transcended the youth exploitation flicks (as few of his colleagues were able to do) and enjoyed a long career as a character actor. The Bluejeans Baby caught between the two was Luana Patten, previously a child star for

Disney in *Song of the South* and *Pecos Bill*. Also in the cast were Shelley Fabares, who would have a lengthy run on TV as Donna Reed's daughter and be a three-time co-star for Elvis Presley, and Rod McKuen, whose famous hoarse voice was a result of one too many rock 'n' roll concerts before turning to poetry.

The film was one of the first made with the emerging (and lucrative) teen audience in mind, standing as the precursor of the popular youth-exploitation picture. It's worth mentioning that the film, though mostly greaser-oriented, also serves as a precursor of the surf 'n' sand picture that, in most people's memory, did not evolve until *Beach Party* (1963); in *Rock, Pretty Baby*, the kids constantly toss off their black leather jackets in favor of

Many of the situations involved the teens in urban settings.

But there was always time for the beach. From left to right, John Wilder, Lucretia Simmons, Sue George, Sal Mineo, and Susan and Caryl Volkman.

Sal Mineo, in a dramatic moment, performs artificial respiration on a drowning pal as Rod McKuen *(center)* and varied teenagers look on.

bikinis. Fay Wray, onetime inamorata of King Kong himself, reintroduced herself to young viewers as the hero's mother, a role she'd play in countless such pic-

tures. Johnny Grant, a real-life West Coast disc jockey who would soon be overshadowed by Dick Clark, appeared as himself. Ed Platt, who had played the sensitive and sympathetic counselor in *Rebel*, here turned up in a role not unlike the one Jim Backus had assayed there, as the confused upper-middle-class father, unable to comprehend his son's motiveless rebellion. Mineo would shortly give up his singing career to be taken more seriously as an actor; in quick succession, he starred in Otto Preminger's *Exodus* (Oscar nominee), George Stevens's *The Greatest Story Ever Told*, and John Ford's *Cheyenne Autumn*. Then, everything fell apart: his drug addiction and flamboyant homosexuality caused his career to crumble; before long he was seen only intermittently, in sordid items like *Who Killed Teddy Bear?* His brutal, lurid death came as a shock to middle-aged adults who had not thought of him in years, but suddenly recalled that for a brief while in the fifties, he'd been a key identification figure.

The film was popular enough to spawn a sequel, though Mineo passed; John Saxon took center stage, courting Molly Bee as the group performed at a lake in *Summer Love*.

172

The Bad Seed

A Warner Brothers Film (1956)

CREDITS:

Produced by Mervyn LeRoy; directed by Mr. LeRoy; screenplay by John Lee Mahin, based on the play by Maxwell Anderson, taken from the novel by William March; running time: 129 minutes.

CAST:

Patty McCormick (Rhoda); Nancy Kelly (Christine); Henry Jones (LeRoy); Eileen Heckart (Mrs. Daigle); Evelyn Varden (Monica); William Hopper (Kenneth); Paul Fix (Bravo); Jesse White (Emory); Gage Clarke (Tasker); Joan Croydon (Miss Fern); Frank Cady (Mr. Daigle).

The postwar era was the period when Hollywood discovered psychoanalysis and made it the basis for films produced in the late 1940s and all through the fifties. There was even one glossy soap opera— *The Cobweb*— which took the premise that had previously been used for *Grand Hotel* and would later be revived in *Airport*, and set it in an insane asylum. Things would not have been complete had someone not made clear that such aberrations extended even to children. *The Bad Seed* was the movie which vividly realized all our worst nightmares by doing just that.

The story takes place in a normal suburban neighborhood where Kenneth and Christine attempt to raise their adorable little girl Rhoda as lovingly as possible: they could be stand-ins for Ozzie and Harriet, only with one girl instead of two boys. The real burden of responsibility

Patty McCormick as Rhoda.

When Rhoda realizes the handyman LeRoy (Henry Jones) is on to her, she begins plotting his demise.

falls upon Christine, since her husband is often away on business. She and the child get along fine: "I've got the nicest mother in the whole world . . .," Rhoda is fond of cooing. But the horrid drowning death of a neighborhood boy will have terrible implications for Christine, as she gradually realizes her daughter killed the child and two other people.

In addition to the absorbing melodrama of a woman discovering her dream child is in fact a monster—resisting this grotesque truth in every way possible until it can no longer be ignored and must be acted upon—the script also exploits the situation for a somewhat simplistic debate on environment vs. heredity. As the dialogue makes obviously clear, the point of this whole thing is that no amount of situational influence can alter the good or bad impulses carried in the blood from birth. Such lines hammer home what was in fact obvious already: this is not so much a film as it is a recording of a stage play (the original Broadway cast was kept almost intact), and *The Bad Seed* suffers from that. Too often, we do not see things happen, only hear about them

afterwards, but when Mervyn LeRoy does take his camera outdoors, as in the lakeside sequence leading up to the boy's drowning, we sense it's a none too subtle "opening up" of the play.

The acting is all a bit arch and overdone, the sort of heightened portrayals so necessary for a stage show to click but antithetical to good movie acting, which is essentially realistic. Today, Nancy Kelly's grimacing as the mother can induce unintentional laughter, while Patty McCormick's eye-rolling portrayal of the murderous child is more than a bit much: in the theater, extreme gestures of feigned innocence may have been necessary to communicate to viewers in the back rows, but on film it seems very much a patent case of play-acting: Rhoda is too obviously faking innocence. Also, what could be disguised on the stage cannot in the larger-than-life medium of movies: Miss McCormick was clearly much older than eight. The static camera set-ups only heighten our realization of the stage origins, though the one departure from the stage play is disastrous. The power of the original show depended on the

174

ending, as we saw Rhoda con her mother and continue her killing spree; for a film made while the Production Code was still in effect and villains (however youthful) had to pay for their crimes, an obligatory ending was necessarily tacked on in which we see Rhoda struck by lightning.

But there was more yet to come; perhaps to acknowledge that this was in effect a filmed play, perhaps to ease the audience's tension and send them home happy, the actors appear for cinematic curtain calls, smiling into the camera and bowing to anticipated applause. There's even an unforgivable bit of business in which Nancy Kelly picks up Patty McCormick, puts the child over her knee, and spanks her while both ladies wink at the audience. As an epilogue to a live theater presentation, such a "cutesy" routine works beautifully; for a film, it's all wrong. Still, if it creaks today, *The Bad Seed* was immensely popular in its time, a film that was very much by, for, and about the psychoanalytic period of picture making. If *Bad Seed* does not have the "legs" necessary to survive its decade and still play effectively today, then at least it still neatly represents the period during which it was produced.

Nancy Kelly and Patty McCormick: "I have the nicest mother in the whole world."

Kenneth (William Hopper) and Christine (Nancy Kelly) cringe when they realize that environment cannot counteract heredity.

Tea and Sympathy

A Metro-Goldwyn-Mayer Film (1956)

CREDITS:

Produced by Pandro S. Berman; directed by Vincente Minnelli; screenplay by Robert Anderson, from his stage play; running time: 122 minutes.

CAST:

Deborah Kerr *(Laura Reynolds)*; John Kerr *(Tom Robinson Lee)*; Leif Erickson *(Bill Reynolds)*; Edward Andrews *(Herb Lee)*; Darryl Hickman *(Al)*; Norma Crane *(Ellie Martin)*; Dean Jones *(Ollie)*; Jacqueline De Wit *(Lilly Sears)*; Tom Lauɡnlin *(Ralph)*; Ralph Votrain *(Steve)*; Steven Terrell *(Phil)*; Kip King *(Ted)*; Jimmy Hayes *(Henry)*; Richard Tyler *(Roger)*; Don Burnett *(Vic)*.

"When you talk about this . . . and you will . . . be kind."

So speaks Laura Reynolds in the last—and most famous—line of Robert Anderson's play *Tea and Sympathy*, as well as in the film version of it. Well, not quite; for if the lights then faded in the Broadway theatre, that was not the case in the movies. The Production Code may have been crumbling, but it had not yet toppled. And since that line of dialogue was spoken by an unhappily married woman to an equally troubled teenage boy she was about to sexually initiate, the filmmakers were forced to tack on an obligatory ending in which, ten years later, the wife at last realizes her horrible mistake and writes a heartfelt letter of apology to her boor of a husband.

But this was, after all, 1956, so *Tea and Sympathy* rates as a pioneer picture for its time. One thing that could not be depicted was homosexuality, and this stands as yet another of the numerous plays in which writers twisted the homosexual experience to make it appropriate for what were then considered mainstream tastes. While the film remains generally true to the play, having been adapted for the screen by the playwright, it did cut away much of what even in the more sophisticated and worldly New York theater could only be hinted at. Though this seems to be the story of a prep school youth whose only real problem is that he has not yet lost his virginity and is waiting for a special woman to share his first sexual experience with, it in fact has another layer of meaning.

The taunts that Tom Robinson Lee suffers at the hands of his jock housemates (they call him a "sissyboy" and a

The "sensitive" youth Tom (John Kerr) observes Laura (Deborah Kerr) at work in her garden.

176

"strange off-horse" in the film, though the language was more pungent and colloquial in the play) are, despite their cruelty, on target. Only by pretending to write about a youth who is not a latent homosexual but is accused of being one could Anderson dramatize the plight of a boy who is, in fact, "different," and is having a horrid time accepting that fact. The moment audiences learned that Tom was "sensitive," they understood what that meant in the existing code by which films then expressed themselves.

One problem with watching the film today is that John Kerr appears incredibly long in the tooth to be playing an 18-year-old; this was, let's recall, filmed only a short while before he went to Hawaii to play the mature young officer Lt. Cable in *South Pacific*, his only other major film role. (Kerr was one of those acclaimed stage actors—Ben Piazza was another, while more recent examples include Frank Langella and Kevin Kline—who for reasons difficult to explain simply do not click on film).

Watching this today, we have to adjust to the convention of the old Hollywood, which held that actors photograph as ten years younger than they actually are, so age adjustments must be made; this notion went unchallenged until 1967, when Franco Zeffirelli dared to cast teenagers as the leads in his film of Shakespeare's *Romeo and Juliet*.

But that problem aside (which *Tea and Sympathy* shares with *The Bad Seed*), the film is effectively adapted for the screen. Though Mr. Anderson retained for most of the film the single set of the dormitory where the boy lives in close proximity to the macho Mr. Reynolds (whose own masculinity is eventually called into question, his raucousness finally seeming so much bravado to cover his fear of a woman like his wife) and the wistful, romantic Laura, that never seems as big a problem here. In part, this is because Vincente Minnelli was a more perceptive director than Mervyn LeRoy (who always functioned best as a creative producer), with a

"When you talk about this . . . and you will . . . be kind!"

Laura's insensitive jock husband Bill (Leif Erickson) grows suspicious.

At a faculty party, Bill makes a fool of himself in front
of the Dean (Edward Andrews).

179

cinematic sensibility that allowed him to shoot on one set without the results appearing static or stagey. When the film included incidents which took place offstage in the play, such as the midnight pajama raid and the visit to a prostitute, this appeared an effective expansion rather than a forced "opening up" of the play. Anderson's script is ultimately more meaningful (even when compromised) and less melodramatic than *The Bad Seed*; and Deborah Kerr played Laura as the kind of unique but believable woman Nancy Kelly was not able to make of the generic mother in *Bad Seed*.

Attack!

A United Artists Release (1956)

CREDITS:

Produced by Robert Aldrich; directed by Mr. Aldridge; screenplay by James Poe, from the play *Fragile Fox* by Norman Brooks; running time: 107 minutes.

CAST:

Jack Palance *(Lt. Costa)*; Eddie Albert *(Capt. Cooney)*; Lee Marvin *(Col. Bartlett)*; Robert Strauss *(Pfc. Bernstein)*; Richard Jaeckel *(Pfc. Snowden)*; Buddy Ebsen *(Sgt. Tolliver)*; William Smithers *(Lt. Woodruff)*; Jon Shepodd *(Cpl. Jackson)*; Peter Van Eyck *(Tall German)*; Strother Martin *(Inge)*.

Like *The Bad Seed, Attack!* was based on a play about a psychologically disturbed character; unlike it, this stands as an example of a drama completely rethought and perfectly restructured for the film medium, never once betraying its stage origins. Robert Aldrich here turned to World War II for the first time; nearly a dozen years later, he would create his blockbuster, *The Dirty Dozen*. There, Aldrich painted a scathingly cynical portrait of the military, where the rare moral man must fight corruption and incompetence on every level to get his job done. By 1967, the public embraced such a vision; in 1956, such a sensibility appeared far ahead of its time. Understandably, *Attack!* did not fare well financially. Yet it rates alongside Lewis Milestone's *A Walk in the Sun*, William A. Wellman's *The Story of G. I. Joe*, and Samuel Fuller's *The Big Red One* as one of the small handful of great films dealing with the ordinary dogface soldier and his attempts to survive the madness of modern war.

Set largely during the Battle of the Bulge, *Attack!* does not attempt to give us an objective overview of combat but instead insists we perceive it from the fragmentary viewpoint of a common soldier, who has no idea of the importance of a particular mission or his own outfit's function in it until afterwards. The drama takes place within an infantry company, after the cold, callous Colonel Bartlett assigns them the near-impossible task of holding a town from the advancing Germans. A far worse problem than the enemy is posed by Captain Cooney, who routinely sacrifices his soldiers owing to fear of death. The men, terrified they will be annihilated owing to their commander's cowardice, turn to the fair-minded Lt. Costa for help. Gradually, he realizes he can rectify the situation only by killing Cooney in cold blood.

Jack Palance as Lt. Costa.

180

Col. Bartlett (Lee Marvin) allows Capt. Cooney (Eddie Albert) to command despite the man's obvious cowardice.

Costa warns Sgt. Tolliver (Buddy Ebsen) that the Germans are moving in on the Bulge.

In an age when movies like *Platoon* unsparingly portray the military, it's sometimes difficult to recall that was not the case in the fifties. As novels, James Jones's *From Here to Eternity*, Norman Mailer's *The Naked and the Dead*, and Herman Wouk's *The Caine Mutiny* literally seethed with bitter resentment toward the army, marines, and navy, but the acclaimed film versions watered down the critical content to win Defense Department cooperation. Which is why those expertly acted films don't have much bite when viewed today; they seem to be forever pulling their punches. It's worth noting, then, that *Attack!* was the first major Hollywood film to be denied such official cooperation. Clearly, there are none of the compromises we note in other

Lt. Woodruff (William Smithers) grows uncomfortable as Costa confronts Cooney.

Costa and Pfc. Snowden (Richard Jaeckel) question a German prisoner, while a Nazi Officer (Peter Van Eyck) looks on.

Unlike such gaudy, glossy (and extremely popular) World War II films as *Battle Cry*, Aldrich's *Attack* took a far grimmer and more realistic approach.

182

films, no laying the blame on a scapegoat so the service itself can escape unscathed. This is brutal, frank, harrowing filmmaking, depicting war without the usual cliché characterizations and stereotypical situations that, say, *Battle Cry* reveled in. No one had ever done this before, and the public was put off by the horrifying and bleak vision. Understandably, *Battle Cry* was an immense hit, marketing heroics and romance, while *Attack!* did dismal business. Understandable too that *Battle Cry* is all but unwatchable now, while *Attack!* remains a classic of gritty naturalism.

Eddie Albert should have won a Best Supporting Actor Oscar (he wasn't even nominated) for his incisive portrayal of a psychologically scarred character, so characteristic of that decade when Hollywood focused on neurotics. At first Cooney seems merely a gutless villain, though he earns a certain amount of sympathy (or at least pity) in the remarkable sequence when he explains how his father, trying to make a man of him, beat him regularly, then finally gave him the bedroom slippers he still carries and fondles. Jack Palance, an effective supporting actor in villainous roles (*Shane*), was briefly

touted as a candidate for crossover to goodguy roles, much as Richard Widmark and Robert Mitchum had done. Though Palance never quite clicked as an offbeat leading man, he did give his best (i.e., most controlled) performances while working for Aldrich, here and in *The Big Knife* and *Ten Seconds to Hell*. Though *Attack!* was not a success in its time, it did serve as a precursor to the grim and realistic war movies which would eventually follow, and which would have been impossible without this groundbreaking film.

Goodbye, My Lady

A Batjac Production (1956)

CREDITS:

Produced by William A. Wellman with Marion Michael Morrison (John Wayne); directed by Mr. Wellman; screenplay by Sid Fleischman, from the novel by James Street; running time: 94 minutes.

CAST:

Brandon de Wilde *(Skeeter)*; Walter Brennan *(Uncle Jesse)*; Phil Harris *(Cash)*; Sidney Poitier *(Gates)*; William Hopper *(Grover)*; Louise Beavers *(Bonnie Dew)*.

When people think back to fifties films about a boy and his dog, they automatically conjure up Walt Disney's *Old Yeller*, the unforgettable tearjerker about a rural youth growing to cherish, then having to face separation from, a pet that's brought love into his lonely life. Certainly, the Disney version of Fred Gipson's Texas tale is a classic, but one year earlier, a virtually unknown film with a similar theme appeared. While it does not have the powerhouse finale of *Old Yeller*, the loss here is more subtle and, in a way, sadder still. *Goodbye, My Lady* is, simply, the best film ever made about a boy and a dog by any studio other than Disney.

Deep in the Mississippi swamps, a boy named Skeeter lives with his elderly Uncle Jesse. One day, Skeeter spies a strange lost dog (the animal can't bark, but makes a laugh-like sound) and takes the animal for his own. With help from their Negro neighbor Gates and the curmudgeonly storekeeper Cash, Skeeter trains the animal to be a fine bird dog, as well as the companion Skeeter has so desperately hungered for. While by day the boy teaches the dog how to hunt and track, in the evening Uncle Jesse—though a total illiterate—teaches

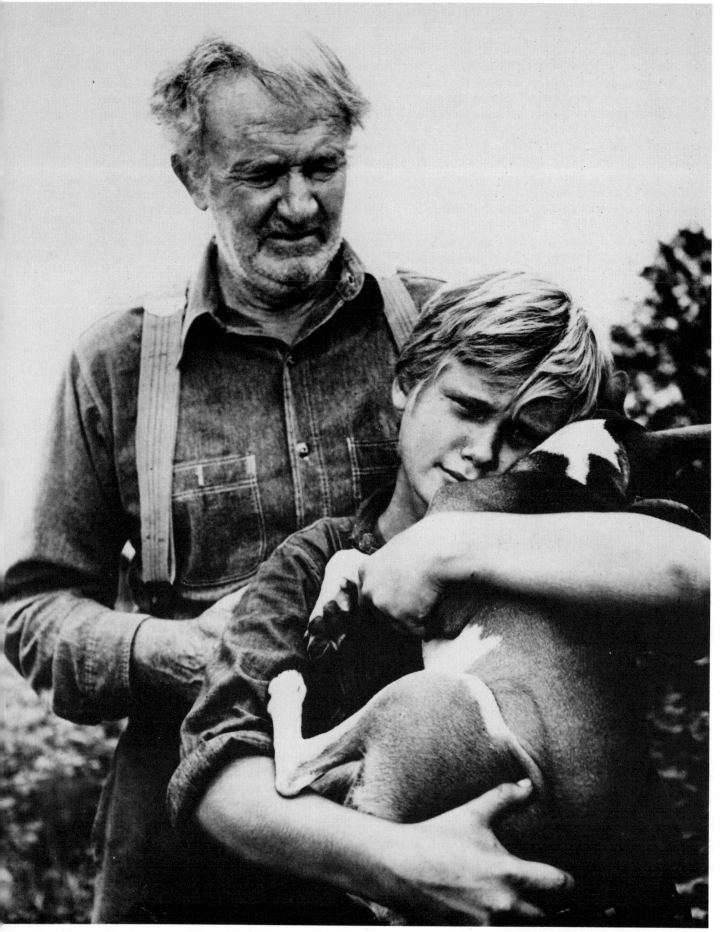

Walter Brennan, Brandon de Wilde, and "lady."

Skeeter and Uncle Jesse discover the "laughing dog" as their friend Cash (Phil Harris) looks on.

Uncle Jesse attempts to resolve Skeeter to the loss of his beloved lady.

The cast of *Goodbye, My Lady*.

that made *Old Yeller* such an instantaneous classic (the dog's fights with a bear, wild boars, and a wolf), but in its quiet, unassuming way, *Goodbye, My Lady* is ultimately a more honest and realistic depiction of the growing bond between a boy and an animal. Though the dog is not destroyed here, *Goodbye, My Lady* comes off as a bit less melodramatic and a touch more tragic. Yeller was, after all, being put out of his misery by Arliss, whereas here Skeeter must give up a healthy, happy animal, a far more heartbreaking experience than ending the life of a once delightful but now mad creature.

the boy moral values, how to display dignity under pressure and do the right rather than expedient thing. After a joyous season with his "lady," Skeeter will have to rely on his uncle's folk wisdom when the dog's true owner (the animal, though mistaken by Jesse and Skeeter for an abandoned mutt, is in fact rare and valuable, a barkless Basenji) shows up to claim him. Drawing strength from Jesse's value system and his own essential integrity, Skeeter hands his beloved pet over to its legal owner and returns to his former lonely life, which is more difficult than ever since he has experienced the taste of honey that "lady" brought to one short, sweet summer in the swamp.

William A. Wellman (*Wild Boys of the Road, The Ox-Bow Incident*) told the story in fittingly anecdotal fashion, concentrating on vividly rendered texture so effectively that "atmospheric" seems an inadequate word for describing his rendering of the life in the wilds. Downplaying the possibilities for sentiment, Wellman's characteristically tender-tough approach (he might be considered the liberal's John Ford) made this a work which charms with its simple surface and underpinning of sensitivity. Likewise, Wellman continued the strong sense of social-consciousness always a hallmark of his work, giving Sidney Poitier one of his best early roles as the dignified, non-stereotypical (Gates is a college grad) neighbor. The film contains whimsical humor and wistful drama. There are none of the spectacular sequences

Brandon de Wilde and Walter Brennan.

186

Three-time Oscar winner Brennan should have received yet another supporting-actor statuette for his delightful portrayal of an ancient, toothless geezer (there are resemblances to his characterization as John Wayne's sidekick in *Red River*) whose idea of Nirvana is to someday get a set of dental plates from Sears Roebuck. De Wilde had captivated Broadway audiences as the charming and in no way clichéd youngster of *A Member of the Wedding*, then went on to repeat that role in the film version, also getting to play the boy in the western classic *Shane*. He starred in the warmhearted live TV comedy-drama *Jamie*, and appeared likely to be one of the few child stars who would breakthrough into adult roles when he won key parts in such early-sixties A pictures as *Blue Denim*, *All Fall Down*, *Hud*, and *In Harm's Way*. But he appeared too clean-cut to have any place in the radical films of the late sixties, and was relegated to the dinner-theater circuit (often performing in *Butterflies Are Free*). Then, while spending a weekend in the woods, his camper rolled over him and claimed his life.

Walter Brennan and Phil Harris.

187

The Lieutenant Wore Skirts

A 20th Century-Fox Film (1956)

CREDITS:

Produced by by Buddy Adler; directed by Frank Tashlin; screenplay by Mr. Tashlin and Albert Belch, from an original story by Mr. Belch; running time: 99 minutes.

CAST:

Tom Ewell (Gregory Whitcomb); Sheree North (Kathy Whitcomb); Rita Moreno (Sandra); Rick Jason (Capt. Sloan); Les Tremayne (Henry Gaxton); Alice Reinheart (Capt. Briggs); Gregory Walcott (Lt. Sweeney); Joan Willes (Joan Sweeney); Sylvia Lewis (Takitoff); Edward Platt (Maj. Dunning); Jacqueline Fontaine (Buxom Date).

The service comedies mass-produced after the resounding success of *Mister Roberts* were essentially male-oriented; *Operation Mad Ball, Don't Go Near The Water, The Wackiest Ship in the Army* all dealt with the problems of servicemen attempting to handle incompetent officers and breathtaking beauties. Which is why *The Lieutenant Wore Skirts* stands out so notably, for as the title suggests, this is a fifties service comedy from the woman's point of view, making an attractive servicewoman the focal character and creating comedy from the way this intelligent, enlightened lady deals with the male-oriented situations presented at face value in other service sitcoms. To the degree that it does concentrate on a man—the husband of the title character—this is also unique. For the genre invariably takes for its central character a brash, youthful fellow, while this movie draws humor from a middle-aged man's attempts to deal with a young man's occupation.

The plot derives from the kind of comic misunderstanding so basic to classic sitcom. Gregory Whitcomb is a successful writer, who shares his upscale life with his lovely wife Kathy, until he receives a telegram informing him that as an inactive member of the Air Force, he's about to be recalled to duty. He dutifully informs his wife of the difficult situation and makes ready to leave. But Kathy is not your old-fashioned stay-at-home type; a pre-feminist believer in total equality, the concept that she can share every aspect of Gregory's life for better or worse, Kathy marches down to the

Sheree North as Kathy Whitcomb.

(Opposite page) Neighbor Gates (Sidney Poitier), an educated and non-stereotypical black.

189

Tom Ewell gives the evil eye to Captain Sloan (Rick Jason) as he dances with "The Lieutenant."

The initial predicament: Greg thinks he's being recalled to active duty, and Kathy is inspired to enlist and join him.

recruiting station and signs up, requesting she be stationed with her husband. Upon arriving home, though, Kathy is informed by a gleeful Gregory that his telegram was all a mistake; he isn't needed, after all. She, however, is now officially in the service, so he—as a civilian—must follow his wife to Hawaii, where she's to be stationed.

The film might better have been titled *I Married a WAF.* Gregory must contend with the fact that, very often, his wife has to attend functions with extremely handsome young flyboys like Capt. Barney Sloan. But what's good for the goose is good for the gander; Gregory escorts such lovelies as the provocative Sandra, who has set her sights on this dapper older man. Tom Ewell was a master at playing such comedy, and his work here with Sheree North might be considered a part of his "blonde trilogy" in which Fox also paired him with Marilyn Monroe *(The Seven Year Itch)* and Jayne Mansfield *(The Girl Can't Help It.)* While his career is all but forgotten today, it's worth noting that Ewell was one of the most popular comic leads of the fifties. A fine stage performer, he lacked the movie star charisma of Tony Randall and Jack Lemmon, with whom he was often in competition for parts.

An even more fascinating career is that of Sheree North. She was one of the many bosomy blondes of the fifties, nurtured by the studios in the wake of Marilyn Monroe's phenomenal popularity. In fact, Sheree's career was cultivated by Fox, who sensed Marilyn's rebelliousness as evidenced by her refusal to take parts she considered beneath her. When Marilyn flatly refused to appear in a routine sex farce called *How To Be Very, Very Popular* that would have paired her with Betty Grable, Fox gave the part (and a big publicity build-up) to Sheree, as an implied threat to their difficult superstar. But if Marilyn was the top blonde, Jayne Mansfield her closest competitor, and Mamie Van Doren the minor league variation, then Sheree seemed nothing more than

a remote bush-league sexy/dumb blonde, the least successful of all. Ironically, she turned out to have the longest career of any of them. As the others aged, their appeal diminished; Sheree, it became clear over the passing years, was a remarkably gifted comic and dramatic actress. Though she often showed up in supporting roles (Sheldon Leonard's wife on the TV sitcom *Big Eddie*, John Wayne's former lover in his final film *The Shootist*), Sheree worked continuously, after her more famous colleague/competitors had met with sad ends or retired. She succeeded for one simple reason: once we got past that immediate image of a second-string blonde bimbo, Sheree North turned out to be a first-rate character actress, which is why she survived.

Doing his bit, Greg blows the bugle to awaken Kathy each morning.

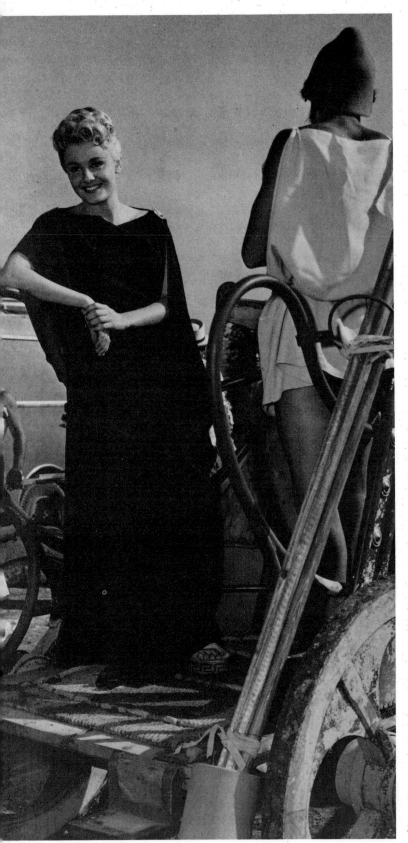

Statuesque Rossana Podesta relaxes on the set.

Helen of Troy

A Warner Brothers Film (1956)

CREDITS:

Produced by Robert Wise; directed by Mr. Wise; screenplay by John Twist and Hugh Gray, inspired by Homer's *Iliad*, running time: 118 minutes.

CAST:

Rossana Podesta *(Helen);* Jack (Jacques) Sernas *(Paris);* Sir Cedric Hardwicke *(Priam);* Stanley Baker *(Achilles);* Niall MacGinnis *(Menelaus);* Nora Swinburne *(Hecuba);* Robert Douglas *(Agamemnon);* Torin Thatcher *(Ulysses);* Harry Andrews *(Hector);* Janette Scott *(Cassandra);* Ronald Lewis *(Aeneas);* Brigitte Bardot *(Andraste);* Eduardo Ciannelli *(Andros);* Maxwell Reed *(Ajax).*

The credits for *Helen of Troy* insisted that this film was based on *The Iliad* of Homer, though the Greek poet would doubtless roll over in his grave several times considering the liberties taken with his somber epic. And not just the elimination of his verse: Homer's heroes, those Greek warriors who courageously sailed off to Troy to bring home their kidnapped princess, were here trashed. The movie's Helen chooses to run away with Paris and is "kidnapped" only in the minds of the pirate-like Greeks, who use this as an excuse to sack the city they've had their eyes on all along. Let's not forget, though, that the fifties was a period of revisionism in terms of popular culture: General Custer had been enshrined as a great American hero in such 1940s films as *They Died With Their Boots On*, but now emerged as the villain in *Sitting Bull, Tonka,* and most every movie made on the subject. It's not surprising, then, that characters from the ancient world received the same sort of reappraisal; this strikingly handsome though sometimes empty romance challenged all the values that the audience brought with them to the theater.

To be fair, the film is never ponderous in the way *The Egyptian* was: the production is slick, the dialogue surprisingly literate, the action sequences involving, the siege of Troy magnificently staged, the final entry into the city via the wooden horse a masterful set-piece. Many of the supporting performances are extraordinary: Stanley Baker's Achilles neatly captures the rage, pompousness, arrogance and bravado but also the majesty of the man; Harry Andrews' Hector is, in perfect contrast,

Cassandra (Janette Scott), Paris (Jack Sernas), and Helen nervously watch as the Greek army advances on Troy.

Spectacular battle scenes marked this Warner Brothers release.

193

The Trojans pull the wooden horse into their city, believing the fleeing Greeks left it as a present.

The city's last great orgy.

genre from spectacle to musical, and you've got the basis for his most famous film, *West Side Story*. With *Helen of Troy*, Wise worked within the emerging international moviemaking scene in which the old discrepancies between Hollywood product and European import became less and less significant, indeed almost impossible to recognize anymore. Though this was a Warner Brothers film, Helen was shot not on a studio back-lot but on location in Italy, with full cooperation from and involve-

quietly courageous, going into battle with his archrival more out of a sense of civic responsibility than any hunger for glory on the field. Their duel outside Troy, while two immense armies sit back and watch, is still a stunner.

Where the film goes soft is in its leads. Jack (Jacques) Sernas was appealing but forgettable, a kind of European Lex Barker. Rossana Podesta was certainly breathtaking enough, but her flawless face and perfect body did not help make her a terribly exciting screen presence. Ironically, the part of her handmaiden is played by an actress whose features may have been less perfect but who projected the vitality and chemistry the part absolutely demands: Brigitte Bardot, who one year later would be catapulted to superstardom in *And God Created Woman*. Amazingly, the woman born to play Helen did appear here, but in the wrong part.

That Robert Wise would make a movie about star-crossed lovers from warring camps, in which the focal couple seem bland compared to the warriors from those camps, should come as no surprise; change the setting from ancient Greece to contemporary America, the

196

ment of the Cinecittà Studio in Rome. Podesta was Italian, Sernas French, Sir Cedric Hardwicke and many of the other cast members British; the director was of course an American.

Here's a minor note, but one that will ring a bell for kids who grew up in the fifties. The movie (like many other films) was preceded by a Dell comic book version; it was the habit of kids to read the comic several times, then go to the movie with the storyline memorized.

Imagine our amazement, then, when at film's end, Paris is killed during the sacking of Troy, and Helen dragged home to Greece by her husband Menelaus; in the Dell edition, to make the story more palatable to youngsters, Paris and Helen had slipped out of the burning city to live happily ever after. People constantly walk out of a movie muttering that they liked the book better; kids, numbed by the film's downbeat ending, were here overheard grumbling that they liked the comic book better.

The Greeks emerge and conquer all.

197

1984

A Holiday Film (1956)

CREDITS:

Produced by N. Peter Rathyon; directed by Michael Anderson; screenplay by William P. Templeton and Ralph Bettinson, freely adapted from the novel by George Orwell; running time: 91 minutes.

CAST:

Edmond O'Brien *(Winston Smith)*; Jan Sterling *(Julia)*; Michael Redgrave *(O'Connor)*; and with: David Kosoff, Donald Pleasance, Mervyn Johns, Carol Wolveridge, Ernst Clark, Patrick Allen, Ronan O'Casey, Michael Ripper, Ewen Solon, and Kenneth Gritfiths.

George Orwell created his masterly combination of social satire, philosophic discourse, and science fiction drama in 1948. Recoiling in intellectual horror from the direction in which our postwar world seemed to be drifting, he merely reversed the two final digits of that year, allowing him to comment on his own time by exaggerating (though not distorting) what he saw for the sake of a more pointed truth through a logical progres-

Edmond O'Brien as Winston Smith.

The last true individualist attempts to flee, but is dwarfed by images of the sumbol of modern technocratic control, Big Brother.

Jan Sterling and Edmond O'Brien attempt to maintain a romance in an age when everyone has been reduced to a number.

One more of director Anderson's marvelously complex shots: Smith is seen only in reflection as the investigating police close in.

sion of present conditions. To Orwell, the modern media appeared ready to conspire with politicians and develop thought-control; stability would be created and maintained through a total repression of individuality. So he combined a melodramatic story of two lovers rebelling against the status quo with an unforgettably detailed portrait of what Huxley had tagged a Brave New World, creating a fable that would involve readers emotionally, then terrify them intellectually. His book became a bestseller, then a classic, though, with its depressing vision, it was hardly the sort of work Hollywood would hurry to option.

This independently produced film, shot in London and distributed in America by Columbia Pictures, captured much of the bite of Orwell's vision: a bleak totalitarian world where the worst aspects of socialism and fascism combine. Workers diligently toil at meaningless jobs for the all-powerful state, while a grotesque caricature of a leader—never experienced in the flesh, but only through endless TV monitors that project his image everywhere—is the Big Brother always watching you. Winston Smith, one more thoughtless working man, lives in Oceana (the earth has been divided into three spheres, the others being Eastasia and Eurasia) where he's employed in the Ministry of Truth. Despite signs everywhere reminding Smith and his fellow workers of such absurdist slogans as "Freedom is Slavery" and "War

Is Peace," Smith finds himself rebelling against this negative Utopia when he spots a functionary worker named Julia, and is unable to control his (illegal) impulses to pursue the lady. But the mind-police are soon on the alert, tracking down the anti-social couple, then elaborately brainwashing them. Smith attempts to remain true to Julia, but he has one weakness, one primal fear, he can't control; since childhood, Smith has been terrified of rats. When Big Brother's emissaries employ their ultra-sophisticated technical equipment to program Smith to believe rodents are crawling all over him, the man cracks. In the final terrifying scene, Smith is seen— fully "rehabilitated"—standing before a larger-than-life poster of the legendary Big Brother, screaming out his undying love and loyalty.

200   O'Connor (Michael Redgrave, standing in black) oversees the intellectual, psychological, and emotional stripping away of people's identities.

Edmond O'Brien neatly captured, in the entire film but especially in that last sequence, the dark vision: absolutely anyone can be broken on the modern rack of technology. The look in his eyes after being completely stripped of his own ideas and emotions—his happiness at having found the "courage" to turn on Julia and surrender at last to the mass idolization of a cipher as empty as Oz in the old children's tale—provides a terrifying warning of the power of the evolving police state; "Ignorance is Strength" has finally won out as Smith's way of life.

O'Brien was himself a unique case, a performer difficult to identify as either a leading man or a character actor. When he played the dashing young hero in his debut film, *The Hunchback of Notre Dame* (1939), he seemed an elegant actor who would rival Ray Milland and Robert Montgomery for the dapper roles. Quickly, though, he gained weight and lost his looks, though his talent allowed him to pick up strong supporting roles in *The Killers* (1946) and *Another Part of the Forest* (1948). Occasionally, O'Brien turned up in leads, as in the offbeat *film noir* (now a cult film) *D.O.A.* (1949), but more often his leads were juvenile westerns *(Warpath, Silver City, The Denver and the Rio Grande)*; for A films of the fifties, he was confined to smaller roles, as in *Julius Caesar* (1953) and *The Barefoot Contessa* (1954), for which he won an Oscar. But the role he should be most remembered for is Smith in *1984*; here, he captured in his performance the hour that Orwell had articulated.

The Search for Bridey Murphy

A Paramount Picture (1956)

CREDITS:

Produced by Pat Duggan; directed by Noel Langley; screenplay by Mr. Langley, from the book by Morey Bernstein; running time: 84 minutes.

CAST:

Teresa Wright *(Ruth Simmons)*; Louis Hayward *(Morey Bernstein)*; Nancy Gates *(Hazel Bernstein)*; Kenneth Tobey *(Rex Simmons)*; Richard Anderson *(Dr. Deering)*; Tom McKee *(Catlett)*; Janet Riley *(Lois Morgan)*; William J. Barker *(Himself)*; Charles Maxwell *(Father Bernard)*; James Kirkwood *(Brian "68")*; Eilene Janssen, Hallene Hill, Denise Freeborn, Ruth Robinson *(Bridey)*.

A craze for hypnosis swept the country in the mid-fifties, following the strange but fascinating "Bridey Murphy case," explained (some would say exploited) in a book by one of the principal players in the story. There, as in this subsequent (and surprisingly stylish) film, Morey Bernstein hypnotized a Colorado housewife, at which point the entranced woman described, in remarkably vivid detail, a series of previous lives, causing people fascinated by out-of-body experiences to cite this as prime proof that reincarnation is a reality. Others scoffed, insisting this appealed only to pseudo-intellectuals who likewise believed in Bigfoot and the imminent arrival of UFOs, insisting the hypnotized lady was merely allowing her imagination to run free. Still, fascination with the case continued, though by the time the film appeared, interest had peaked as the fickle public, sated with Bridey and convinced it had been the greatest hoax since The Cardiff Giant, moved on to other mat-

Morey Bernstein (Louis Hayward) hypnotizes Ruth Simmons (Teresa Wright).

202

He finds himself confronting
the spirit of Bridey Murphy.

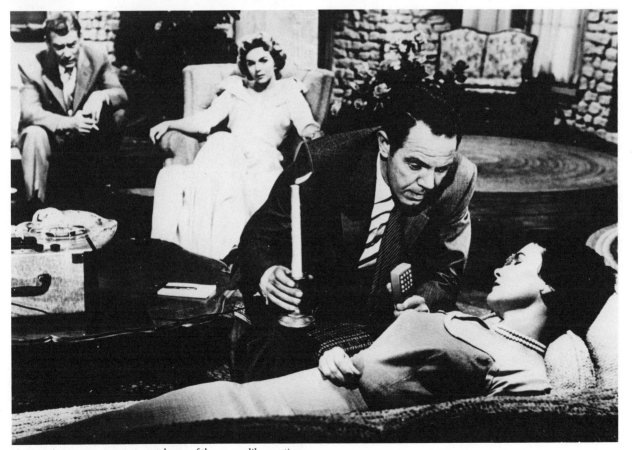

Various witnesses congregate to watch one of the seance-like meetings.

While under Bernstein's spell, Ruth takes on a succession of personalities, all radically different from her own.

In a flashback, Brian (James Kirkwood) is married to the original Bridey (Ruth Robinson).

ters. Bridey remains a vaguely recalled oddity in the cultural flotsam of the fifties, momentarily stirring loud debate before being relegated to the junkpile of passing popular history.

Bridey Murphy, the most vividly recalled of all the housewife's former lives, was a woman who supposedly lived and died in Ireland during the mid-nineteenth

204

century. The script was closely drawn from precise recordings of Mrs. Simmons' sessions with Bernstein, adding a sense of authenticity. Unfortunately for the film version, studies of supposed reincarnation conducted after the book's brief but noisy run as a bestseller revealed a considerable amount of thought transference can take place between hypnotist and subject, while the press had loudly proclaimed that Mrs. Simmons—however sincere—had been tricked into combining vague childhood memories with imperfectly recalled films and semi-digested novels she had consumed and, on a conscious level, forgotten. Mr. Bernstein, who had been obsessed by hypnosis and went into the experiment hoping to find something worth writing a book about, was pronounced a sham who had manipulated the lady into saying what he wanted her to say, and was never heard from again.

One reason why the film was more impressive than the usual cheapjack exploitation item is that writer-director Noel Langley (working closely with special ef-

Dr. Deering (Richard Anderson) and Rex Simmons (Kenneth Tobey) are among those amazed by what they see and hear.

fects expert John P. Fulton) moved effectively from realistic, near-documentary depictions of Ruth being hypnotized in her parlor to bizarre, surreal, dreamlike images that borrowed heavily from avant-garde cinema, introducing many of their distorted effects to the commercial cinema for the first time, conveying to the viewers a sense that we are watching Ruth's mental meanderings through an imagined universe rather than a depiction of what actually happened. Another is the conviction that Teresa Wright, a fine character actress, brought to the role; her ability to slip back and forth between Ruth's American accent and Bridey's Irish brogue made this an acting tour-de-force. In fact, the entire film was made with an aesthetic rather than exploitive tone, which may explain why it did not do as big business at the box-office as had been hoped for; clearly, this was a serious endeavor, not sensationalism.

Yet the contempt that most critics felt for the entire Bridey Murphy affair caused them to be unfairly condescending to the picture. For this was a case of style transcending substance. The Bridey Murphy incident may have been a ruse, but this film was the real thing: the images of an "astral life" in which the dead Bridey wanders between two worlds might easily have become ridiculous, but are surprisingly effective as visualized.

The popularity of the book caused a sudden spurt of amateur hypnotism parlor games, some of which ended quite disastrously. No wonder, then, that Louis Hayward, in the role of Bernstein, didactically if politely explained at the movie's end that such actions were dangerous. The producers feared that the film—with its immediate impact—might influence an even larger portion of the public toward such irresponsible actions.

The Killing

A United Artists Release (1956)

CREDITS:

Produced by James B. Harris; directed by Stanley Kubrick; screenplay by Stanley Kubrick, with additional dialogue by James Thompson, adapted from the novel *Clean Break* by Lionel White; running time: 83 minutes.

CAST:

Sterling Hayden *(Johnny Clay)*; Coleen Gray *(Fay)*; Vince Edwards *(Val Cannon)*; Jay C. Flippen *(Marvin Unger)*; Marie Windsor *(Sherry Peatty)*; Ted DeCorsia *(Randy Kennan)*; Elisha Cook, Jr.

Elisha Cook, Jr. is to Hayden's right, Jay C. Flippen to his left.

(George Peatty); Joe Sawyer *(Mike O'Reilly)*; Timothy Carey *(Nikki Arane)*; Jay Adler *(Leo)*; Kola Kwarian *(Maurice Oboukhoff)*; Joseph Turkell *(Tiny)*; James Edwards *(Parking Attendant)*.

Stanley Kubrick would emerge, by the decade's end, as the darling of serious critics who favor heavyweight projects. The tremendously powerful anti-war melo-drama *Paths of Glory* and the thinking man's spectacle *Spartacus*—both starring the estimable producer/actor Kirk Douglas—would establish Kubrick as a director able to shift back and forth between intimate little black-and-white films and immense full-color epics without losing his unique cinematic vision. Then, in the late sixties and early seventies, he emerged as a kind of American Bergman with such critical and commercial ground-breakers as *Dr. Strangelove, 2001: A Space Odyssey,* and *A Clockwork Orange.* In time, the lustre would wear off Kubrick's mantle. Film fans sharply divide on whether *Barry Lyndon* and *The Shining* were daring aesthetic experiments that courageously undercut audience expec-tations or merely cold, clinical examples of an ever more aloof filmmaker's descent into self-indulgence, movies that are all style and no substance, rating as nothing more than emotionless, meaningless exercises.

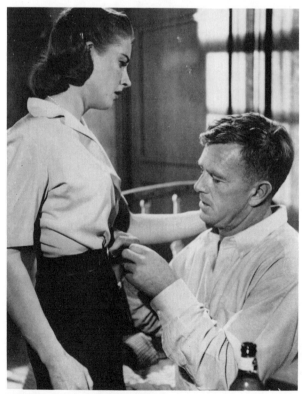

Johnny briefly plays with Fay (Coleen Gray) in their sordid setting before heading for the racetrack.

But somewhere back there in the fifties, this difficult, obscure expatriate—an American who chooses to live and work in London, whose decision to make only one film every five years is taken by some as his dedication to true art, by others as evidence of a pompous and pretentious approach to filmmaking—began one of the most controversial careers in contemporary cinema. The beginnings were humble indeed. *The Killing*, Kubrick's third feature film (the first two, *Fear and Desire* and *Killer's Kiss*, were barely-released low-budget items, though not without interest), was generally written off in its time as a cheapjack *Asphalt Jungle*, starring the actor who had headlined that John Huston crime classic. Even then, though, there were critics who noticed a panache to the playing of what might have been an ordinary exercise in crime melodrama, a directorial signature still in the process of developing but already most intriguing and quite unmistakable. For better or worse, the unique vision of Stanley Kubrick was upon us.

The story concerns Johnny Clay, an ex-con who has one last hope of hitting the big time: he will lead a sad assortment of losers on an attempted big take at a race track, walking off with a cool two million dollars for their afternoon's efforts. But as is so often the case in such a tale, the intricately developed strategy falls apart owing to the human element which the leader could not have foreseen, especially the advances of Sherry, the sluttish wife of the group's most nervous and neurotic member. Marie Windsor was never more effectively used than she is here; the Joan Crawford of B features, she made the cheap, sordid, undeniably attractive Sherry a moderately sympathetic character without ever sentimentalizing her. Elisha Cook—the nasty little creep Bogart grinningly knocked about in *The Maltese Falcon*—likewise has a field day as Georgie, the pathetic racetrack cashier who enters into the desperate plan in hopes of stealing enough money to satisfy his wife, unable to realize that if they succeed, she'll merely run off with Val Cannon, her nasty stud of a boyfriend.

Unrelenting is the way to describe Kubrick's delineation of their complex plan; there is, of course, a double meaning to the title, as their planned "killing" (making a killing at the racetrack, figuratively speaking) transforms into a very different sort of "killing" (the deranged gunman, Nikki Arane, will ruin everything by turning the title into a terribly literal truth). Throughout, we watch the unpleasant but arresting tale of these unhappy little people, scrambling about in their ever more desperate shot at the big time, as fate closes in and seals off their chances and hopes. We view a routine tale of sordid action directed with more style than anyone could have guessed possible by a man who was clearly, even at this point, someone to note. Concepts of filmmaking were changing; Stanley Kramer was about to make way for Stanley Kubrick.

The Brave One

A Universal-International Release (1957)

CREDITS:

Produced by Maurice King and Frank King; directed by Irving Rapper; screenplay by Harry Franklin and Merrill G. White, based on a story by Robert Rich (Dalton Trumbo); running time: 100 minutes.

CAST:

Michel Ray (*Leonardo*); Rodolfo Hoyos (*Rafel Rosilio*); Elsa Cardenas (*Maria*); Carlos Navarro (*Don Alejandro*); Joi Lansing

Sterling Hayden as Johnny Clay.

Leonardo (Michel Ray) cares for his little pet.

But baby bulls have a tendency to grow up and become candidates for the ring.

(Marion); Fermin Rivera (Fermin); George Trevino (Salvador); Carlos Fernandez (Manuel).

One of the great legends of Hollywood in general and the Academy Awards in particular surrounds this film, which was honored with a statuette for Best Original Screen Story. That Oscar would have rightly gone to Robert Rich, who did not step up to claim his due when the envelope was ripped open and his name called out. The reason, simply, is that Robert Rich did not exist, the name being a pseudonym for blacklisted screenwriter Dalton Trumbo. People are sometimes shocked to learn that, though Joseph McCarthy had long since fallen from power, his influence hung over Hollywood like a poisonous cloud for years. Once the blacklist had been set into operation, it continued, as a force unto itself, long after the motivation for it had passed out of the public consciousness. It would not be until 1960, when producer Kirk Douglas insisted the screenwriter's proper name be listed in the credits for *Spartacus*, that Dalton Trumbo was recognized once more as existing. It's worth

noting too that, at that time, the film was picketed as "communist propaganda" during its initial run in some major cities.

The writing Oscar for *The Brave One* went unclaimed until 1975, when it was at last acknowledged that this was Trumbo's work. And while his blacklisting seems an outrageous over-reaction to the man's modest liberalism, *The Brave One* does indeed—in the guise of a children's film—illustrate the populist values that run through all of Trumbo's work, from his own anti-war novel *Johnny Got His Gun* to his screen adaptation of Edward Abbey's *Lonely Are the Brave*: a strong and sincere concern for the common people, an angry criticism of the way they are mostly dealt a losing hand by society at large. If in much of his work, including the films *Tell Them Willie Boy Is Here!* and *Papillon*, Trumbo tended to over-articulate rather than subtly suggest such ideas, *The Brave One* stands as his modest masterpiece, an under-stated film that avoids overt preaching. Instead, it involves us emotionally with the characters, then allows the working out of their plight to carry the message home.

The American Marion (Joi Lansing) and her cohorts take an interest in Leonardo and his problem.

209

Leonardo desperately searches for his beloved bull.

Leonardo is a small, poor Mexican boy who loves only one thing: the bull he has cared for since the animal's difficult birth. But his relationship with Gitano is doomed, since the beast is marked for the bull ring. The child will do anything—repeat, anything—to save Gitano. He attempts to steal the animal and run away with it; he forces his way in to see the president of Mexico and reason with him; he elicits the aid of a beautiful American woman, Marion; he rushes out into the bull ring itself, confronting his bloodied best friend in front of the crowd, just after Gitano has flipped a matador about with his horns.

Part of the film's appeal comes from its being the first movie to try and make audiences see bullfighting in a different light. Previous pictures like *The Bullfighter and the Lady* and *The Brave Bulls* clearly took the humans' side, portraying the animals as nothing more than ferocious creatures to be thoughtlessly slaughtered for sport and spectacle. Trumbo's movie assumes, of course, the opposite approach; instead of attempting to elicit screams when Hollywoodized matadors (played, in fifties films, by such stalwarts as Robert Stack, Anthony Quinn, and Mel Ferrer) are skewered on the beasts' horns, this film had its audiences cheering at just such sights. It also had viewers in tears when the child darted out into the arena and hugged the bleeding beast; instead of goring him, as we expect a "dumb" creature to do, Gitano responds by nuzzling the boy who once cared for him.

The point of the film is to make us see bulls differently than we have before. And it works. This is the Dalton Trumbo vision: a head of state who is so far removed from the people he is supposed to serve that he cannot perceive the boy in front of him in fact represents mankind at its most humane. The melodrama is intensely emotional, the Jack Cardiff color photography quite exceptional, and the variety of expressions that cross Michel Ray's face rate this, along with *The Bicycle Thief*, as a film containing one of the great unaffected child performances.

The Three Faces of Eve

A 20th Century-Fox Film (1957)

CREDITS:

Produced by Nunnally Johnson; directed by Mr. Johnson; screenplay by Mr. Johnson, adapted from the book by Drs. Corbett H. Thigpen and Hervey M. Cleckley; running time: 91 minutes.

CAST:

Joanne Woodward (Eve); David Wayne (Ralph White); Lee J. Cobb (Dr. Luther); Edwin Jerome (Dr. Day); Alena Murray (Secretary); Nancy Kulp (Mrs. Black); Douglas Spencer (Mr. Black); Terry Ann Ross (Bonnie); Ken Scott (Earl); Vince Edwards (Eve's Lover); Mimi Gibson (Eve, Age 8); and with narration spoken by Alistair Cooke.

The two major innovations of 1950s filmmaking—a feeling of documentary realism owing to the telling of actual stories in low-key styles and the emphasis on psychological characterization to provide movies relating to the most neurotic period in our nation's history—converged with *The Three Faces of Eve*. Based on the actual case of a Georgia woman harboring three distinct personalities, the project allowed filmmaker Nunnally Johnson to educate the public, through a fact-based drama, on the ways in which a clinical psychiatrist works in helping a person adjust to problems of the psyche. Though this is best remembered as the film that won Joanne Woodward an Oscar, establishing a lady previously thought of as one more pretty blonde as one of our heavyweight actresses, the film's great significance for its time of release can best be understood in its combining

Joanne Woodward as Eve.

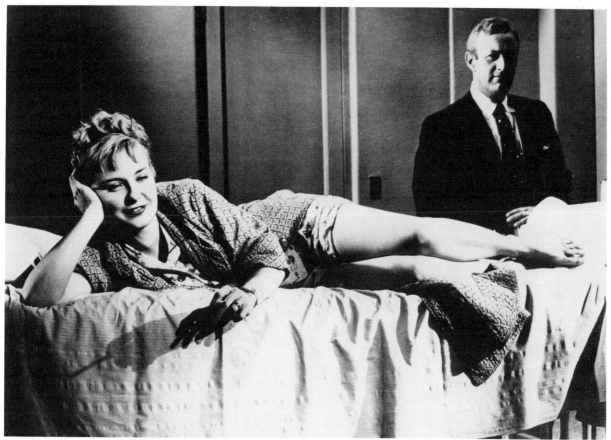

Eve slips into her slut personality before the eyes of Dr. Luther.

the newly developed realistic moviemaking approach with the single subject which most characterized the films of the decade. For in the fifties, the public—living under the shadow of a nuclear cloud and troubled by Cold War fears of instantaneous oblivion—saw mental health emerge from the old *Snake Pit* notion of a bizarre aberration into something that seriously affected us all.

In the opening sequence, Dr. White is introduced to a new patient who enters his Georgia office, complaining of severe headaches and bouts of depression. At first, she doesn't seem different from other troubled women he meets, so the doctor sends the nervous Mrs. White and her boorish husband home, insisting there's nothing severely wrong. Before long, though, she's back again, at least in terms of physical presence. For inhabiting that same body is now a sluttish woman who refuses to accept that her child is her own and laughingly talks about wild nights on the town. While the doctor is watching, this brassy, bitchy personality recedes, leaving the intense, quiet, confused woman he first encountered once more in front of him. Fascinated, the doctor realizes that on command, the woman before him can flip—literally in a split second—back and forth from the conventional Mrs. White to the catty Eve.

The prim, proper Eve confronts the doctor with her husband (David Wayne), though he will shortly absent himself from the scene.

213

The doctor confronts Eve as she slips into a third personality.

Her husband Ralph watches this but, unable to comprehend what's happening, rushes off for a divorce. In his limited view, the wife must be faking, to have an excuse for going out without him; the doctor can't break through, make the man see that mental illness is, like any other form of sickness, something the patient has no control over. As doctor and patient continue working, a third personality emerges: an incredibly bright woman, as perceptive as she is self-possessed. The film's great moments come when Woodward whisks back and forth from one to the other; audiences were dazzled, and Hollywood honored her with its highest accolade.

Eve does not date well. Its importance had to do with the timing of release in terms of style and substance, and the overwhelming presence of Woodward in the title role(s). A retrospective viewing of the picture makes painfully clear the only complex thing about it is Woodward's performance. The film seems surprisingly literal minded, both in terms of what it says about psychiatric

A specially prepared studio shot that allowed Joanne Woodward to demonstrate the subtle reactions of her eyes, suggesting which of Eve's personalities was dominating at any one point.

disorders and the flat visualization with which it was mounted. Eventually, the doctor draws from Eve a long-repressed childhood memory; as an eight-year-old, she was forced by her mother to kiss her deceased grandmother just before burial. The notion that all Eve's problems stem from this single incident—and that her conscious recognition of it will immediately cure her, so she can shortly go off to live a normal life with a nice, conventional man named Earl—seems at best naive, at worst simplistic. Today, most psychiatrists would rather hold that this disclosure would only serve as a starting point for a long, troubled journey toward a hopeful (though less than likely) total recovery. And what seemed honest journalistic filmmaking at the time looks a bit dull today; this surprisingly short and uninvolving film plays more like a routine programmer than a movie classic.

Time Limit

A Heath Production (1957)

CREDITS:

Produced by Richard Widmark and William Reynolds; directed by Karl Malden; screenplay by Henry Denker, based on the play by Mr. Denker and Ralph Berkey; running time: 96 minutes.

Carl Benton Reid (Gen. Connors) and Richard Widmark (Col. William Edwards) find themselves in an impossible Cold War situation.

Edwards shares his problems with his lovely assistant, Corp. Jean Evans (Dolores Michaels).

215

Edwards conducts a complicated set of interviews in hopes of determining the guilt or innocence of his client.

CAST:

Richard Widmark *(Col. William Edwards)*; Richard Basehart *(Maj. Harry Cargill)*; Dolores Michaels *(Cpl. Jean Evans)*; June Lockhart *(Mrs. Cargill)*; Carl Benton Reid *(Gen. Connors)*; Martin Balsam *(Sgt. Baker)*; Rip Torn *(Lt. George Miller)*; Yale Wexler *(Capt. Joe Connors)*; Alan Dexter *(Mike)*; Manning Ross *(Harvey)*; Kale Deel *(Kim)*; Skip McNally *(Poleska)*; James Douglas *(Steve)*.

Time Limit was the finest of the many Cold War thrillers turned out during the 1950s. This exasperatingly complex courtroom tale took all our then-current concerns—the confusing war in Korea, the psychological make-up of a human being, the inability to tell where courage ends and cowardice begins, the sense that black-and-white judgment calls were no longer possible since all life now appeared to be painted in morally ambiguous shades of gray—tying them together in a drama that was both emotionally absorbing and intellectually stimulating. While Henry Denker based the screenplay on his own controversial stage piece, *Time Limit* was every inch a movie; and for anyone wanting to experience what amounts to a case study of fifties angst, *Time Limit* is one for the time capsule.

William Edwards is the investigating colonel in what at first appears a clear case scheduled for court martial proceedings: Harry Cargill, during his service in Korea,

Sgt. Baker (Martin Balsam) discovers Edwards in a compromising situation.

216

was captured and held prisoner by the North Korean Army. There seems no doubt he completely collaborated with the enemy, going so far as to defect, supplying them with information they asked for, willingly appearing in radio broadcasts during which he proclaimed his own belief in the communist doctrine and his hatred for the "imperialist" attitudes of America. There's plenty of proof Cargill did indeed participate in such activities, and the man—now back home and ready to stand trial—openly admits everything.

But the case is too pat for the fair-minded Edwards not to grow suspicious. Working with a pretty WAC officer, Jean Evans, he delves deep into the situation, discovering there's more under the surface than anyone cared to note. One possible defense is that Cargill was the victim of an elaborate brainwashing by his captors; some officers believe this in itself makes him innocent despite his actions, while others would hold him accountable anyway. The real capper comes, though, when Edwards realizes to whatever degree Cargill aided and abetted the enemy, he did so to save the lives of men immediately within his command, including the son of General Connors.

As far as Edwards is concerned, the altruism of Cargill's motives is enough to redeem him. Not everyone in the military agrees. Ironically, it is General Connors who, despite the realization that Cargill's actions saved his own son's life, wants to press forward. A believer in the notion of sacrificing the few to save the many, Connors holds firm to the attitude that Cargill must be prosecuted to the full limit of the law, to discourage others (by making this man an "example") from likewise embarrassing their country through complicity. For Connors, the fate of a single human being (however wrongfully maligned) means nothing; it is the system that he must preserve at all costs.

Edwards' own personality crisis comes when he attempts to bridge the two points of view; as a good soldier, he too wants to save the system, but as a sensitive and intelligent man, he cannot resolve himself to doing so at the expense of a person he now understands to have been under pressure no one could resist. There has to be, he finally decides, a time limit: a point beyond which a normal human being cannot be expected to retain a sense of loyalty or the values he has always lived by. This was likewise the theme of Rod Serling's *The Rack*, which appeared at about the same time and featured Paul Newman as a deeply troubled soldier suffering through similar problems.

Good as that movie is, *Time Limit* rates as the superior work. For Widmark, formerly a Fox contract player, *Time Limit* represented a first attempt at following in the footsteps of Wayne, Lancaster, and Douglas by picking out appropriate vehicles and independently producing them himself. The laconic manner and dangerous eyes that relegated him to villainous supporting roles in the forties made Widmark a natural for jaded good guy parts in the fifties. For Karl Malden, *Time Limit* offered a chance to direct a film; considering the critical acclaim he won, it's surprising he has never gone that route again. For both, its their least known film; it's also one of their very best.

The Story of Mankind

A Warner Brothers Film (1957)

CREDITS:

Produced by Irwin Allen; directed by Mr. Allen; screenplay by Mr. Allen and Charles Bennett, based on the book by Hendrik Willem van Loon; running time: 100 minutes.

CAST:

Ronald Colman (*The Spirit of Man*); Vincent Price (*The Devil*); Cedric Hardwicke (*High Judge*); guest stars, Groucho Marx (*Peter Minuit*); Harpo Marx (*Isaac Newton*); Chico Marx (*Medieval Monk*); Hedy Lamarr (*Joan of Arc*); Virginia Mayo (*Cleopatra*); Helmut Dantine (*Anthony*); Agnes Moorehead (*Queen Elizabeth*); Peter Lorre (*Nero*); Charles Coburn (*Hippocrates*); Cesar Romero (*Spanish Envoy*); John Carradine (*Khufu*); Dennis Hopper (*Napoleon*); Marie Windsor (*Josephine*); Marie Wilson (*Marie Antoinette*); Edward Everett Horton (*Sir Walter Raleigh*); Reginald Gardiner (*Shakespeare*); George E. Stone (*Waiter*); Cathy O'Donnell (*Early Christian Woman*); Melville Cooper (*Major domo*); Henry Daniell (*Bishop of Beauvals*); Francis X. Bushman (*Moses*).

In 1956, Mike Todd released *Around the World in 80 Days*, an Oscar-winning hit which, among other things, introduced the latest lure-them-from-television tactic: an all-star/cameo cast. Todd persuaded such venerable superstars as Frank Sinatra and Marlene Dietrich to do walk-ons in his witty combination of romance and spectacle, but other filmmakers didn't fare so well. In particular, Irwin Allen—long before *The Poseidon Adventure* was a glimmer in his eye—mounted a disaster epic of a different order. *The Story of Mankind* represents Allen's attempt to assemble a remarkable cast of walk-on stars, in a vehicle that certainly seemed to offer a stunning array of bit parts. Unfortunately, he mostly ended up

Celestial antagonists: Vincent Price as a dandified devil, Ronald Colman as the softspoken Spirit of Man.

B-movie villainess Marie Windsor was strangely teamed with aspiring James Deanish youth-cult star Dennis Hopper as an ersatz Josephine and Napoleon.

with older has-beens and young hopefuls, neither of whom spelled excitement at the box-office. But that was the least of his problems, for this is surely one of the worst movies ever made, at once vulgar and pretentious.

Critics have long debated whether Hendrik Willem van Loon's lengthy discourse was the definitive study of man's history on earth or only a sometimes oversimpli-

fied, sometimes longwinded attempt that finally fails to bring its mammoth subject into comprehensible focus. Certainly, though, the more impressive aspects of that undertaking were not in evidence in this flaccid, facile film, which reduces great events to cardboard costume film clichés or—more surprising still—bizarre comedy sketches. There is also a framing device of the sort one expects to encounter in a high school play written by the students themselves, as in a celestial courtroom the Spirit of Man presents the greatest of mankind's achievements, while the Devil offers up our most horrid happenings. The High Judge (apparently God Himself) must ultimately decide whether or not mankind should continue.

The film jumps from period to period, and the choices of what to include seem dictated by no more intelligent a rationale than whether or not Warner Brothers had mounted an expensive color film on the subject; if so, then that era was included, and if not, it wasn't. Movie-

218

Peter Lorre as a disgruntled Nero, surrounded by Hollywood starlets as his courtesans, and even a child to suggest the decadence of ancient Rome.

The original Dumb Blonde, Marie Wilson (of *My Friend Irma* fame), commands the peasants to eat cake as a giggly Marie Antoinette.

Groucho Marx, as Peter Minuit, appears less interested in cheating the Indian Chiefs than in slipping out of eyesight with a comely maiden.

goers who had paid to see *Helen of Troy* only three years earlier now had the opportunity to see stock footage from that film—a massive Greek army marching on Priam— though for the close-ups of Helen, another actress was substituted in the role. Intriguingly, though, Helen— who had been transformed into a heroine for the 1954 film—now reverted to the stereotypical temptress/villainess, since that suited the filmmaker's purpose here.

The film is initially intriguing, thanks to the outrageous casting. When we see Groucho Marx rolling his eyes as Peter Minuit or Harpo (as Sir Isaac Newton) dazed after an apple bounces off his head, we can't help but wonder if perhaps this is going to be a cult item, a sophisticated precursor to *Saturday Night Live* style contemporary humor. Such hopes do not last long, for in due time the film becomes almost numbing, as incident after incident is tossed onto the pile of historical-situations-reduced-to-stereotypes. Then again, you haven't

219

The Final Summing Up: with all the artistry and subtlety of a director of a Junior High School play, filmmaker Irwin Allen sets the problem before the audience and God himself, fading out with a huge question mark as to whether man will receive another chance.

lived until you've seen Dennis Hopper doing a second-hand method actor approach to Napoleon, apparently unaware of how comic his James Dean imitation appears when presented as a costumed cameo. At least that distinguished star of bygone years Ronald Colman got to play his dignified persona for the last time, while film-makers realized how hammily effective Vincent Price could be in devilish roles. If nothing else, *The Story of Mankind* is a one-of-a-kind movie, almost beyond normal conceptions of good taste and bad. And considering that cast (beginning with Hedy Lamarr as Joan of Arc, everyone is cast against type), this at least rates as a true conversation piece.

Twelve Angry Men

A United Artists Release (1957)

CREDITS:

Produced by Henry Fonda and Reginald Rose; directed by Sidney Lumet; screenplay by Reginald Rose, from his teleplay; running time: 95 minutes.

CAST:

Henry Fonda (*Juror Eight*); Lee J. Cobb (*Juror Three*); Ed Begley (*Juror Ten*); E. G. Marshall (*Juror Four*); Martin Balsam (*Juror One*); John Fiedler (*Juror Two*); Jack Klugman (*Juror Five*); Edward Binns (*Juror Six*); Jack Warden (*Juror Seven*); Joseph Sweeney (*Juror Nine*); George Voskovec (*Juror Eleven*); Robert Webber (*Juror Twelve*); Rudy Bond (*Judge*); John Savoca (*Defendant*).

Like Rod Serling, Paddy Chayefsky, and Sterling Silliphant, Reginald Rose was one of the bright young serious writers of the fifties who made their mark on television during the so-called "golden age," when their original plays—*Requiem for a Heavyweight, Marty, Days of Wine and Roses, The Hustler, Judgment at Nuremberg*—were "premiered" on such shows as *Playhouse 90* and its equally impressive though lesser known competitors. Today, people kindly forget that the vast majority of original plays were so dreadful they were never heard from again; less than ten percent were superb, and these were bought by Hollywood and turned into major motion pictures. Since those films have been endlessly rerun on TV over the years, we tend to remember them as representative of the golden age TV fare, though in truth they were the exceptional works. Perhaps none was quite so exceptional as *12 Angry Men*, the film that marked the directorial debut of Sidney Lumet, whose best work (*Serpico, Dog Day Afternoon, The Verdict*) would always effectively capture the gritty feel of New York reality.

As in the TV version, this follows a jury as they enter their private room having just left a courtroom situation, almost all convinced that the defendant (a boy accused of killing his own father) is guilty. But one man, a quiet and unassuming fellow, softly but doggedly insists that despite all the evidence against the boy, he is innocent. One by one, the other jurors begin to doubt their initial belief in the boy's guilt, though one belligerent man, Juror Three, grows ever angrier that the others are turning away from their initial conclusion. Even he, though, changes his mind in due time, for certain details, when discussed at length, make it clear that the defendant could not possibly, under any circumstances, have done the deed. At last, all twelve men come around to the opposite of the conviction they had planned on calling for, and march back into the courtroom to clear the boy.

In theme, *12 Angry Men* resembles a contemporary version of Fonda's famous indictment of lynch-mob mentality, *The Ox-Bow Incident* (1943). It's worth noting that while he is today considered in retrospect one of the

Henry Fonda as Juror Number Eight.

The major conflict occurs between Juror Eight and Juror Three (Lee J. Cobb).

Henry Fonda and the cast of the century.

great movie stars, Fonda did not think highly of Hollywood movies, preferring to live in the East and work on Broadway, returning to films only when a particular project captured his fancy. When he saw *12 Angry Men* on TV, he knew it was something he would like to do, though getting it made was not easy. Most studio bosses passed on it, and not unreasonably, for with its use of realistic time (this is one of those ultra-rare movies where the duration of the film's running time and its story-time

are precisely the same, without any of the "cheating" *High Noon* employed) and claustrophobic setting (there are no flashbacks to get us out of the jury room) did not lend itself to cinematic treatment as easily as, say, *Marty* (with its natural progression to many places) or *Requiem* (with its elaborate boxing matches). Which helps explain why, as doggedly determined to get it made as his character in the finished film is to unearth the truth, Fonda turned producer and, with author/co-producer

Juror Eight breaks through, convincing the others of the defendant's innocence.

Rose, beat the bushes until they came up with the money necessary to complete the picture.

They gave fine roles to a remarkable variety of character actors, some well known then (Lee J. Cobb, E. G. Marshall), others who would soon become important staples of film and TV (Jack Klugman, Martin Balsam); all offered finely etched portraits of well-rounded, believable men. The concept of "reasonable doubt" and the necessity of logic winning out over emotion if the jury system is to function properly has never been so admirably dramatized. Several of the actors had appeared in the TV version, where Robert Cummings portrayed the focal role. A competent light comedian for a weekly series like *Love That Bob*, Cummings lacked the depth, sensitivity, and intelligence to make the role work; certainly, no actor could convey those qualities as well as Henry Fonda.

223

Beau James

A Paramount Picture (1957)

CREDITS:

Produced by Jack Rose; directed by Melville Shavelson; screenplay by Mr. Rose and Mr. Shavelson, based on the book by Gene Fowler; running time: 105 minutes.

CAST:

Bob Hope *(Jimmy Walker)*; Vera Miles *(Betty Compton)*; Paul Douglas *(Chris Nolan)*; Alexis Smith *(Allie Walker)*; Darren Mc-Gavin *(Charley Hand)*; Joe Mantell *(Bernie Williams)*; and featuring guest appearances by Jimmy Durante, Jack Benny, and George Jessel; narrated by Walter Winchell.

Every dramatic actor secretly desires to do a comic role, just as every comic has a repressed urge to at least once be taken seriously. When the dramatic actors try comedy, they usually fail; comedy may look easy, but it's in fact considerably harder to do well than drama. Understandably, then, the opposite does not hold true: the comic—because of his command of pacing—invariably surprises the skeptic by doing just dandy in a serious part. Cary Grant in *None But the Lonely Heart*, Jackie Gleason in *The Hustler*, Ed Wynn in TV's *Requiem for*

Bob Hope as Beau James, tossing in a baseball for the beginning of the season.

a Heavyweight, and Art Carney in his Oscar winning *Harry and Tonto* are only a few of the numerous examples. Another is Bob Hope in the title role of this witty, ironic, but essentially serious biographical film about Manhattan's onetime Mayor James Walker, the controversial and high-living "heart of the people" during his 1920s reign. Though the film was a disaster at the boxoffice, Hope turned in a performance that—had the film been more financially successful—might have won him the Oscar he has so often half-kiddingly coveted.

Hope incarnates the myth of Walker, that legendary playboy-politico who lived the good life to the hilt, managing for longer than anyone would have guessed possible to avoid contamination by the incredible stench of dirty politics that plagued his administration. Beloved

Scenes such as this one showed Jimmy's willingness to wheel and deal with the Old Boy network.

by the people, Walker—who according to legend danced his way into public office—maintained his popularity even as events around him threatened to tarnish his reputation. The film's approach to Walker—that he was "honest and dumb"—may be heatedly debated by historians, many arguing that was a guise, a shield the cagey Walker presented to protect himself from implication in scandals, until 1928 when Albany's Seabury Committee's simultaneous disclosure of three questionable activities conspired to bring Walker down.

It's fascinating to note, too, how the movie casually depicts Walker's own casual division of his time between wife Allie and showgirl Betty Compton, openly escorting the latter to public places, the political Gentleman's Agreement mindset of the time holding that this is the man's private life. Walker—had he lived in our time—would doubtless have been a casualty of the *National Enquirer* long before Seabury got to him.

Paramount's VistaVision process (their answer to the competition's CinemaScope) handsomely captured, in

225

Walker visits a poor neighborhood where he campaigns with his wife (Alexis Smith).

an elaborate full-color reconstruction, the bygone New York, while an excellent jazz-drenched musical score added neatly to the nostalgic effect. The most perfect sequence features Hope/Walker, riding about his beloved city in a horsedrawn Hansom Cab with his beautiful blonde companion, enjoying the way the starlit sky and the lights of the city blend; in that moment of ecstasy—The Good Life in all its glory—he almost forgets the scandals that threaten to bring him down. Hope's famous flippant delivery of lines, the brashly roguish and ever-boyish charm, here lends a strong sense of bravado mixed with stoicism to his characterization of Walker. Even if there's the possibility he will be politically destroyed tomorrow, he's going to enjoy this magnificent evening to the fullest—adding a poignancy to the man's fate. For finally, an investigation into "irregularities" in his administration forces Walker to resign (over the protest of his loving supporters) after leading one final St. Patty's Day parade and dancing with Jimmy Durante (playing himself) one last time, ending as he began.

One final note for trivia fans: Walter Winchell's terse, incisive narration of this film so impressed producer Desi Arnaz that, a year later, when he wanted to create an immediate sense of authenticity for TV's *The Untouchables*, he offered the role of narrator to Winchell, whose voice became as inseparable from that series' success as was Robert Stack's tough, tight-lipped portrayal of Eliot Ness.

He dons top-hat and tails for a night out on the town with his elegant mistress (Vera Miles).

Jimmy only wants to enjoy himself with his beautiful mistress (Vera Miles) but has to contend with political cronies Chris Nolan (Paul Douglas, *far left*) and P. R. man Charley Hand (Darren McGavin).

228

Slaughter on 10th Avenue

A Universal Picture (1957)

CREDITS:

Produced by Albert Zugsmith; directed by Arnold Laven; screenplay by Lawrence Roman, based on "The Man Who Rocked the Boat" by William J. Keating and Richard Carter; running time: 103 minutes.

CAST:

Richard Eagan (William Keating); Jan Sterling (Madge Pitts); Dan Duryea (John Jacob Masters); Julie Adams (Dee); Walter Matthau (Al Dahlke); Charles McGraw (Lt. Anthony Vosnick); Sam Levene (Howard Rysdale); Mickey Shaugnessey (Solly Pitts); Harry Bellavar (Benjy Karp); Nick Dennis (Midget); Joe Downing (Cockeye); Amzie Strickland (Mrs. C.); Mickey Hargitay (John).

The Kefauver Commission on organized crime led to an entire cycle of films during the early fifties, reviving the *film noir* style of darkly lit black-and-white urban tales but grafting onto that format an influence of Italian neorealism with its strong documentary flavor. The impact of Elia Kazan's *On the Waterfront* led to other films dealing with longshoremen and dockworkers, including the powerful *Edge of the City* and *Slaughter on Tenth Avenue*. Though the latter will be forever remembered for its stirring musical track, which won accolades and became a best-selling jazz album, few recall that the magnificent music was adapted for a movie that must be considered B+ in budget but rates nothing less than an A− in quality.

Slaughter proceeded from the point of view of William Keating, who penned the book this film was fash-

William Keating (Richard Egan) slugs Al Dahlke (Walter Matthau).

229

ioned from. Like Kazan's better known movie, *Slaughter* deals with the problem of a conspiracy of silence among longshoremen, who may not like infiltration of their livelihood by racketeers but nonetheless refuse to divulge any dirt to outsiders. Whether or not this "code of honor" is indeed honorable is a question Kazan debated in his film, where he came out on the side of those who finally agree to name names (perhaps in a self-justifying way, since Kazan controversially agreed to name names during the McCarthy-era investigations into supposed Hollywood infiltration by communists). But whereas Kazan and Budd Schulberg attempted to make an epic hero of the man who breaks the conspiracy of silence, Terry Malloy (Marlon Brando), Keating and filmmaker Arnold Laven naturally took the outsider's approach.

"These waterfront cases tend to get involved," lawyer Keating is told when, working as a deputy assistant district attorney, he's assigned to cover an attempted murder in which Solly Pitts, a boss longshoreman, has been shot under highly questionable circumstances.

Keating is amazed when the mortally wounded man refuses to tell what he obviously knows about who did this, causing Keating—stunned to realize a man who knows he's dying would remain silent rather than insure his killers are brought to justice—proceeds to question the man's wife Madge and his best friends, Benjy and Midget. They too are tight-lipped. Stymied, he does happen upon a suspect, who certainly appears guilty and has a long dirty record, only to learn that Al Dahlke, a corrupt labor leader, will use a squad of tough "body-guards" to defend this obviously guilty character.

When Keating attempts to prosecute that suspect, the defense lawyer, Masters, turns out to be a Jim Dandy of a dresser who makes an extremely comfortable living defending thugs with strong labor/racket connections; Keating is amazed that this man, in his more idealistic days, served in the D.A.'s office as a prosecutor, and still maintains close ties with many of his one-time colleagues. Before long, Keating begins to suspect there may be a terrible tie-in between certain parties in his

230

For the first time since the decade's beginning the labor unions were portrayed as something other than misguided communist dupes.

Dan Duryea was one of the screen's classic sleazy/silky villains; here, as a corrupt lawyer, he interrogates Madie Pitts (Jan Sterling).

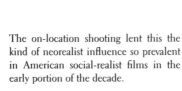

The on-location shooting lent this the kind of neorealist influence so prevalent in American social-realist films in the early portion of the decade.

own office and the racketeers, that the good guys and the bad may be linked. He also realizes that should he choose to proceed, he'll do so without support, since his own boss Rysdale clearly has been bought off.

Gritty and unsparing, the film is a fine example of the fifties crimebusting genre, featuring Walter Matthau in one of the many bad guy roles he played early in his career, at a time when no one could have guessed he would eventually emerge as one of our more beloved comic actors. Jan Sterling, always effective as a dreary, dour, washed-out blonde, was at her best here, playing a woman who understands that to reveal what she knows about her husband's death would insure that she promptly join him. Richard Egan, always searching for the role that would catapult him into the Big Leagues, certainly had a strong one here, though Dan Duryea stole the show with another of his slimey/silky villains. He remains one of the great character people in the history of Hollywood: had Richard Widmark been a spineless B-movie whiner instead of a strong A-movie snarler, he would have been Dan Duryea.

Will Success Spoil Rock Hunter?

A 20th Century-Fox Film (1957)

CREDITS:

Produced by Frank Tashlin; directed by Mr. Tashlin; screen story and screenplay by Mr. Tashlin, based on the stage play by George Axelrod; running time: 94 minutes.

CAST:

Jayne Mansfield (*Rita Marlowe*); Tony Randall (*Rock Hunter*); Betsy Drake (*Jenny*); Joan Blondell (*Violet*); John Williams (*La Salle Jr.*); Henry Jones (*Rufus*); Lili Gentle (*April*); Mickey Hargitay (*Bobo*); Georgia Carr (*Calypso Number*); Dick Whittinghill (*TV Interviewer*); and guest star Groucho Marx.

Jayne Mansfield as Rita Marlowe.

Tony Randall is the glib young executive Rock Hunter, using Rita Marlowe to sell a new form of bra.

232

When Jayne Mansfield enjoyed her first starring vehicle in Fox's *The Girl Can't Help It*—an exploitation film designed to show off her 40-inch bustline—critics carped she looked like a cartoon version of Marilyn Monroe. In fact, that presentation may have been intentional, for the writer-director of that film and Miss Mansfield's next—*Will Success Spoil Rock Hunter?*—was Frank Tashlin, a cartoonist turned feature film director. Mansfield proved (like the more recent Bo Derek) a sex symbol whose popularity was as brief as it was intense, so once the public had gawked, they felt no compunction to return. Like *Tarzan, The Ape Man, The Girl* did brisk voyeuristic business; *Bolero* and *Rock Hunter* did not. In the case of the Dereks, that may not be much of a loss, but the Mansfield-Tashlin story is a different matter. For *Rock Hunter* is not, like *The Girl*, merely another quick, clever exploitation flick but a sharp satire. Based on a

Rita models the new bra as she breaks into an impromptu striptease.

play by George *(The Seven-Year Itch)* Axelrod, it contains enough commentary on the fifties to rate as a perceptive analysis of the sort one expects only in retrospect.

Most movies of the fifties were filled with rampant Bosomania, what feminist critic Marjorie Rosen eventually labelled Mammary Madness. But Rock Hunter rates as the only film of the fifties to be *about* Bosomania and its absurdity. It's also about everything else that most distinctly characterizes the 1950s: the button-down executive mentality and television's ability to turn modern advertising techniques into a form of mass brainwashing. Axelrod's play had concerned a mousey writer for fanzine type movie magazines who sells his soul to the devil to live out his wildest fantasy, growing attractive and seducing a Hollywood screen queen. Tashlin happily changed the entire focus of the piece by making the subject of the humor not Hollywood movies but their

233

Rock's girlfriend Jenny (Betsy Drake) wonders if perhaps by buying the controversial bra, she will be able to win her errant man back.

Was the film biographical? Having Mansfield's own musclebound boyfriend, Mickey Hargitay, play a similar role in the picture suggested Tashlin had improvised his script around what he saw in this couple's Pink Palace life-style: the vulgarity of his extreme caricature approach was, unbelievably enough, a kind of realism. But the failure of this fine film at the box-office spelled a quick end to Jayne Mansfield's run as a star at Fox; she next appeared in *Kiss Them For Me*, generally considered Cary Grant's worst vehicle; Mansfield bragged she was playing opposite the world's handsomest man, though that distinction went to Suzy Parker, while Jayne provided half the low-comedy relief, playing opposite Mickey Shaugnessey. Convinced she was no longer exploitable, Fox quickly dropped her; Mansfield went off to Europe, where she and Mickey made *Hercules in Love*, a dreadful Italian costume epic that (amazingly enough) still shows up regularly on the late show, while *Rock*—easily her finest hour—goes almost unseen today.

new and bitter competition, TV. Tashlin dumped the metaphysical morality play element, transforming Rock into a brash young executive hoping to land a major account. His problem is to somehow persuade a bona fide movie star, Rita Marlowe, to appear in a television endorsement of a particular brand of lipstick. If he succeeds, he will be the first to get a major movie personality to acknowledge and accept TV, resulting in a major breakthrough.

Rita finally agrees, though only if he'll transform himself into Lover Boy, escorting Rita everywhere to make her boyfriend Bobo jealous so he'll pay her more attention. Eager to get the endorsement, Rock goes along with the gag, though "success' changes his life drastically: his superiors at the ad agency are stunned that he could be the lover of one of the world's great beauties, and promote him to vice president; his pretty but modestly built girlfriend Jenny begins wearing falsies in hope of luring him back. Though Randall would shortly become most famous for his supporting roles in the Rock Hudson/Doris Day comedies, he here created a part not so different from the one that won Jack Lemmon fame in *The Apartment*: the fundamentally decent guy trying to adjust to the amoral world of late fifties corporate structure mentality.

She learns what it's like to be a large-busted woman; clearly, Rock's interest has been piqued.

234

China Gate

A Globe Enterprises Production (1957)

CREDITS:

Produced by Samuel Fuller; directed by Mr. Fuller; screenplay by Mr. Fuller; running time: 97 minutes.

CAST:

Angie Dickinson (Lia/"Lucky Legs"); Gene Barry (Sergeant Brock); Nat "King" Cole (Goldie); Paul Dubov (Captain Caumont); Lee Van Cleef (Major Cham); George Givot (Corporal Pigalle); Gerald Milton (Private Andreades); Neyle Morrow (Leung); Marcel Dalio (Father Paul); Maurice Marsac (Colonel De Sars); Warren Hsieh (the Boy); Paul Busch (Corporal Kruger); Sasha Hardin (Private Jaszi).

If the fifties was the era when the independents took over Hollywood, then Samuel Fuller is the filmmaker who best represents the fifties. Coming to film as he did from journalism, Fuller brought the rules of a good newspaperman with him, for his inexpensively made movies play like the cinematic equivalents of tabloid

Angie Dickinson as Lia ("Lucky Legs").

Why Are We in Viet Nam? Fuller was the first American filmmaker to tackle the theme. Singer-turned-actor Nat "King" Cole played an equal with (rather than sidekick to) Gene Barry.

235

After losing Lia, Sgt. Brock finally overcomes his hostility to the Oriental appearance of his son and accepts the boy as his own.

Angie Dickinson relaxes on the set between takes.

columns. Topical in their subjects, blunt and at times brutal in their approach, strikingly economical in style, slambang in technique, more emotional than intellectual in impact, they represent the screen's own yellow journalism transformed, through a natural understanding of imagery and editing, into a primitive but viable art form. Fuller was the first filmmaker to deal with the morally ambiguous issue of the Korean Conflict, rushing in (with *The Steel Helmet* and *Fixed Bayonets*) where more reserved Hollywood traditionalists initially feared to tread.

There followed a string of films dealing with such domestic issues as racism, the Cold War, neo-Naziism, prostitution, and mental health institutions, movies as colorful as their titles: *House of Bamboo, The Crimson Kimono, Verboten!, Shock Corridor, The Naked Kiss.* In 1957, Fuller returned to the subject of war, once more leaping into the fray ahead of everyone else, and all but singlehandedly fashioned the earliest screen depiction of yet another evolving conflict. *China Gate* is the first film to deal with American involvement in Vietnam. More remarkable still, it remains one of the very best.

The plot involves a patrol by French and Vietnamese rangers to blow up an immense Communist cache of weapons, hidden away deep in the mountainous hill country of Southeast Asia. Leading the group is an American "advisor," Sgt. Johnny Brock. A Korean War vet, he's a surly, unhappy fellow who finds himself attracted to his guide, a half-caste woman named Lia but nicknamed "Lucky Legs" for her singularly beautiful limbs that have established her as one of the most sought-after street girls in Saigon. Along with them is a seasoned fighting man, Goldie, and a former Paris cop, Pigalle, both happy to fight against the communist threat. Others include international soldiers-of-fortune: the Greek expatriate Andreades, the former German combatant Kruger, the onetime Czech military man Jaszi. Together, they form a makeshift microcosm: tarnished warriors of the free world, attempting to become white knights by fighting the Red Menace.

With them too is a child, whom we learn is Brock's own son by Lia; she turns out to be his estranged wife. The way in which their emotional relationship rekindles during the mission—how sexual passion grows out of political commitment—is basic to Fuller's point-of-view in this and other films as diverse as the oddball western *Run of the Arrow* (1957) and the incisive World War II drama *The Big Red One* (1980). In *China Gate*, Fuller once more deals with significant social issues more by implication than overt statement; never one to make an obvious message movie, he instead tells a gripping story that wordlessly suggests the filmmaker's attitudes. The break-up of the couple, we learn, happened because their child looked totally Oriental, which Brock could not deal with; but by agreeing to serve as guide on the mission, Lia insures that her son will at last leave this hellhole and escape to America. Though during the mission Lia and Brock rekindle their romance—and, significantly, Brock comes to see how silly and spurious his previous attitude was—Lia is killed, their hope for reconciliation forever dashed. Ironically, though, Brock is now able to accept the boy as his own.

When, during the auteurist heyday of the sixties, Fuller was singled out as one of the underrated artists of the previous decade, he laughed, insisting his films were nothing more than slapdash programmers. His admirable unpretentiousness and humility notwithstanding, there is clearly a single vision that unites Fuller's films, as well as a spontaneous, unstudied understanding of how best to tell a story in the movie medium. Like his other finest films, this is a violent and sometimes sensationalized picture, but one which hits the viewer hard. If actions speak louder than words, then *China Gate*—like Fuller's other films—speaks loudly indeed.

Jeanne Eagels

A Columbia Release (1957)

CREDITS:

Produced by George Sidney; directed by Mr. Sidney; screenplay by Daniel Fuchs, Sonya Levien, and John Fante; running time: 109 minutes.

CAST:

Kim Novak *(Jeanne Eagels);* Jeff Chandler *(Sal Satori);* Agnes Moorehead *(Mme Neilson);* Charles Drake *(John Donahue);* Larry Gates *(Al Brooks);* Virginia Grey *(Elsie Desmond).*

What would the fifties have been without Kim Novak and Jeff Chandler? Or, for that matter, without an eventual coupling of the two? At the time of its release, critics complained that *Jeanne Eagels* was superficial,

Kim Novak as Jeanne Eagels.

The forgotten couple of the fifties: Kim Novak and Jeff Chandler, here in a posed studio publicity shot.

lacking the substance a biopic about the stage actress of the 1920s ought to feature. Basically, they were correct. Still, this film is at the very least irresistible trash, and at moments something more than that, providing a showcase for two of the most attractive and enigmatic stars of that delirious decade.

The film's plot follows the basic pattern of Miss Eagels' life, from her childhood in Kansas City through an acclaimed career as a New York stage actress. In time, though, she was done in by her weaknesses for expensive men and cheap liquor, finally meeting a sordid end on narcotics. But as many reviewers of the time pointed out, the script takes the most tawdry approach to the woman's real problems, while adding fictitious melodramatic elements. In the film, Jeanne is portrayed as entering show business when Sal Satori gives her a job as a hoochie-coochie dancer in his carnival; in actuality, Eagels was a child prodigy who performed in serious Shakespearean productions when only six years old. Pathetically trying to marry into class, she becomes the bride of John Donahue, a Princeton graduate (whereas Jeanne actually married a Yale graduate).

If the contrived love sequences at Coney Island between Jeanne and Sal allow for some torrid moments, the film reached its lowpoint of vulgar sensationalism when it showed Jeanne turning to drink after a pathetic

Hoochie-koochie dancer Jeanne reveals she only wants to have some fun and is a good, simple girl at heart.

238

star-on-the-skids, Elsie Desmond (any relation to Norma?), commits suicide because she held the legal rights to a great play but was forced out by the producers so they could showcase Jeanne instead. Like the competing biopics about Jean Harlow made during the mid-sixties, featuring Carroll Baker and Carol Lynley, this film blows its blond star's seamy personal life out of all proportion while failing to effectively portray the very thing that makes her worthy of such a filmed tribute: the lady's greatness as a performer.

In *The Stars*, Richard Schickel tagged Kim Novak The Somnambulist, a breathtaking sleepwalker, the female equivalent of Alan Ladd. Just as Ladd, wooden actor that he was, could be brilliantly used by George Stevens in *Shane* (where the character is less a real man than a child's dream of a perfect hero), so could Novak's similar presence (properly understood, she was not the weak actress she has been called but a non-actress, a magnificent inanimate object to be photographed) be strikingly exploited by Alfred Hitchcock in *Vertigo*, where her character turns out not to be a character at all but the hero's idealized vision. Understandably, that's the film she's best remembered for, while her attempts at heavy drama (*Picnic, Man With the Golden Arm, The Eddie Duchin Story*) and light comedy (*Pal Joey, Bell, Book and Candle, The Notorious Landlady*) seem curi-ous indeed, the drama overwrought and the comedy underplayed. Novak has likewise been tagged "the slut goddess," owing to a quality on display in *Jeanne Eagels*. When the camera captures her at precisely the right angle, her looks appear almost classic, and at such moments she seems a Greek goddess; but the slightest change of angle reveals something seamy under that surface, suggesting a slum woman feigning the role of an elegant upperclass ice-goddess; that, of course, is what Hitchcock's *Vertigo* was all about.

Born Ira Grossel, Chandler was handsome in a distinguished way, appealingly gray-haired throughout most of his career. He's still best remembered for his dignified portrayal of the Apache chief Cochise in *Broken Arrow* (1950), mainly because most of his later roles were in respectable but undistinguished projects: *East of Sumatra, Away All Boats, A Raw Wind in Eden*. Though Chandler was always on the verge of becoming a major star on the order of Charlton Heston, he remained locked in B+ pictures, never finding the A movie role that would have propelled him to superstardom. All but forgotten today, the late Mr. Chandler might—had he been allowed to play the leads in, say, *The Ten Commandments* or *Ben-Hur*, showing what a Jewish actor can do in a Jewish role—have become a true screen legend.

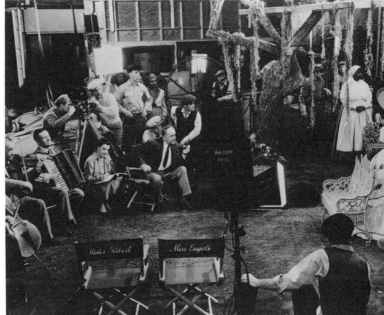

Jeanne *(far right)*, in costume, shoots a scene for one of her films.

At last, Jeanne achieves Broadway stardom.

The D.I.

A Mark VII Picture (1957)

CREDITS:

Produced by Jack Webb; directed by Mr. Webb; screenplay by James Lee Barrett: running time: 106 minutes.

CAST:

Jack Webb (T/Sgt. Jim Moore); Don Dubbins (Pvt. Owens); Jackie Loughery (Annie); Lin McCarthy (Capt. Anderson); Monica Lewis ("Burt"); Virginia Gregg (Mrs. Owens); Cpl. John R. Brown (S/Sgt. O'Neill); Barbara Pepper (Woman).

Jack Webb as T/Sgt. Jim Moore.

Jack Webb's "acting" has long been an object of derision, with some justification; stiff, wooden, and at best two-dimensional, Webb will never be confused with Marlon Brando, though they did begin together in *The Men*. But this much must be said for Mr. Webb: he apparently sensed his own limitations as a performer, so as a producer wisely chose vehicles well suited to his narrow low-key style. In the radio and two separate TV incarnations of *Dragnet* (as well as a feature film version), Webb found in the LAPD's Sgt. Joe Friday a terse, intense character demanding no less and no more than the performer could bring to the part. Indeed, what once seemed laughable came to be considered quite charming with the passage of years, as the warm, gentle satire of Dan Aykroyd in the 1987 hit comedy *Dragnet* made clear.

But if *Dragnet* was Webb's canniest and more enduring choice, others worked just as well. In particular: *The D. I.*, with Webb as Sgt. Jim Moore, a Parris Island drill instructor who whips raw recruits into full-fledged marines. Refusing to coddle his charges, Moore presents to them a one-note facade: loud, harsh, and unbending. That tough guy stance perfectly suited Webb, who strutted, shouted, and snarlingly berated the grunts, endlessly inspecting their equipment in search of the slightest speck of dirt, seeming to take a terrible pleasure in running these boys ragged. Yet the men come to sense that what Moore does, he does for the sake of their eventual survival in combat.

The film only falters when producer/director/star Webb follows James Lee Barrett's screenplay off the base and into town, where Moore and other non-coms head for an occasional evening out. The romance between Moore and Anne, a perky dress saleswoman, seems contrived and flat. Though these scenes are added to allow some human dimension to Moore—to show us that, after hours, a D. I. is, after all, human like the rest of us—they are unconvincingly played and unimaginatively filmed, diffusing the near documentary vision of boot camp.

In contrast, though, the scenes detailing his unsentimental education of the boys are terrific, easily Webb's best work ever as a director. The pacing is whirlwind, the editing razorsharp, the overall portrait of a typical marine barracks unquestionably authentic. For drama, there's a contrived relationship between Moore and Pvt. Owens, a spoiled, psychologically troubled compulsive quitter. Owens' motivations are kept from the audience for too long, so we watch most of the movie unable to sympathize with him; then, when revealed, his reasons are too familiarly formulistic to dramatically involve a viewer. Still, their conflict provided one classic bit: after

Owens slaps a sandfly during a maneuver calling for the men to freeze, Moore has the entire platoon spend the night searching for the "murdered" bug to give it a proper burial.

Clearly, what brings out the best in Webb is a situation allowing him to share with his audience the inner workings of some institution which fascinates him; most often, that's a public service agency where solid professionals labor for the general good, usually without proper recognition. This was certainly the case with most of the popular TV shows Webb produced under the auspices of his Mark VII company, not only *Dragnet* but also *Adam 12* and *Emergency!*, as well as the film "-30-" (about a single night in the operation of a metropolitan newspaper). It's also less than coincidental that in the early sixties, Webb hosted a forgotten series called *True*, fea-

Though outwardly gruff, Moore is teaching the grunts what they need to know if they are to survive some future combat.

Private Owens (Don Dubbins) cannot stand the grueling pace, breaking down in front of Moore and Capt. Anderson (Lin McCarthy).

turing scripts based on stories from the magazine of the same name. "True" might have been a working title for all the Webb shows and films, for, his acting limits aside, Webb was the Hollywood person who most fully understood the implications of the docudrama form. Understandably, then, with the exception of the small handful of leads, all roles of servicemen in *The D. I.* were portrayed by actual marines, "recruited" during the on-location filming at Parris Island.

For trivia buffs, one detail is irresistible: Don Dubbins, who played Owens, had attracted Webb's attention with a small but strong role in an earlier film about the training of servicemen, *From Here to Eternity*. Dubbins' character's name in that 1953 classic? Friday.

Moore finds himself making an awkward visit to the dress store where Annie works; Jackie Loughery, beauty contest winner and Mrs. Jack Webb at the time, had her only major film role here.

The Young Stranger

A Universal-International Release (1957)

CREDITS:

Produced by Stuart Millar; directed by John Frankenheimer; written by Robert Dozler; running time: 84 minutes.

CAST:

James MacArthur (Hal Ditmar); Kim Hunter (Helen Ditmar); James Daly (Tom Ditmar); James Gregory (Sergeant Shipley); Whit Bissell (Grubs); Jeff Silver (Jerry); Jack Mullaney (Confused Boy); Eddie Ryder (Man in Theater); Jean Corbett (Girl in Theater); Charles Davis (Detective); Marian Seldes (Girl).

James MacArthur as Hal Ditmar.

An endless string of youth-oriented melodramas about decent teenagers unfairly tagged as juvenile delinquents were rushed into production following the surprise success of *Rebel Without a Cause* (1955). Following James Dean's death that same year, Hollywood witnessed a scramble among young actors eager to assume his position as cult hero to the teen audience. Few of those actors were ever heard from again (anyone out there remember Ray Stricklyn or Mark Damon?), in part because they tried too hard to ape Dean's unique screen quality, in part because the vehicles they appeared in were such facile imitations of *Rebel*. But one film excelled, largely because it instead opted for a unique story of a lonely, alienated misunderstood youth. Which is why the debuting star—along with his debuting director—would enjoy long, successful careers, even if the fine film they jointly premiered with has unaccountably disappeared.

The Young Stranger was yet another of the late 1950s/ early sixties films based on "live" teleplays which proved, in their impact on audiences and critics, to be of more than passing interest. In this case, it was Robert Dozier's poignant, quietly powerful drama which sounds more than a little autobiographical. While it deals with yet another upper-middle-class father trying to understand the rebellious son he has not made enough of an effort to know, this time the father in question happens to be a TV and film writer.

Tom and Helen Ditmar live comfortably in their Hollywood home, certain they have given their son everything he could possibly want. But like so many other boys his age, Hal is vaguely disgruntled, though like the James Dean character, he cannot quite articulate a cause. One day, while Hal is at the movies (by implication, watching James Dean's incarnation of fifties

As Sgt. Shipley, James Gregory played the kind of sincere, understanding police officer Ed Platt had portrayed in *Rebel Without a Cause* two years earlier.

style youth-rebellion, making clear how thoroughly *Rebel* provided the typical American teenager with an idealized image of his own emotional bewilderment), he gets into a minor argument that causes him to be reprimanded by the theater manager. Slightly embarrassed, the boy returns home and breaks the news of the scuffle to his father. Instead of dealing calmly with the news, Tom overreacts, blaming Hal for the scene, refusing to listen to the boy's version of the story, blowing the incident out of all proportion. Like a snowball rolling downhill, the situation escalates, with Hal growing ever more infuriated at his father's refusal to give credence to his own son's point-of-view, Tom in turn becoming outraged that his son is not more apologetic, Helen caught between them. The son realizes for the first time how little his father trusts him, so there's a growing tension in the family as suppressed anger and repressed resentment slowly begin to boil over. Finally, a well-meaning detective lectures Tom on his insensitivity toward his son, leading to a tenuous reconciliation.

There is nothing in the film to compare with the switchblade fight at the planetarium, the chicken race toward the edge of the cliff, or the shooting of Sal Mineo

that, taken together helped to make *Rebel Without a Cause* such a memorable movie. But in its own less spectacular, less melodramatic manner, *The Young Stranger* simply, effectively breathes life into a more believable everyday example of familial confusion, fifties style. The movie features fine performances by James Daly and Kim Hunter, expert stage performers here attempting to establish themselves as movie character people, and a knockout of a debut by James MacArthur (son of Helen Hayes), who shortly thereafter played the lead in Walt Disney's *Light in the Forest*, then went on to a dozen other film roles before becoming a sympathetic detective (on TV's *Hawaii Five-O*), not unlike the one who helped his character in this film. Frankenheimer well represents the new breed of director who first proved himself with live TV plays, then went on to adapt the successful movie version, thereby carving himself a niche in Hollywood. His next two films—*The Young Savages* and *All Fall Down*—likewise dealt with alienated youth, though he will forever be best remembered for his classic 1963 political thriller, *The Manchurian Candidate*. Still, *The Young Stranger* has been too long out of sight and out of mind.

Tom Ditmar (James Daly) attempts to approach his rebellious son, who has suddenly become "a young stranger."

The Strange One

A Horizon Picture (1957)

CREDITS:

Produced by Sam Spiegel; directed by Jack Garfein; screenplay by Calder Willingham, based on his novel and play *End As a Man*; running time: 100 minutes.

CAST:

Ben Gazzara *(Jocko de Paris)*; Pat Hingle *(Harold Knoble)*; Mark Richman *(Cadet Corger)*; Arthur Storch *(Simmons)*; George Peppard *(Marquales)*; Paul E. Richards *(McKee)*; Larry Gates *(Major Avery)*; Clifton James *(Col. Avery)*; Geoffrey Horne *(Georgie Avery)*; James Olson *(Roger Gatt)*; Julie Wilson *(Rosebud)*.

The cadets, from left to right: Pat Hingle, James Olson, Arthur Storch (in shadow, wearing glasses), Ben Gazzara, Mark Richman.

The womanhater Jocko picks up a girl in a bar to use and abuse her in vicious ways.

Harold (Pat Hingle) and Jocko (Ben Gazzara) harass Simmons (Arthur Storch) while Marquales (George Peppard) grows upset at the ugliness he sees.

Released within a week of *The Young Stranger*, this similarly titled film offered a score of young actors, all at the time considered hopefuls in the Next James Dean competitions. Otherwise, it had little in common with other movies about troubled teenagers. Though less popular than many of the more blatant *Rebel Without a Cause* ripoffs, this probing, powerful drama about life in a Southern Military Academy was based on Calder Willingham's much praised novel and play. The central character was anything but another Wild One, for Jocko de Paris—strutting about the dorm in his yachtsman's cap, loud Hawaiian shirt, undershorts and gartered socks with a huge cigar hanging from his mouth—remains one of the most terrifying portraits of a psychotic yet captured on film.

Nasty and manipulative, Jocko plans to destroy one of the cadets he considers an enemy by creating the appearance that the boy became drunk, against the school's strict rules. To achieve this, he weaves a remarkably intricate web of Machiavellian proportions, corrupting one boy with a prostitute, constantly attempting to deny his own latent homosexuality as, Iago-like, he sets out to destroy an innocent fellow-student. Jocko has been allowed to run rampant because the headmasters fear his powerful father, but after seeing one too many of their fellows' lives ruined by Jocko's insane cruelty, the cadets decide on their own to teach him a lesson, dragging Jocko out late one night vigilante fashion, proving the cocky kid is actually a coward by threatening to place him directly in the path of an oncoming train.

But is this intended as an indictment or a celebration of the cadets' Klan-like approach to their problem? That's hard to tell (in the novel, it was the headmasters who resolve the situation), owing to the approach of director Jack Garfein. Here, as in his follow-up feature *Something Wild* (1961) starring his then-wife Caroll Baker and Ralph Meeker, Garfein provided intense drama that initially seemed to bristle with impact but, on second consideration, doesn't make much sense. Presenting a lurid approach to sordid subjects (repressed homosexuality here, the aftereffects of an attempted rape in the second feature), Garfein focused on confused, almost dazed characters; but as a director he seemed confused, almost dazed, himself, never allowing us to understand the meaning of the story, perhaps because he failed to comprehend it.

The cast introduced a striking assortment of young actors, most from the Broadway play, the majority here making their film debuts. Ben Gazzara seemed a natural for Brando-ish stardom, though the movies proved a tough nut to crack; occasional roles in lesser films like *Convicts 4* and *The Young Doctors*, alternated with Broadway roles, allowed him a certain exposure until the popular *Run For Your Life* TV series in the mid-sixties finally won him a larger following. George Peppard, playing the idealistic new cadet who refuses to abide by Jocko's edicts, quickly moved into the major leagues with such items as *Breakfast at Tiffany's*, *How The West Was Won*, and *The Carpetbaggers*, though he never quite became a superstar of the Steve McQueen/Paul Newman order; by the mid-seventies, with several failed action-adventure TV shows behind him, Peppard was lucky to find himself in the lucrative hamburger hit, *The A Team*. Geoffrey Horne, as the headmaster's son, won the coveted role of the young British guerilla in *Bridge on the River Kwai*, but not much happened for him after that; Mark Richman ended up on the intriguing TV crime series *Kane's Hundred* in the late fifties, then drifted into dreadful movies like *Agent for Harm*; Paul Richards likewise went to TV, with a good show about psychiatrists called *The Breaking Point*, though that proved the end rather than the beginning of his career; James Olson enjoyed some success as a character lead in *Rachel, Rachel* and *The Andromeda Strain*. Pat Hingle became one of the most popular character actors in the history of movies, and Arthur Storch left acting behind (except for his notable cameo as Regan's psychiatrist in *The Exorcist*) for a long, still successful career as a theater director.

The all-night card game: Arthur Storch (standing, holding bottle), George Peppard, James Olson, Ben Gazzara, Pat Hingle.

245

A Hatful of Rain

A 20th Century-Fox Film (1957)

CREDITS:

Produced by Buddy Adler; directed by Fred Zinnemann; screenplay by Michael V. Gazzo and Alfred Hayes, based on the play by Mr. Gazzo; running time: 109 minutes.

CAST:

Eva Marie Saint *(Celia Pope)*; Don Murray *(Johnny Pope)*; Anthony Franciosa *(Polo)*; Lloyd Nolan *(John Pope, Sr.)*; Henry Silva *(Mother)*; Gerald O'Loughlin *(Chuch)*; William Hickey *(Apples)*.

Drug addiction is usually recalled as a problem that came to the public's attentions during the psychedelic sixties, when the new freedom of the screen was born. In fact, though, Hollywood began to deal with the problem as early as the mid-fifties. Otto Preminger's *Man With the Golden Arm* (1955), featuring Frank Sinatra as an addict attempting to kick the habit, was considered so harrowing that the film had to be released without the usual Production Code seal of approval. In 1957, there were two striking screen depictions of junkies suffering through hell: Cameron Mitchell in the low-budget *Monkey on My Back* (based on Barney Ross's autobiographical *No Man Stands Alone*) and Fox's entry into the emerging genre, a major movie directed by Oscar-winner Fred Zinnemann from the hit Broadway play everyone had believed was too volatile for screen treatment, at least not without compromise. But Zinnemann, who had successfully translated the sensational blockbuster *From Here to Eternity* to the screen only four years earlier, once again did a marvelous job of turning a major literary work into a powerhouse of a picture.

Like *Monkey*, *Rain* tells the story of a veteran who is addicted to hard drugs not by choice but by chance; having been wounded in combat and given drugs to ease his pain, he is now hooked. Johnny Pope has a beautiful wife, Celia, and a loving brother, Polo. But he is a slave to his habit, though he cannot bring himself to tell his pregnant wife why he constantly slips out at night. She becomes convinced he's seeing another woman, and

Don Murray as Johnny Pope, drug addict.

Celia (Eva Marie Saint) attempts to help, but believes Johnny is seeing another woman.

"Mother" (Henry Silva) and his fellow hoodlums threaten Johnny.

Polo Pope provided Anthony Franciosa with his best film role.

turns to Polo in her desperate need for some emotional help. But Polo, though devoted to his brother, is also secretly in love with Celia, and finds himself torn by conflicting emotions.

For the documentary look that marks so many of the best films of the fifties, Zinnemann chose to shoot the film in the streets of New York, bringing vividly to the screen the social situation that could only be suggested on stage. We see the humble housing project where the Popes live on the ravaged East Side; when the pushers (led by Henry Silva, in one of his early roles establishing him as the most menacing screen villain to emerge in the late fifties) move toward Johnny, we sense the threat as real rather than theatrical.

Yet there's more to A Hatful of Rain than just documentary realism. With its story of sibling rivalry—John Pope, Sr., has always favored Johnny and downplayed Polo, considering him a loser and blaming him for all Johnny's problems, even though it is Polo who quietly holds the family together—Rain moves beyond the valuable though simple level of social commentary and takes on the dimensions of a Greek tragedy. This is not just a "problem picture" about drug addiction but a movie about the gradual, inexorable admission of truth on the part of a family of characters who cannot know whether such an admission will save or destroy them, but finally must face the most terrifying knowledge if they are ever to be free.

Eva Marie Saint, though elegant and intelligent in appearance, managed here (as in Elia Kazan's On The Waterfront, which won her an Oscar) to believably curtail her natural glamour (which Hitchcock would shortly use to great effect in North by Northwest) and convincingly come across as a lower-middle-class woman, threatened by the thought of her husband cheating on her during what is a vulnerable time for any woman, completely oblivious to the true nature of their situation. Don Murray, who had been introduced as a star opposite Marilyn Monroe in Bus Stop, here effectively took on the role that Ben Gazzara played on the stage. Murray would shortly slip into lesser films and then out of sight completely, only to stage a remarkable comeback a quarter-century later thanks to the prime-time TV soap, Knot's Landing. Franciosca would shortly settle in as a light comedy leading man, enjoying his greatest popularity on television thanks to such shows as The Name of the Game, though here (as in Kazan's A Face in the Crowd) he appeared interested in (and effective at) heavy dramatics.

Bleak and upsetting, A Hatful of Rain stands as a barely remembered example of how the "majors" were gradually daring to tackle the kinds of themes that had been considered too terrifying for serious screen treatment only a few years earlier.

Bonjour Tristesse

A Columbia Film (1958)

CREDITS:

Produced by Otto Preminger; directed by Mr. Preminger; screenplay by Arthur Laurents, from the novel by Francoise Sagan; running time: 94 minutes.

CAST:

Jean Seberg (Cecile); Deborah Kerr (Annie); David Niven (Raymond); Mylene Demongeot (Elsa); Geoffrey Horne (Philippe); Walter Chiari (Pablo); Martita Hunt (Philippe's Mother); Jean Kent (Mrs. Lombard); David Oxley (Jacques); Elga Anderson (Denise); Juliette Greco (as herself).

Like this film version of her most famous novel, author Francoise Sagan is all but forgotten today, at least on these shores. But in the fifties, this literary lady emerged as something of a *cause célèbre*. A shockingly liberated woman in those pre-feminist times, the Frenchwoman confounded critics who divided on whether her writing represented so much precious sentimental nonsense or serious and sensitive social observation. Sagan offered portraits of young, headstrong, confused women struggling for a sort of emancipation. Though they were hardly fighting for equal rights in the workplace, more often merely demonstrating that a woman ought to enjoy the same sexual options as a man, Sagan's heroines—and their real-life counterparts—seemed a necessary precursor to the more intellectualized and politicized forms of Women's Liberation.

Understandably, Sagan wrote at length about the social significance of Brigitte Bardot; in films like *And God Created Woman*, the star symbolically captured the essence of Sagan's ideas. B. B.'s wild abandonment appeared not so much a superficial surrender to the senses as a statement, a woman's insistence she will experience and enjoy men the way they have traditionally sampled women. Surprisingly, it was not Bardot but an American actress who provided the screen incarnation of Sagan's most provocative and appealing heroine.

The story, set on the French Riviera, concerns a

Jean Seberg as Cecile.

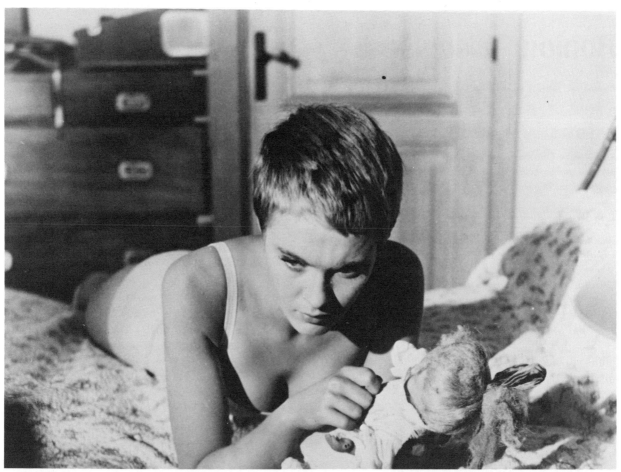

A tragic beauty, Seberg resembled Brigitte Bardot's child-woman who hit the screens in *And God Created Woman* at the same time that *Bonjour Tristesse* was released.

Jean Seberg as the new reckless youth, David Niven as the condemning father.

250

fascinating if psychologically disturbed young creature, Cecile, pursued by all the young men, including handsome Philippe. But she cannot form a lasting relationship because (unbeknownst to herself) she is desperately in love with her own father, Raymond, a handsome playboy. Thus far, Cecile has barely subliminated her intense feelings, but they rise to the surface when he announces his intentions to marry Anne, a mature woman. Coldly and clinically, Cecile sets out to destroy the union, employing and exploiting Elsa—her father's cast-off mistress—to serve her own purposes.

The material seems an unlikely project for Anglos; Francois Truffaut would seem the proper filmmaker, considering his brilliant screen treatises on obsessive/compulsive love *(Jules and Jim, The Story of Adele H.)*. Recall, though, that Truffaut was at that time making his transition from critic to director, while Otto Preminger had not yet degenerated into an assembler of ever-more empty overblown epics *(Exodus, The Cardinal, In Harm's Way)*, but was still best known for his atmospheric, mood-drenched psychological studies *(Laura, Daisy Kenyon, Where the Sidewalk Ends)*. In 1957, while assembling *Saint Joan*, Preminger had searched for a young unknown talent to play the doomed Joan, and settled on Jean Seberg. The film was a critical and commercial disaster. But Jean Seberg bounced back, the following year, as Sagan's self-indulgent, strangely seductive heroine; if she did not seem likely to find mainstream superstardom, Seberg was well on her way to being a cult heroine. Shortly thereafter, Jean-Luc Godard cast this expatriate in his landmark New Wave item, *Breathless*, and the image of her as a transatlantic beatnik, surviving in Paris by selling the *Herald Tribune*, became an indelible image: the breathtaking bourgoise American bitch-goddess playing at being a bohemian.

In time, Seberg would return to America, though with an ironic twist: at the very moment when, after *Easy Rider*, the Hollywood cinema seemed about to adapt to a gritty European-style realism, just her style, Seberg chose to appear in (of all things) the most reactionary movie of 1970, *Airport*, playing a Lana Turnerish part in this ultra-Establishment formula film. Inside, though, Seberg was still something of a radical; her interest in Black Panther politics has been cited as the motivation for a long, cruel period of hassling by agencies of the federal government, who apparently set out to "get" her. That, compounded by Seberg's own inner problems, led to her suicide. Seberg's story—that of a remarkable but doomed woman, as strange, self-indulgent, and seductive as Cecile—sounds like a Francois Sagan novel come to life.

The New Bohemians: Jean Seberg joins The Beat Generation.

Joseph Dufresne (Anthony Perkins) is dominated by his mother (Jo Van Fleet).

Joseph's sister Suzanne (Silvana Managano) is courted by Michael (Richard Conte).

This Angry Age

A Dino De Laurentiis Production (1958)

CREDITS:

Produced by Dino De Laurentiis; directed by Rene Clement; screenplay by Mr. Clement and Irwin Shaw, based on the novel *The Sea Wall* by Marguerite Duras; running time: 110 minutes.

CAST:

Anthony Perkins *(Joseph Dufresne)*; Silvana Mangano *(Suzanne Dufresne)*; Richard Conte *(Michael)*; Jo Van Fleet *(Mme. Dufresne)*; Nehemiah Persoff *(Albert)*; Yvonne Sanson *(Carmen)*; Alida Valli *(Claude)*; Chu Shao Chuan *(Caporal)*; Guido Celano *(Bart)*.

This practically unknown film stands not only as a lost masterpiece but also as proof of an aborted attempt to develop an international cinema in the fifties. That would, in fact, transpire a decade later, when *Blow-Up* was shot in England by an Italian director for an American company. The commercial as well as critical success of that film began a rage for pictures combining elements of the European art film with aspects of Hollywood

252

entertainment, but there had been those who experimented in this direction earlier: *Indiscretion of an American Wife* (1953) was shot in the manner of an Italian neorealist film by Vittorio DeSica, but starred Montgomery Clift and Jennifer Jones. *This Angry Age* went even further in assembling a truly international array of talent for this fascinating forerunner of a cinema in which old, rigid distinctions between various types of movies no longer applied.

Set in Indochina, the story concerns a small, tight European family attempting to keep their failing rice plantation (located on the Thai River) going at all costs, despite an endless series of natural catastrophes. The main problem is the river itself, symbolizing the unmanageable force of nature in the raw; its unpredictable changes in current tear away at the family's pathetic attempts to tame and thereby claim this small piece of land for civilization. Though unconscious of it, they are attempting to prove the superiority of man over nature, but are as doomed to eventual failure as Captain Ahab was in his pursuit of Moby Dick.

In addition, there are problems within their little circle. The mother believes she is a woman with a mission, but unbeknownst to herself is a frightened,

She is nearly assaulted by Legros (Nehemiah Persoff).

The girl is thrown into an intense conflict with her mother.

lonely creature. Unable to face the fact that her offspring must venture into the world to make their own ways, she exploits the problems of their plantation as a means of keeping the two teenagers close—and under her loving but frightful domination. The hint of an incestuous love between brother and sister gives way to their desperate choices of lovers from the outer world, as Suzanne takes up with Michael, a shamed sailor, while Joseph becomes involved with Claude, a mature and experienced older woman. Their mother sadly, desperately begs them to stay and build up the sea wall, the only thing that keeps nature at bay. Each of her children must decide whether or not to surrender a chance for a healthy life on the outside to comply with their mother's obsession. In fact, it is the apparently stronger boy who will find he cannot shake off his mother's influence: she willfully dies, knowing he will succumb to a sense of responsibility, breaking off with his lover and remaining on the plantation, forever building up the sea wall, wasting his life by doing what his mother would have wanted. From the grave, she dominates him still.

253

The stunning final sequence: Joseph escorts his sister to the bus, where she will rejoin the real world following her mother's death.

The part of the son serves as a forerunner to the role Perkins would play two years later, in Alfred Hitchcock's *Psycho*. That movie would, of course, forever associate him with horror roles; but it's important to note that at this point in his career, Perkins was perceived as a cross between James Stewart and James Dean, a tall, gawky, traditional boy next door with some fifties style complicated shadings. France's Rene Clement *(Forbidden Games, Gervaise, Purple Noon)* was hired by producer De Laurentiis (who cast his wife, Silvana Mangano, in a plum role) owing to that director's previous success with subtle, poetic studies of complex psychological relationships. The movie, like the well-regarded Marguerite Duras novel on which it was based, was to have been called *The Sea Wall*, but Columbia—uncertain as to how they should "sell" such a film—instead opted for passing Perkins off as yet another "new James Dean," tagging this with a title that was supposed to remind teenagers of *Rebel Without a Cause*. Though the movie had been shot as an A feature, it never premiered on Broadway but was double-billed (with a cheap action-adventure item called *Screaming Mimi*, starring Anita Ekberg and Gypsy Rose Lee) at neighborhood showcase theaters. Given the proper respect and a suitable distribution, this mesmerizing movie might well have hastened the new style of international cinema which, as things turned out, was still ten years off.

The Witches of Salem

A Kingsley International Release (1958)

CREDITS:

Produced by Arthur Miller and Jean-Paul Sartre; directed by Raymond Rouleau; screenplay by Mr. Sartre, adapted from the play *The Crucible* by Mr. Miller; running time: 104 minutes.

CAST:

Simone Signoret *(Elizabeth Proctor)*; Yves Montand *(John Proctor)*; Mylene Demongeot *(Abigall Williams)*; Raymond Rouleau *(Danforth)*; Francoise Lugagne *(Jane Putnam)*; Jean Debucourt *(Parris)*; Jeanne Fuster-Gir *(Martha)*; Alfred Adam *(Thomas)*; Yves Brain-ville *(Hale)*; Miss Darling *(Tituba)*; Pierre Larquey *(Francis)*; Chantal Gozzi *(Fancy)*; Alexandre Rignault *(Willard)*; Pascal Petit *(Mary)*.

At first glance, *Witches of Salem* would seem to have little in common with *This Angry Age* other than the fact that both are forgotten masterpieces; this is, after all, a costume film set in the darkest days of America's Puritan era but shot in France, with European performers playing the American characters. *This Angry Age* was a contemporary story of Europeans (mostly played by Americans) set in Indochina. If anything, the two films seem the opposite of one another. In fact, though, *Witches* likewise represents the push for an international cinema in the late fifties which, owing to lack of public response, was aborted until, one decade later, the time was ripe for such a new cinema.

Set in 1692 Salem, the film accurately follows the

Abigall Williams (Mylene Demongeot, second from left) and her blond, innocent-appearing "sisters" pose on a bleak, existential beach.

In John Proctor (Yves Montand), playwright Arthur Miller found a real-life hero able to express the concerns of thinking Americans at the height of the McCarthy-mania.

Mylene Demongeot (a Brigitte Bardot lookalike) proved a solid choice for Abigall, though one wishes Marilyn Monroe might have played the part: the wife of playwright-producer Miller at that time, she did in fact seduce Yves Montand, who had to contend with the guilt and pain it caused his wife Simone Signoret, who plays his wife in this picture. While it seems odd that

Simone Signoret, real-life wife of Montand, played Proctor's wife Elizabeth.

general outline of events which began with the sexual frustrations of some teenage girls and inexorably led to a widespread mass hysteria in which some of the finest people of that time and place were destroyed. But the screenplay does allow for plenty of psychological drama that derives from both Arthur Miller and Jean-Paul Sartre having freely interpreted the possible motivations and meaning behind a given historical set of circumstances. Abigall Williams is an irresistibly breathtaking blonde nymphet, a colonial Candy; John Proctor is a fine, good man who nonetheless gives way to his impulses, and sleeps with the Lolita after she sets her sights on him. Out of respect for his intelligent, loving wife Elizabeth, Proctor breaks off the forbidden relationship. But Abigall, her source of sex cut off, diverts her intense emotions into an evil urge for revenge. Taking up with a voodoo-practicing slave, Tituba, the charismatic Abigall draws other teenage girls under her spell; before long, their midnight practicing of dark arts has led to a terrifying witch hunt. John Proctor will be the eventual target, and he emerges here as a tragic man, strong in many ways but doomed by one fatal flaw, his single weakness that threatens to bring not only him but his entire society down. In the end, like a true Greek tragic hero, Proctor will sacrifice himself so his society can survive.

this representative American tale would be shot in France, that did allow for a sexual frankness that would never have been possible in a Hollywood picture, and in fact had been overly subdued in the Broadway play by Mr. Miller. It's worth noting, though, that Miller did not decide to illustrate this particular dark moment from our nation's history by chance. Like most other liberals of the time, he was astounded and outraged by the Joe McCarthy inspired period of communist witch hunting and, as an artist, wanted to criticize it through drama. But the atmosphere of heightened fear did not easily allow for a play that would directly confront McCarthy and the madness he inspired. So McCarthyism had to be criticized in disguised ways. *High Noon* (1952) still

Mylene Demongeot as Abigall, here played as a Brigitte Bardot type teen temptress.

stands as the great example of a movie that initially seems nothing more than a psychological western but which in fact was designed by writer Carl Foreman to comment on the blacklist, whereby the residents of Hollywood forsook old friends who had been targeted, letting them stand alone; in the film, when Frank (McCarthy) comes to Hadleyville (Hollywood), all the good citizens desert their beloved lawman. Miller's play was the stage equivalent, adapting a story from the past in order to indirectly comment on a problem in the present.

And while it seems a condemnation of Hollywood that the studios were so gutless that Miller had to take his play to Paris to get it filmed, it did in the long run work out for the best, for playwright-philosopher Sartre, in his screenplay-rewrite, lent the tale an existential sensibility which broadened its appeal and deepened its impact.

The mass hysteria finally claims the lives of all involved.

Thunder Road

A United Artists Release (1958)

CREDITS:

Produced by Robert Mitchum; directed by Arthur Ripley; screenplay by James Atlee Phillips and Walter Wise, from an original story by Robert Mitchum; running time: 94 minutes.

CAST:

Robert Mitchum *(Lucas Doolin)*; Gene Barry *(Troy Barrett)*; Jacques Aubuchon *(Kogan)*; Keely Smith *(Francie Wymore)*; Trevor Bardette *(Vernon Doolin)*; Sandra Knight *(Roxanne Ledbetter)*; Jim Mitchum *(Robin Doolin)*; Betsy Holt *(Mary Barrett)*; Francis Koon *(Sarah Doolin)*; Randy Sparks *(Guitarist)*; Mitch Ryan *(Jed Moultrie)*; Peter Breck *(Stacey Gouge)*; Peter Hornsby *(Lucky)*.

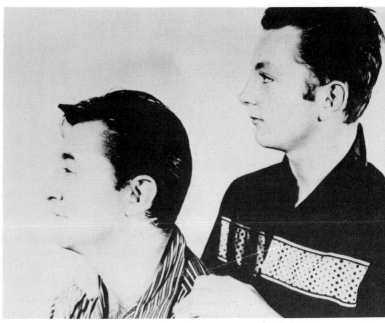

Robert Mitchum as Lucas Doolin and Jim Mitchum as Robin Doolin.

Thunder Road allowed Robert Mitchum his chance to go independent, but there was in fact no producer listed anywhere on the credits, a unique situation which adds to the film's long-held reputation as a cult item. Whereas his contemporaries were careful to develop class items for themselves (Kirk Douglas's *The Indian Fighter*, John Wayne's *Hondo*, Burt Lancaster's *The Kentuckian*), Mitchum—always something of a maverick—chose to do what was, ostensibly, a B movie of the sort then being marketed to the Drive-Ins, where this cheaply-shot dé-

As Roxanne Ledbetter, Sandra Knight enjoyed her only significant lead.

At home with The Moonshiners.

classé curio (it was never even reviewed in the newspaper of record, *The New York Times*) enjoyed astounding success, especially in the South. Revived every summer, *Thunder Road* was annually anticipated, playing to packed theaters. It was the first of the moonshine movies, and though hillbilly histrionics would enjoy great popularity in redneck areas of the country for the next several decades, none ever came even close to equalling *Thunder Road*; artistically, it may be awful, but just try and deny its appeal!

Mitchum penned the original story, creating in Lucas Doolin a role clearly intended for himself. Doolin is truly a man who stands alone, a Kentucky moonshiner targeted both by the feds, led by idealistic agent Troy Barrett who wants to clean up the area, and by the crime syndicate, run by the cold-blooded Carl Kogan, anxious to rid themselves of such pesky "independents" as Lucas. His last name, of course, carries shades of old-time western badmen, and Doolin is certainly something of an anachronism; riding his car down the lonely roads, never knowing whether he's being pursued by the police or the mob, always sure there'll be someone close behind.

Such chases are not staged all that well: the photography is slack, so what should be exciting sequences are generally without tension. And there's endless uninspired talk, between Mitchum and his colleagues (such scenes try for quaint Americana, but the results are less than convincing), with his two girlfriends, a pretty young thing (played by Sandra Knight in her only major role, though she'd soon be glimpsed opposite then-husband Jack Nicholson in *The Terror*) and an old flame (Keely Smith, in her only dramatic part, typecast as a roadhouse singer).

Yet that's all beside the point; like other cult favorites, including *The Little Shop of Horrors*, this film weaves a

spell far in excess of any obvious qualities. It may not be good, but it sure is memorable, a "great bad movie" that leaves you wondering why you're so touched at the end by Mitchum's death in a blazing car crash when for a goodly amount of the viewing time you were bored stiff. Perhaps it's partially the appeal of getting to hear Mitchum himself warble the title ballad as the opening credits roll (he also wrote the music), or the way in which as an actor he gives the movie everything he's got instead of condescending to the script, or the fascination of seeing his son Jim play Bob's younger brother.

So the film seduces even a viewer who is aware that it's all rather sloppy, with fast cars bogged down in gushy melodrama. And the ending is a bit much, as Roxanna Ledbetter, whom we are asked to believe is devoted to Lucas, begins holding hands with Lucas's younger brother Robin even before word has reached her that the older Doolin is dead. Though Jim Mitchum looked amazingly like his dad, the contrast between their performances made clear how subtle an actor Robert Mitchum is; though he's occasionally been mocked as a stiff barely able to keep his sleepy eyes open, the proximity to his lookalike son (who spoke his lines emotionlessly and added no facial reactions at all) served, however unintentionally, to point up Mitchum's marvelous abilities as an actor, even in a junk movie like this.

When teenage boys who'd mindlessly enjoyed this while in high school reached college age, they were amazed to discover that their dorm mates felt the same way, so this silly vision of hillbilly heaven ended up being the topic for endless late night discussions. In those midnight rap sessions, a dumb drive-in movie was transformed into a cult favorite.

No Time for Sergeants

A Warner Brothers Film (1958)

CREDITS:

Produced by Mervyn LeRoy; directed by Mr. Leroy; screenplay by John Lee Mahin, from the play by Ira Levin, based on the novel by Mac Hyman; running time: 111 minutes.

CAST:

Andy Griffith *(Will Stockdale)*; Myron McCormick *(Sgt. King)*; Nick Adams *(Ben)*; Murray Hamilton *(Irvin)*; Howard Smith *(Gen.*

Bush); Will Hutchins *(Lt. Bridges)*; Sydney Smith *(Gen. Pollard)*; James Milhollan *(Psychiatrist)*; Don Knotts *(Manual Dexterity Cpl.)*; Jean Willes *(WAF)*; Bartlett Robinson *(Capt.)*.

When in 1955 John Ford stormed off the set of *Mister Roberts* after less than a week's shooting following a legendary punching match with star Henry Fonda, Mervyn LeRoy finished the film. The result, an instant classic, kicked off a cycle of service comedies (including *Operation Mad Ball* and *The Wackiest Ship in the Army*, both starring *Roberts'* Oscar winner, Jack Lemmon). The popularity of service comedies did not abate until the disastrous *Ensign Pulver* (1964), a long-delayed sequel to the film that had begun the genre, and which all but ended it. In the meantime, LeRoy himself mounted one of the most popular entries, and if in *No Time For Sergeants* he did not have his Lemmon for good luck, LeRoy did at least give a strong role (and third billing) to an actor who three years earlier had premiered in a bit role as one of *Roberts* crew.

Nick Adams as Ben and Andy Griffith as Will.

Ben and Will find themselves put in their place by a pretty WAF (Jean Willes).

That was Nick Adams, who here assayed the part Roddy McDowall played on Broadway: Ben, the mousey and much put-upon Air Force inductee who helps a hayseed survive, as they form one of the most pleasing odd couples in movie history. The hillbilly Will Stockdale was portrayed, in the film as onstage, by Andy Griffith, who early in his career attempted to balance his work as a light comic actor specializing in rural characterizations (as was the case here) with heavy dramas, in which he hoped to emerge as the countrified equivalent to Marlon Brando. His best serious role came in Elia Kazan's *A Face in the Crowd*, yet it was as a comic actor that the public most took to Griffith: here,

Will and Ben parachute down to earth at the end of one of their comically misguided missions.

263

and in his long-run *Mayberry* TV series, where his genial, naive, but never stupid country boy elicited warmhearted laughter.

After being conscripted into the service (something others dread but which he considers a great honor, bestowed on him by a magnanimous Uncle Sam), Will Stockdale discovers his lack of guile may prove his undoing. Truly a natural innocent quite incapable of lying or playing any of the games that are ordinarily a part of service life, Will throws an Air Force base into a tizzy owing to his direct answers and honest actions. He all but exhausts Sgt. King (who is positive Will's friendly attitudes must be a trick), and is lucky to have the ultra-nervous Ben Whitledge around to rescue Will from near-disasters; unfortunately, the slick, snide Irvin is also there, cruelly and contemptuously causing trouble.

The film could reach back beyond the popular stage play to the original novel, actually showing things that had to take place offstage on Broadway. There is, then, a depiction of Will and Ben in their wild parachute jump, when they've managed to get themselves deep into trouble despite their good intentions. The film was zesty and sometimes outrageously funny, managing the not so easy task of kidding Will's country origins without becoming nasty or condescending. Though the main character was a hayseed, and much humor was had at

his bequest (though not, importantly, at his expense), this was hardly what could be typed as simple hayseed humor.

The film does not have the kind of almighty reputation which has always surrounded *A Face in the Crowd*, yet it's worth noting that the more serious Griffith vehicle was never a box-office success, while this all-but-forgotten film was a big draw, an immense popular hit in its time. The film also began a long and happy association between Griffith and Don Knotts; though he appeared here in a small (if memorable) role, Knotts made enough of an impression on Griffith that when Andy began his long-run CBS series in October, 1960 (after being disappointed to learn there were simply not that many strong movie vehicles for someone of his unique personality, his popularity notwithstanding), Griffith encouraged Knotts to play the role of his deputy, Barney Fife, and their comic chemistry was sustained for the first five years of the series. There was, incidentally, a *No Time for Sergeants* series on ABC, premiering in 1964 but lasting only a year. Though newcomer Sammy Jackson tried hard, no one could ever make the public forget the perfect casting of Andy Griffith as Will Stockdale. Andy Taylor on TV may have been written expressly for Griffith, but Will Stockdale was the role he'd been born to play.

Emily Ann Faulkner (Kim Stanley) seduces serviceman John Tower (Steve Hill).

The Goddess

A Columbia Picture (1958)

CREDITS:

Directed by John Cromwell; produced by Milton Perlman; screenplay by Paddy Chayefsky; running time: 104 minutes.

CAST:

Kim Stanley *(Emily Ann Faulkner)*; Lloyd Bridges *(Dutch Seymour)*; Steve Hill *(John Tower)*; Betty Lou Holland *(The Mother)*; Joan Copeland *(The Aunt)*; Gerald Hiken *(The Uncle)*; Patty Duke *(young Emily)*; Elizabeth Wilson *(Secretary)*; Bert Freed *(Lester)*; Joan Linville *(Joanna)*; Gail Haworth *(Emily's Daughter)*.

The problem with most film biographies of Marilyn Monroe, however ambitious *(Marilyn: The Untold Story)* or exploitive *(Goodbye, Norma Jean)*, is that they fail to see the forest for the trees; attempting to depict precisely specific moments of Monroe's life, those movies miss the greater meaning of Marilyn. Paddy Chayefsky had a

In Hollywood, Emily Ann (read Norma Jean?) hangs out at the popular joints.

She reads the trade papers with other Hollywood hopefuls.

better idea when, for his first original screenplay (he had adapted the Oscar winning *Marty* from his own earlier TV script), he fashioned a *cinéma-à-clef*, loosely based on the actress's rise and fall. As in the classic *Citizen Kane*, which tells us more about William Randolph Hearst than any official biography would ever dare reveal, Chayefsky was able to feature controversial facts by disguising them as fiction. Except for Arthur Miller's stage play *After the Fall*, this is easily the most impressive dramatization of the M.M. story, though that is something it never explicitly claims to be.

Rather than attempting to chronicle the entire life of a smalltown girl who becomes a world famous movie star, then succumbs to tragedy brought on by insufficient emotional development, Chayefsky offers three slices of Emily's life, each capturing her at a telling juncture. The opening introduces Emily as a child, earning good grades in school but receiving no attention from a mother who wishes the little girl had never been born. This causes the impressionable Emily to emulate the very mother she hates, becoming a local tramp who escapes her tawdry life as a plaything for boys by dreaming of becoming a Hollywood star. That's accomplished following a calculated marriage to John, the drunken serviceman son of an actor; eventually, Emily abandons her own child born of that disastrous coupling.

Section Two deals with Emily's entrance to Hollywood, where as a struggling starlet she marries a well known athlete, Dutch Seymour, only to drive him to despair with her constant posing for nude photographs and trysts with producers in a position to offer her a contract. In the conclusion, Emily attempts to reconcile with her mother (who, having passed through her young slut period, now thumps the Bible self-righteously, giv-

She marries an over the hill athlete, Dutch (Lloyd Bridges).

ing her daughter no more love or emotional contact in the present guise than in the previous one); when the mother dies, Emily falls into an emotional dependency on drugs. Most tragic is that Emily, near death though only in her mid-thirties, cannot show any more love for her own daughter than she received from her mother.

265

As Emily Ann withdraws from reality, she convinces herself a screenwriter and casual friend (Werner Klemperer) is actually the closest person to her.

A quarter century before the publication of Nancy Friday's *My Mother, Myself*, Chayefsky fashioned a disturbing drama with a similar theme.

In a sense, then, he used the basic outline of Marilyn Monroe's meteoric rise and foregone fall to create not a film biography but something less specific, more symbolic, employing the sketchiest outline of the actual tale as a means for illustrating themes and concerns that pervade his work, from *Marty* to *Network*. Here lost, lonely characters strive to forge their own futures but are held back by the genetic realities of who are they and what they come from. Still, we finish this film with a conviction we've just experienced the essence of what Monroe was really about, even though the surface of events has been somewhat rearranged and/or fabricated. Certainly, no one would have dared imply some of these things while Marilyn was still alive or if they had chosen to use her actual name.

Chayefsky's dialogue is scintillating: the late writer's greatest gift lay in his ability to find a kind of poetry in popular cadences, to write lines that initially ring true in terms of slang usage but, on closer examination, are tightly constructed to express the individual characters' and the author's own ideas. Director John Cromwell (*Algiers*, *Since You Went Away*) brought the script to life with a vivid sense of scene. Kim Stanley, a remarkable stage actress, offered a fine performance, though in truth she never communicated the glow of a Monroe, simply because—though far more talented—she was not blessed with a similar charisma. Though Stanley would forever be in demand as a character actress, she was not in fact movie star material, and this remains her only significant screen lead.

God's Little Acre

A Security Pictures Presentation (1958)

CREDITS:

Produced by Sidney Harmon; directed by Anthony Mann; screenplay by Philip Yordan, based on the novel by Erskine Caldwell; running time: 118 minutes.

CAST:

Robert Ryan *(Ty Ty Walden)*; Aldo Ray *(Bill Thompson)*; Tina Louise *(Griselda Walden)*; Buddy Hackett *(Pluto Swint)*; Jack Lord *(Buck Walden)*; Fay Spain *(Darlin' Jill)*; Vic Morrow *(Shaw)*; Helen Westcott *(Rosamund Thompson)*; Lance Fuller *(Jim Leslie)*; Rex Ingram *(Uncle Felix)*; Michael Landon *(Dave "The Albino" Dawson)*.

Robert Ryan as Ty Ty Walden.

Darlin' Jill (Fay Spain) watches as Pluto Swint (Buddy Hackett) and Ty Ty make small talk.

With his graphic depictions of the sordid sex lives of Southern "poor white trash" rural folk, Erskine Caldwell has always been perceived as a lowbrow Faulkner; if readers notice none of the deep symbolism and complex themes in Caldwell that so clearly form Faulkner's meaningful subtext, they at least grasp Caldwell's ability to tell a tawdry tale with enough wry humor that the result never degenerates into mindless exploitation. That, during the period of the Production Code, made Caldwell difficult to adapt for film. But by the post-*Peyton Place* late fifties, Caldwell could at last be lensed without compromise, as *God's Little Acre*—which reached the screen intact following a 25-year delay—proved.

Caldwell Country—which combines elements of Faulkner's Yoknapatawpha County with Al Capp's Dogpatch—is brought vividly to life in this story of unshaven but not entirely unsavory Ty Ty Walden's relentless search for a legendary cache of gold, supposedly hidden somewhere on his farm. Ty has to contend with his son-in-law, Bill Thompson, a citified type who wants to drag the populace into the twentieth century by getting them away from the farm and into a cotton-mill, where they can join the Machine Age by working assembly-line style. Yet even the modern man Bill is subject to base emotions: though married to Walden's plain daughter Rosamund, he can't keep his eyes off his sister-in-law, Buck's vixenish wife Griselda, half Baby Doll and half Daisy Mae. Others, including the would-be sheriff Pluto, lust after the younger daughter, Darlin' Jill, a kind of backwoods Lolita.

Owing to the series of eight westerns he made with James Stewart, as well as others with Gary Cooper, Henry Fonda, Victor Mature, and Barbara Stanwyck, all

Ty Ty notices the tension between Buck Walden (Jack Lord) and Griselda (Tina Louise).

numbing in their overt violence, impressive in the way that violence is made to seem more existential than exploitive, Mann has come to be considered a close also-ran to John Ford as the all-time great practitioner of the

Griselda goes the way of all Poor White Trash and heads for the hay with a handsome stranger, Bill Thompson (Aldo Ray).

western. More than to Ford, though, the unavoidable comparison is to Nicholas Ray. Like Ray, who had his first great success in 1949 with a *film noir* starring Farley Granger and Cathy O'Donnell called *They Live By Night*, Mann that same year directed *Side Street*, a similar *noir* featuring the same stars. Like Ray, who was responsible for *Run for Cover, The Lusty Men, Johnny Guitar* and *The True Story of Jesse James*, Mann did make a string of singular westerns. Ray turned out fascinating glimpses of offbeat alternative American lifestyles *(On Dangerous Ground, Bigger Than Life, Hot Blood)* throughout the late forties and fifties, then found himself directing ever more elaborate and ever more empty European spectacles *(King of Kings, 55 Days at Peking)* in the early sixties; Mann also went the Chuck Heston/Sam Bronston route *(El Cid, Fall of the Roman Empire)* during his final days as a commercial filmmaker. But like Ray, Mann was more of an artist than either the fans of his westerns or detractors of his ancient-world epics would allow. For both directors, their great work resides in their esoteric Americana: peering percep-

tively into the hidden cul-de-sacs of American existence, presenting them unsparingly but sensitively onscreen, providing vivid and vital cinematic treatments of ordinarily unappreciated lifestyles. For Ray, it was Florida game wardens, rodeo cowboys, and gypsies; for Mann, the reservation Indians *(Devil's Doorway)*, Louisiana shrimp fishermen *(Thunder Bay)*, jazz musicians *(The Glenn Miller Story)*, presidential bodyguards *(The Tall Target)*, and jet pilots *(Strategic Air Command)*. No Anthony Mann movie offers more striking proof of his abilities in that direction than *God's Little Acre*. What might, in lesser hands, have become simply sensational (and some of the huge crowds that assembled for this much-hyped wallow in the affairs of poor white trash did doubtless show up for that reason) is redeemed from such base appeal by Mann's intelligence and humor. United Artists may have sold this film back in 1958 on the basis of its sexy situations, but *God's Little Acre* remains a minor masterpiece (and an all-too-overlooked one) owing to the fascinating sensibility of its underappreciated filmmaker.

When the sexy stuff stops, the gougin' and swingin' begins; that's Vic Morrow wielding the shovel.

Wind Across the Everglades

A Schulberg Production (1958)

CREDITS:

Produced by Stuart Schulberg; directed by Nicholas Ray; screenplay by Budd Schulberg; running time: 93 minutes.

CAST:

Burl Ives *(Cottonmouth)*; Christopher Plummer *(Walt Murdock)*; Gypsy Rose Lee *(Mrs. Bradford)*; George Voskovec *(Aaron Nathanson)*; Chana Eden *(Naomi)*; Tony Galento *(Beef)*; Howard I. Smith *(Bob)*; Emmett Kelly *(Bigamy Bob)*; Pat Henning *(Sawdust)*; Curt Conway *(Professor)*; Peter Falk *(Writer)*; Fred Grossinger *(Slowboy)*; Sammy Renick *(Loser)*; MacKinlay Kantor *(Judge)*.

Canadian actor Christopher Plummer had his first crack at movie stardom in this little opus; playing opposite him was Israeli born beauty Chana Eden.

Was there ever a cast stranger than the oddball assortment presented here? A Canadian stage actor, a folksinger, a circus clown, a former stripteaser, a jockey, a prizefighter, a noted author, and an Israeli beauty were among the "stars" of this singular, eccentric, unlikely item. Colorful and curious, this is a strange, seductive

Gypsy Rose Lee was among the diverse public figures (others included clowns, novelists, and prizefighters) recruited by offbeat filmmaker Nicholas Ray.

Christopher Plummer (wearing the Star of David given him by the young Jewish immigrant) and Burl Ives each found his finest screen role in this iconoclastic item.

film. The forceful team of writer Budd Schulberg *(On The Waterfront, What Makes Sammy Run?)* and director Nicholas Ray *(Rebel Without a Cause, Johnny Guitar)* understandably resulted in a bizarre, brilliant brew, offering a provocative peek into an ordinarily overlooked aspect of American history. *Wind Across the Everglades* is every bit as intriguing as its evocative title would

269

suggest. If ever a movie seemed appropriate for cult interest, this is that film. Yet it's all but gone today, a remarkable if only fitfully successful experiment at imposing avant-garde values on a mainstream movie that is long overdue for revival.

Walt Murdock is a conservationist sent to the Florida wilds to establish a game preserve, but his weakness for alcohol causes him to collapse in a stupor in the Miami fancy-house run by Mrs. Bradford. He's redeemed, though, by the friendship of Jewish immigrant Aaron Nathanson and the love of the man's beautiful daughter Naomi; revitalized by the older man's intellectual and the young woman's emotional interest in him, Murdock sets about his duty, journeying deep into the natural world to confront Cottonmouth, the reclusive poacher who lives off the land. When they at last come into contact, there is an ironic struggle between the man of Civilization who wishes to preserve nature and the Natural Man who is inadvertently destroying his own habitat. It is a struggle that necessarily leads to the death of one of them, though before that happens, they have come to respect, even love, one another.

In retrospect, *Everglades* can be considered one of the first ecological films, a movie which, like *Savage Innocents*—Ray's 1961 adaptation of *Top of the World*, the best book ever written about Innuit existence—failed commercially owing to its being so far ahead of its time. Though the original critical reaction in the dailies was lukewarm at best, *Everglades* was briefly revived a decade later, in part owing to the ecological orientation, in part the auteurist interest in its iconoclastic director. But with the waning of auteur criticism in the seventies, Ray— and, with him, this fascinating if flawed film—passed

out of the public consciousness once more. That's too bad, because his striking sensibility as a filmmaker— visual, thematic, and philosophical—is worthy of consideration beyond the ever-popular youth-cult film *Rebel* and the outlandish Freudian/feminist western *Johnny Guitar*. Teenagers and cowboys have always been box-office, whether treated with Ray's offbeat brilliance or a more modest mainstream approach. Ray ought to be recalled for letting us look into hidden avenues and secret alleys that, were it not for him, would have gone all but unrepresented so far as the cinematic distillation of reality is concerned. Authentic visions of Hollywood screenwriters (*In a Lonely Place*), suburban drug addicts (*Bigger Than Life*), rodeo cowboys (*The Lusty Men*), professional dancers (*Party Girl*), career soldiers (*Bitter Victory*), gypsies (*Hot Blood*), and press agents (*A Woman's Secret*) all preceded this esoteric study of a little-known though fascinating corner of existence.

To a degree, *Everglades*—though written by Schulberg—serves as a disguised autobiography for its director. In *Johnny Guitar*, Sterling Hayden confesses to being "a stranger here, myself"; Ray scholars have long noted that statement is as true of all the Ray heroes as it is of Ray, who found himself as much at odds with his Hollywood surroundings as they all are with their varied environments. Like Walt Murdock, Ray was a brilliant young "comer" who, owing to inner demons, wasted much of his talent through drink and drugs; but at odd and unpredictable moments, each reveals a dazzling potential for positive performance, managing to momentarily throw his act together and perform striking deeds under great duress.

It is finally Cottonmouth who is bitten by an element of the nature he is part of but has betrayed, while the inexperienced civilized man survives.

Night of the Quarter Moon

A Metro-Goldwyn-Mayer Film (1959)

CREDITS:

Produced by Albert Zugsmith; directed by Hugo Haas; screenplay by Frank Davis and Franklin Coen; running time: 96 minutes.

CAST:

Julie London *(Ginny Nelson)*; John Drew Barrymore *(Chuck Nelson)*; Agnes Moorehead *(Cornelia Nelson)*; Nat "King" Cole *(Cy Robbin)*; Anna Kashfi *(Maria Robbin)*; James Edwards *(Asa Tully)*; Dean Jones *(Lexington Nelson)*; Robert Warwick *(Judge)*.

In recent years, Edward Wood, Jr., has emerged as the fifties' great purveyor of sleazy cinema, owing to

Julie London as Ginny Nelson; that's James Edwards as Asa Tully to her left.

Rehearsing one of the film's dance numbers.

271

Ginny finds herself surrounded by reporters as she tries to tell her story.

such junk-movie classics as *Glen or Glenda* and *Plan 9 From Outer Space*. But other, forgotten filmmakers rivalled Wood, and two of the most significant were producer Albert Zugsmith and director Hugo Haas. Zugsmith began as a mainstream moviemaker, responsible for such respectable items as Doug Sirk's Dorothy Malone/Rock Hudson vehicles, *Written on the Wind* and *The Tarnished Angels*. But when, in 1958, he

helmed *High School Confidential*, Zugsmith found his true calling, as the latent sleazeball side of this formerly serious producer came out of the closet. There followed a succession of ever more garish, sensationalized vehicles for the inimitable Mamie Van Doren, among them *The Beat Generation, Girl's Town, College Confidential, Sex Kittens Go to College*, and *The Private Lives of Adam and Eve*, as well as *Platinum High School*. Zugsmith films starred insane ensembles: Conway Twitty, Ray Anthony, Tuesday Weld, Walter Winchell, Terry Moore, Paul Anka, Yvette Mimieux, Ray Danton, Sheilah Graham, and Steve Allen and Jayne Meadows. In the late sixties, Zugsmith created the film his cultists consider the man's final masterpiece, *LSD I Hate You!*

As an actor/director, meanwhile, Hugo Haas likewise begun in the big leagues, but after striking out with the major studios turned instead to such tepid, tawdry items as *Pickup* and *Paradise Alley*; apparently, he hoped anything downbeat or depressing would provide an enlightening alternative to Hollywood's typical tinsel. Haas never grasped that the terms "sordid" and "street realism" were not interchangeable. At any rate, it seemed a foregone conclusion that sooner or later these two giants of the junk movie would collaborate, and *Night of the Quarter Moon* was the result.

This is a grotesque and incongruous film, representing one of Zugsmith's final assignments for MGM before he went independent and low-budget; solidly (and at moments extravagantly) mounted thanks to Metro's second-string production unit, this stands as an embarrassed Big Studio effort at assembling the kind of shrill, lurid item usually associated with Poverty Row. It was, understand-

Ginny finds herself excluded from the town's society.

ably, the last time either Zugsmith or Haas would get a foot inside a major studio door.

Civil Rights, the key social issue of the time, was treated with great dignity in such fine films as *The Defiant Ones* and *Raisin in the Sun*. *Night of the Quarter Moon*, on the other hand, offered only an exploitation film approach, studying the effect of a marriage between Chuck, a member of a leading San Francisco family, and Ginny, a beautiful quadroon. They meet while he's vacationing in Mexico, and immediately fall in love. Ginny, who could easily pass for white, openly admits her mixed blood to Chuck, though he flippantly dismisses this information. Unfortunately, when he brings her home to his mansion on the hill and the up-tight family inhabiting it, Ginny will learn that not all the Nelsons are so devoid of prejudice. These are, after all, bluebloods, who loathe and fear the admission of a woman with even a touch of black blood into their family.

The local newspaper announces the arrival of a woman who is one fourth Portuguese-Angolan into the upper strata of their city's high society as if heralding the beginning of World War III; the girl's black relatives are attacked by whites while the boy's family tries every trick in the book to have the marriage annulled. Eventually, Ginny is dragged into court, forced to disrobe publicly to prove her flesh is indeed white. In the meantime, Chuck—who, in the tradition of other fifties film heroes, is an emotionally scarred Korean War vet—suffers from sudden fainting spells.

This represented one final attempt to make a movie star out of the statuesque, sultry torch singer Julie Lon-don, who though a competent enough actress seemed onscreen something of an elegant iceberg. Barrymore (who earlier billed himself as John Barrymore, Jr.) tried valiantly but vainly to live up to his family's great theatrical tradition. The most sympathetic roles were assayed by Nat "King" Cole and Anna Kashfi (then wife of Marlon Brando) as the nightclub performers Ginny feels at home with, and James (*Home of the Brave*) Edwards as her earnest lawyer.

Tarzan's Greatest Adventure

A Paramount Release (1959)

CREDITS:

Produced by Sy Weintraub and Harvey Hayuting; directed by John Guillerman; screenplay by Mr. Guillerman and Bernie Giler, based on a story by Les Crutchfield; running time: 90 minutes.

CAST:

Gordon Scott *(Tarzan)*; Anthony Quayle *(Slade)*; Sara Shane *(Angie)*; Niall MacGinnis *(Kruger)*; Sean Connery *(O'Bannion)*; Al Mulock *(Dino)*; Scilla Gabel *(Toni)*.

Gordon Scott as Tarzan.

Superb performances by Sean Connery and Anthony Quayle as the villains lent this film an aura of adult suspense rather than the usual kiddie jungle melodramatics.

Tarzan finds himself taken with the beautiful contemporary woman (Sara Shane) he meets.

Like the heroine, the villainess (Scilla Gabel, far right) was also played as a sleek, sensuous modern woman.

Tarzan has been a staple of Hollywood movies ever since 1918, when Elmo Lincoln played the Lord of the Apes in the first screen incarnation of Edgar Rice Burroughs' enduring hero. But for most fans, Tarzan did not reach greatness until portrayed onscreen by Johnny Weissmuller in the big-budget 1932 MGM production. This success led to ever less-spectacular sequels, until the character was farmed out to Poverty Row studios and other actors assumed the role. In the fifties, though, several producers introduced youthful performers, added color and replaced Weissmuller's artificial studio-bound jungle sets with on-location filming, in hopes of reviving interest. Lex Barker fared decently enough in several tepid items, and is second only to Weissmuller in terms of association with the role. But it was Gordon Scott who appeared as the Ape Man in the best Tarzan movie ever made.

In fact, even so strong a superlative may be an unfair assessment, for *Tarzan's Greatest Adventure* is not so much a superior series entry as a remarkably well paced and stunningly atmospheric suspense story, borrowing the Tarzan character for a believable tale about diamond smugglers being pursued through the jungle. Indeed, Tarzan seems less the conventional character he'd become in previous pictures (Jane and Boy are not only missing from the plot, but appear never to have existed) than a kind of silent, primitive avenging force. Importantly, though, Tarzan's antagonists, as played by such excellent actors as Anthony Quayle and Sean Connery, never become cliché villains but are psychologically complex. Likewise, the women are total departures from any females previously seen in a Tarzan film. Rather than the deliciously deadly Amazon queens and the good, heroic ladies like Jane, the two breathtaking women on view here are flesh-and-blood women, and

274

not all that different from one another, since the "good girl" seems even lustier than the bad girl, a far cry from the formula, where a woman's erotic potential immediately characterized her as a killer.

Tarzan does not grunt and roar and devastate the English language, but—in what was a breakthrough move—speaks perfect English. And while the traditional chimp sidekick was on hand for the first several scenes, Tarzan sent him home early. When he calls out, "So long, Cheetah!" the line seems symbolic, acknowledging that while the film began with a nod to the more traditional Tarzan series' entries, it would stalwartly move in other directions. There was even a hint of tongue-in-cheek humor when, at one point, Tarzan fights a crocodile in a marvelous stunt sequence that never looks phony (as do so many parallel scenes in the older pictures), only to have his pretty companion blink her eyes ingenuously and ask: "What do you do for an encore?" The blond playgirl then attempts to provocatively put her hands all over the body of the jungle lord, as though Angie belonged in a 1960s spy flick. A less pleasant fate lay in store for the equally stunning blond companion of the villains; when they attempt to lure Tarzan over a covered trap that consists of a deep hole with spears, Toni is frightened by a lion and, running hysterically from the beast, finds herself impaled.

Scott had already starred in several Tarzan films—*Tarzan's Hidden Jungle, Tarzan and the She-Devil*—but they were mediocre series entries. Then a dreadful 1959 cheapie remake of *Tarzan the Ape Man* with Denny Miller suggested to some that for all intents and pur-

poses, Tarzan was done as a movie item. It was producer Sy Weintraub who was inspired to make an intelligent, exciting and ultra-realistic adult-oriented film, graphically violent and daringly erotic, but never exploitively so, and without a single stock-footage shot of animals.

The CinemaScope images composed by Ted Scaife immediately made clear to viewers that the fairy tale world of the MGM Tarzans was a thing of the past. Sean Connery so impressed the powers that be that, as a result of his secondary role here, he was chosen to play a new kind of screen hero, James Bond, in a series of movies that would eventually outstrip even Tarzan as the most popular series of all time.

Compulsion

A Darryl F. Zanuck Production (1959)

CREDITS:

Produced by Richard D. Zanuck; directed by Richard Fleischer; screenplay by Richard Murphy, based on the novel by Meyer Levin; running time: 103 minutes.

CAST:

Orson Welles *(Jonathan Wilk)*; Diane Varsi *(Ruth Evans)*; Dean Stockwell *(Judd Steiner)*; Bradford Dillman *(Artie Straus)*; E. G. Marshall *(State's Attorney Horn)*; Martin Milner *(Sid Brooks)*;

Orson Welles as Jonathan Wilk.

Ruth Evans (Diane Varsi) confers with Wilk.

Richard Anderson *(Max Steiner)*; Robert Simon *(Lt. Johnson)*; Ed Binns *(Tom Daly)*; Voltaire Perkins *(Judge)*.

At the decade's end, one film managed to capture the key tendencies of cinema drama in the fifties. Combining elements of psychological analysis of the characters, a fact-based story and corresponding journalistic technique, an adult approach to human sexuality which evidenced the new maturity of the screen, striking performances by young method actors able to convincingly communicate the confusion of rebels without causes, and a socially-oriented message with a liberal bias, *Compulsion* stands as one of the fifties formidable (if least often cited) films.

Based on Meyer Levin's personal recollections of the infamous Leopold-Loeb case, *Compulsion* traces the story of two boys born with too much, too soon. Judd and Artie hail from wealthy Chicago families, are both brilliant enough to have graduated from college at age 18, and are now in law school, where they're considered

Dean Stockwell, Bradford Dillman, and Orson Welles prepare their defense.

For most viewers, Welles' explicit anti-capital punishment sentiments did not ring true.

young men with great leadership potential. But each secretly has his problems: Artie likes to dominate his friend, perhaps as compensation for having always been something of a mama's boy, and while he is egregious and outgoing, these are more signs of his immaturity than an easygoing nature. Judd is a born submissive, confused and unsure of himself, introverted when it comes to sexual matters. He has attempted to rape a classmate, Ruth, and now has begun to realize with dread that his feelings for Artie may be at least in part physical. Their ever-more-intense bond, which they here appear unable to consummate sexually, pushes them to express their anguished passion through the negative flip-side of sex, violence. Since they have been reading Nietzsche, the two are fascinated with the idea of The Superman, an elite subdivision of men so far beyond the norm that they can literally get away with murder, since conventional morality does not apply to them.

Early, they are seen driving drunk late one night, attempting to run over a vagrant. Later, they carefully plan the abduction and death of one of their friends, an act that seems in the context of the story to be a substitute for the homosexuality they repress. Artie and Judd are so certain mere mortals can never comprehend (much less apprehend) them that they go out of their way to help the police with their investigation, knowing they are beyond suspicion and the law. But they "know" wrong; immediately, the police find Judd's eyeglasses at the scene of the crime. In short time, the boys are arrested and the crime of the century—as motiveless as it is malignant—heads for trial.

Their defense lawyer, Jonathan Wilk, is clearly modelled after Clarence Darrow, and only an actor of Orson Welles's stature could effectively bring him to life. As the crowds call out for the death sentence for the two, he enters into an elaborate speech exhorting everyone against giving in to mob hysteria. But his diatribe against capital punishment did not convince moviegoers: after seeing the spoiled boys indulging themselves in what they considered the enjoyable experiment of taking an innocent lad's life, viewers had a hard time accepting this speech as intended (Wilk serves as a kind of author's spokesman, his words none-too-subtly verbalizing the film's major thrust), and rather hoped these two smug, overgrown brats would get what they deserved.

Welles was, by this point, appearing in practically any film he was offered to continue financing the pictures he himself directed; though his role here was not lengthy, it did allow him a fine cameo. Bradford Dillman and Dean Stockwell emerged from the film as younger versions of Anthony Perkins and Montgomery Clift. Diane Varsi, slated for big things after *Peyton Place*, never found another effective vehicle; that, coupled with serious personal and psychological problems, caused her to all but drop out of sight. In the mid-1970s, she returned as an attractive middle-aged lady and starred in TV's *Eight Is Enough*; her comeback was cut short when cancer claimed her life. One great irony is that as Welles's hard-bitten opponent, E. G. Marshall turned in a striking if strident performance that helped him eventually earn the role of a lawyer on the other side of the fence when, in the sixties, he starred in TV's well-received *The Defenders*.

Paul Muni as Dr. Sam Abelman.

While Myron (Joby Baker) looks on, Dr. Abelman is interviewed by Woodrow Wilson Thrasher (David Wayne) in the broadcasting studio.

The Last Angry Man

A Columbia Release (1959)

CREDITS:

Produced by Fred Kohlmar; directed by Daniel Mann; screenplay by Gerald Green, from an adaptation by Richard Murphy of his own novel; running time: 100 minutes.

CAST:

Paul Muni *(Dr. Sam Abelman)*; David Wayne *(Woodrow Wilson Thrasher)*; Betsy Palmer *(Anne Thrasher)*; Luther Adler *(Dr. Max Vogel)*; Joby Baker *(Myron Malkin)*; Joanna Moore *(Alice Taggart)*; Nancy R. Pollock *(Sarah)*; Billy Dee Williams *(Josh)*; Claudia McNeil *(Mrs. Quincy)*; Godfrey Cambridge *(Nobody Home)*.

By the time he made this, his final film, Paul Muni was all but forgotten. That may not seem earth-shattering until one considers the significance with which his career was initially considered. Muni (born Muni Weisenfreund) came to films during the transition to sound, when an accomplished, acclaimed stage actor could all but call the shots as he saw fit. When, after a few early talkies for Fox, he assayed the lead in Howard Hawks's searing gangster-tragedy *Scarface* (1932), Warner Brothers considered themselves lucky to afterwards get Muni under contract. Whereas Bette Davis engaged in endless bitter feuds with Jack Warner to convince him she deserved better roles than *Parachute Jumper* and *Housewife*, Muni literally had the studio's red carpet rolled out for him. Warners' acclaimed biographical films—*The Story of Louis Pasteur, The Life of Emile Zola, Juarez*—were literally created for Muni to portray historical char-

Dr. Abelman learns from his old friend Dr. Max Vogel (Luther Adler) that he is far from well.

acters of grand enough stature to be worthy of his presence. *I Am A Fugitive from a Chain Gang* was rightly considered the greatest of the 1930s social protest films, while John Steinbeck's *Bordertown* and Pearl Buck's *The Good Earth* rated as high-prestige literary adaptations. No one doubted Muni was to the 1930s what Lon Chaney (Sr.) had been to the twenties, what Brando would be to the fifties—a man of a thousand faces, the great actor-star of his era.

But while the mythic stature has not diminished for those two (and while, incidentally, the lustre of Bette Davis's hard-earned legendary status grows ever brighter), Muni was all but passé even as the thirties drew to a close. His career resembles that of Greer Garson in the forties or Jose Ferrer in the fifties; each was immediately acclaimed as a class act, only to have people wonder if what had at first seemed an imposing presence might be merely a pretentious one. Revisionism was not kind; in retrospect, Muni's performances receded in the memory, seeming more self-important than socially important. Had anyone suggested during the mid-thirties that Humphrey Bogart, fourth-billed gun-wielding punk in the assembly line gangster epics, would some 30 years later

Dr. Abelman holds his own in an arm-wrestling match with tough street kid Josh (Billy Dee Williams).

Thrasher surveys the slum surroundings where Dr. Abelman tries to perform some good for his fellow man.

be remembered as one of the greatest actor/stars in the history of movies, the very idea would have drawn condescending laughter; had anyone suggested Muni, Warner Brothers' greatest status-star, would be shortly forgotten, the listener would have refused to believe such a preposterous idea. But popular culture has a way of sorting out what lasts from what doesn't, and if Bogart was enshrined, Muni proved a casualty.

Having been all but absent from the screen for more than a decade (Muni's only other 1950s performance was in *Stranger on the Prowl*, a lurid little crime drama directed in Italy by blacklisted filmmaker Joseph Losey), he at least exited in style with this frankly sentimental tale of a beloved and crusty old doctor who, despite his age and infirmity, still makes house calls in the decrepit Brooklyn neighborhood where he lives. The man's dedication—and his oncoming death—persuade a TV reporter to do a documentary on the neglected fellow's lifelong service. Clearly, Muni found in this tribute to a worthwhile and once admired though too long overlooked man a kind of parallel to his own plight as an actor.

Parents in the village begin to realize their seemingly pluperfect children are actually "midwich cuckoos."

There's a great irony to the title, for ever since *Rebel Without a Cause*, films with titles suggesting "angry men" were generally thought to be about the alienated members of the Beat Generation who were invariably extremely young, though this film concerned itself with a septuagenarian. And his "anger" was hardly that of a rebel without causes; what Dr. Sam Abelman is angry about is the way in which neighbors no longer seem, in the "lonely crowd" atmosphere of the fifties, to care about one another. This aged Jewish doctor certainly cares about the blacks who now inhabit the once predominantly Jewish neighborhood. His goodness and kindness are enough to transform Thrasher, the producer making a video about Abelman's life, from a calculated media man interested only in his story to a decent human being who like the doctor cares about people on something other than a lip-service level. In making a film about a *mensch*, Thrasher becomes one himself.

The Village of the Damned

A Metro-Goldwyn-Mayer Release (1959)

CREDITS:

Produced by Ronald Kinnoch; directed by Wolf Rilla; screenplay by Mr. Rilla, George Barclay, and Stirling Silliphant, based on John Wyndham's novel *The Midwich Cuckoo*; running time: 78 minutes.

CAST:

George Sanders (*Gordon Zellaby*); Barbara Shelley (*Anthea Zellaby*); Michael Gwynne (*Major Bernard*); Martin Stephens (*David*); Laurence Naismith (*Dr. Willers*); John Phillips (*General Leighton*); Jenny Laird (*Mrs. Harrington*); Richard Warner (*Mr. Harrington*).

"Father, I want to talk to you."

That was the line that hit home when people caught this offbeat, inventive, entirely original British import. As dialogue, it might not sound like much, but in context, it packed a wallop. For this was spoken to a father convinced he must kill his beautiful, intelligent son, an act that sounds like the ultimate derangement, but which is made to seem logical and necessary as a conclusion to the unfolding story. Part horror tale (though with none of the conventional trappings) and

The Children of the Damned.

part science-fiction (though certainly far from the main-stream), *Village of the Damned* was a low-key, artistic thriller by daylight, featuring none of the stereotyped spook show contrivances. There are no living carrots, no prehistoric thingamajigs, no flying saucers full of monster machinery. Here, all the science-fiction was suggested, all the horror psychological. And the only major special effects were those necessary for the children's eyes.

The film begins on a quiet day in a quaint English town. Everybody goes about their normal business, but the routine is interrupted by a strange occurrence: for several hours in the afternoon, the inhabitants of the village fall into a kind of deep sleep, from which they wake with no apparent ill after-effects. They kiddingly comment that they were subject to a mass paralysis, like the one in the old fairytale Sleeping Beauty, though theirs lasted a considerably shorter time. There is never a recurrence, and they write it off as one of those bizarre, inexplicable happenings that show up in curiosity books as fascinating if unimportant footnotes to history.

Gordon Zellaby (George Sanders) senses his child David (Martin Stephens) is too perfect.

281

But a number of the women, including Mrs. Zellaby, realize in a short while that they are pregnant. Most do not make much of that fact, though Anthea, being the wife of a scientist, does suffer from nervous anxiety: could there have been more to that deep sleep than anyone realized? But when the child is born, both Zellabys briefly breathe a sigh of relief. For the child is more perfect, more beautiful than they could have hoped . . . with a shock of blond hair and the most penetrating eyes anyone has ever seen. . . .

Yes, their boy is perfect. Too perfect, for the Zellabys come to sense he is not quite human. There is, of course, no way they could convince anyone of this. If they went to the authorities and tried to suggest their delightful little boy is a monster-mutant, they would be the ones who'd be put away some place where there are padded cells. Yet each knows what they hardly dare to utter even to one another. Gordon begins some research into the day of the deep sleep, learning there were similar occurrences at the same moment in isolated small towns all over the world. Gordon and Anthea notice that every child born to a woman nine months following that event has the same blond hair and penetrating eyes as their own.

In time, there are suicides in the village, and murders. What Gordon comes to realize is that the children are able to hypnotize people and, through the power of their minds, force anyone whom these emotionally empty creatures consider their enemies to kill one another or take their own lives. This is, clearly, the first babystep in the beginning of an invasion from outer space, though it's handled quietly and without fanfare—no creatures coming down to blow away New York or stomp on Tokyo, but rather some seed to begin a new life-form on earth, right in the midst of a humanity that remains blind to what is happening.

Most people, perhaps, but not Gordon, who sets out to stop the children and finds himself confronted by his own little boy, whom he realizes will kill him if he does not kill the boy first. Like the American classic *Invasion of the Body Snatchers*, this was a sci-fi/horror thriller without any of the usual baggage; like *The Exorcist, The Omen*, and so many genre pieces of the 1970s and eighties, it is perversely powerful owing to the sympathetic image of a father planning to kill his own child for what he believes to be the greater good of mankind. At least a decade ahead of its time, this is a classic waiting to be rediscovered.

He tries to comfort his wife Anthea (Barbara Shelley).

The Tingler

A Columbia Release (1959)

CREDITS:

Produced by William Castle; directed by Mr. Castle; screenplay by Robb White; running time: 89 minutes.

CAST:

Vincent Price (Dr. Chapin); Judith Evelyn (Mrs. Higgins); David Morris (Darryl Hickman); Patricia Cutts (Mrs. Chapin); Philip Coolidge (Ollie Higgins).

The crazed Dr. Chapin (Vincent Price) corners his beautiful cheating wife (Patricia Cutts).

In the unique world of 1950s B movies, William Castle is the great forgotten man. He never acquired a reputation as the American Fellini of junk films, as did Roger Corman (*Pit and the Pendulum, The Trip*), nor were his pictures so outrageously awful that they developed a cult following devoted to the worst movies ever made, as was the case with Ed Wood, Jr. (*Plan 9 from Outer Space, Glen or Glenda*). But Castle was a unique schlockmeister, the filmmaker who first realized that in reaching his teen audience, the manner of sell could be more significant than either style or substance. Disdaining conventional newspaper ads, Castle effectively exploited TV (with brief, intensely effective spots placed on local *Bandstand* shows) and radio (relentlessly hyping his new film on rock 'n' roll stations) for a week prior to the opening. At local high schools, everyone on the cafeteria lines was buzzing excitedly about the upcoming Castle film, then lining up for the Friday evening premiere. The "hook" was always some great gimmick, which made a mediocre feature sound exciting. In *Thirteen Ghosts*, Castle had theater managers provide special glasses for the teens, without which it was impossible to see the creatures; supposedly, the images were so horrible that viewers had to be allowed an opportunity to escape by removing the glasses, though the ghosts turned out to be more comical than creepy.

Going to a Castle film evolved as an adversarial experience: realizing he was out to take you, you adjusted and learned how to take him instead. For *Homicidal*, Castle employed a much publicized gimmick of stopping the screening of the film for one minute before the supposedly frightening finale, so viewers could exit the theater and get their money back if they felt they simply couldn't take it. That approach had to be quickly scrapped when the savvy kids (getting wise to Castle and

He pretends to forgive, seduced by her beauty.

beating him at his own game) attended an early evening show, watched the movie all the way through, stayed in the theater for the late screening, then left five minutes before the second show ended after receiving a full refund.

Castle would try anything: "ghosts' (bedroom sheets) whisked on wires over a screaming, giggling audience; registered nurses on duty in the lobby, to check the blood pressure of people entering; free insurance policies promising a fortune for your heirs if you should die of fright while watching. Castle himself proved to be an irrepressible ham, on the order of Alfred Hitchcock or Salvador Dali, introducing his pictures with filmed messages. But when removed from their contexts, the movies themselves thud, clomp, and drag along.

Typical of Castle's approach was *The Tingler*, a dull, dumb, dreary item which nonetheless caught on big owing to a brilliant gimmick: some theater seats were wired so whenever the characters experienced a "tingle" of fear, so did selected viewers. Vincent Price, a latter-day Lionel Atwill, played a scientist who isolates an invisible aspect of the human make-up he calls "the tingler," which gives us a tingling sensation of fear along our spines. We release it by screaming, but what would happen if we were unable to? The obsessed doctor cannot resist experimenting when he comes across a woman who is mute, and he obsessively studies her reactions after administering L.S.D. to her (seven years ahead of its time, this was the first film to acknowledge

But his diabolical plan is to make her the next victim of The Tingler!

"The Tingler is loose in *this* theater . . . it may be under *your* seat at this very moment . . . so scream, scream for your lives!"

"acid" and attempt a visualization of a "trip"). The woman writhes in agony of imagined horrific occurrences.

When we see the tingler, it's laughable rather than scarey: a rubber facsimile of a crustacean, dragged along the floor on a string. But Castle's dedication to breaking down the barriers between what was happening on screen and what was taking place in the audience was brilliantly demonstrated at the finale. The mute woman works as a cashier in a movie theater, and the tingler gets loose there. Just as the lights went out in the theater onscreen, they also did in the theater where people were watching *The Tingler*; in the total darkness of the "two theaters," Vincent Price screamed out: "The tingler is loose in *this* theater. It may be under *your* seat at this very moment. So scream! Scream for your lives!" Hundreds of thousands of gleeful teenagers were only too happy to oblige. Making moviegoing an active rather than passive theatrical experience, Castle could be seriously analyzed today as the Brecht of B Movies.

Peter Sellers as (from left to right) Tully Bascmombe, Grand Duchess Gloriana, and Prime Minister Count Montjoy.

The Mouse That Roared

A Highroad Picture (1959)

CREDITS:

Produced by Walter Shenson, and presented by Carl Foreman; directed by Jack Arnold; screenplay by Roger MacDougall and Stanley Mann, from the novel by Leonard Wibberley; running time: 83 minutes.

CAST:

Peter Sellers (Grand Duchess Gloriana/Prime Minister Count Montjoy/Tully Bascombe); Jean Seberg (Helen); David Kossoff (Prof. Kokintz); William Hartnell (Will); Timothy Bateson (Roger); Monty Landis (Cobbley); Harold Krasket (Pedro); Leo McKern (Benter); Colin Gordon (B.B.C. Announcer).

For 1959, the sleeper of the year was this offbeat little comedy which won the hearts of not only arthouse audiences (where it originally played) but also a larger, broader cross-section of the public when *Mouse* moved over to neighborhood theaters and did surprisingly well there. While *Dr. Strangelove* (1963) is often considered the crossover film that changed the shape of movies, bringing the Underground up to the surface while knocking down previous barriers between art films and entertainment movies, *Mouse* can correctly be considered a significant predecessor which broke significant ground in that direction. Like *Strangelove*, it none-too-coincidentally featured Peter Sellers in three roles; he would gradually ease out Alec Guinness as the most beloved British actor, a man of a thousand comic faces.

The concept is as simple as it is deft: a small, peaceful, poverty stricken European country (called Grand Fenwick, it's a contemporary equivalent of a mythic land from Ruritanian romance) maintains the life-style of several hundred years ago. But Grand Duchess Gloriana realizes they can no longer sustain their old-fashioned ways in the current world climate, for the financial situation is bleak, and no one can see a way out. Not until, that is, the Prime Minister notes that any country defeated by the United States in a war is, immediately following the signing of a peace treaty, rehabilitated and refinanced by the U.S. He comes up with a brainstorm: declare war on the U.S., send the Hereditary Field Marshal and Grand Constable, Tully Bascombe, with a single longboat full of viking-like warriors into New York harbor, enter into a brief and bloodless conflict in which

After "invading" New York harbor, Tully and his bowmen attempt to surrender and reap the benefits of American aid, though there is no one to be found.

The American authorities are quickly seduced by the ladies of Grand Fenwick.

Peter Sellers, in his first major role for American audiences.

The way in which they win neatly identifies *Mouse* as a film of the fifties: when Tully's boatload of mail-clad men arrive, the city appears deserted, because nearly everyone's involved in an elaborate air raid drill. The threat of an atomic war was one of the two great bugaboos of the fifties, and anyone who lived through that era can certainly recall such preparations for World War III. The other was the fear of an invasion by creatures from Mars, and that's precisely what the authorities assume Bascombe and his men are. Accidentally, they come into the possession of a new explosive so powerful it makes the atomic bomb look like a child's firecracker. An element of conventional screen romance is involved when Bascombe meets Helen, the beautiful daughter of the inventor.

Jean Seberg regained the attention of American audiences with her portrayal of the nonconformist lady, but the lion's share of interest in this film was due to Sellers. During the next decade, he would emerge as the comic actor who defined his times: what Harold Lloyd had been to the twenties, Sellers would be to the sixties, sporting a Beatle wig in Woody Allen's *What's New, Pussycat?* and spoofing the James Bond craze in *Casino Royale*. Mostly, though, he would be remembered as the bumbling Inspector Clouseau from the *Pink Panther* films, where he created a comic persona which allowed him plenty of opportunity to slip into an endless series of disguises.

Fans of film comedy still heatedly debate the career of the late Mr. Sellers; while some consider him a comic Everyman on the order of Charlie Chaplin, others insist he only hid behind a succession of masks, opting for numerous cameos in any single picture because he was unable to develop a single character in depth. *Mouse,* though, certainly reveals a remarkable talent: the haughty grandeur of the Duchess, the aristocratic pompousness of the Prime Minister, and the wide-eyed innocence of the bespectacled Bascombe stand out as razorsharp if rather broadly etched sketches in a film that veers from lighthearted spoof to dark satire.

a few arrows are harmlessly shot in the air, then quickly surrender and reap all the benefits that the American conquerors bring to little Grand Fenwick. But, through a bizarre set of circumstances, they win the war without a person being harmed, then find themselves legally bound to support the entire United States population.

Douglas Brode divides his time between working as a film critic, radio announcer, T.V. talk show host, college professor, regional theatre actor, free-lance writer, playwright, and husband and father of three.

Professor Brode is seen here with legendary filmmaker Nicholas Ray when, in the mid-seventies, they jointly delivered college lectures about contemporary and classic films.

Professor Brode's previous books for Citadel Press include *Films of the Fifties, Films of the Sixties, The Films of Dustin Hoffman, Woody Allen: His Films and Career,* and *The Films of Jack Nicholson.*

Brode's first original screenplay *Midnight Blue,* was recently optioned by Holiday Films for their premiere production.